TEXAS DOCUMENTATION HANDBOOK

Appraisal, Nonrenewal, Termination

FIFTH EDITION

By

Frank R. Kemerer

and

John A. Crain

TEXAS DOCUMENTATION HANDBOOK
Appraisal, Nonrenewal, Termination

FIFTH EDITION

First printing: August 2011

Texas School Administrators' Legal Digest
1601 Rio Grande, Ste. 455
Austin, Texas 78701
512-478-2113
Fax: 512-495-9955
E-mail: info@legaldigest.com
www.legaldigest.com
www.texasdocbook.com

The focused observation instruments in Appendix B and the forms in Appendix D are available on CD for computer downloading and completing. The CD is now included in the *Texas Documentation Handbook* purchase price. For ease of purchase, order additional copies of both through the www.texasdocbook.com website or by contacting the *Texas School Administrators' Legal Digest.*

NOTE: The information provided in this handbook is intended to be accurate and authoritative at the time of printing. The handbook is published and marketed with the understanding that neither the publisher nor the authors are rendering legal advice. If specific legal advice or assistance is required, the services of a competent professional should be sought. Readers should be aware that with the passage of time, some of the information contained in this handbook may become out of date.

ISBN 1-4243-0680-9

TABLE OF CONTENTS

PREFACE

We are pleased to present the Texas school community with the new fifth edition of the *Texas Documentation Handbook*. Over the years, this handbook has become an indispensable user-friendly desktop resource for administrators and supervisors across the state. In the five years since the last edition was published, new legal developments and expanding knowledge about classroom documentation have prompted us to produce this new edition.

As with previous editions, the fifth edition begins with an overview of the legal framework within which documentation takes place. Clearly, the first step for effective documentation is to make sure that it is done in accord with employment law. We then address the basic principles for effective documentation of both professional and auxiliary employees. We illustrate our points through samples of both good and bad documentation. Thereafter, we shift to address how documentation can be used to facilitate improvement in the marginally effective teacher's performance or to prepare for contract nonrenewal or termination. We discuss how important the choice of supervisory style is to accomplishing either goal effectively.

In succeeding chapters, we explain how classroom walk-through data gathering can be simplified by using one or more of our five focused observation instruments. In this new edition, we have fine-tuned these instruments to make the process of gathering information even easier than before. We provide illustrations of how to complete the instruments and then use the information to write follow-up memoranda anchored in district expectations for effective teaching and linked to desired changes in student performance.

The process we describe complements and is independent of the Professional Development and Appraisal System (PDAS) or a locally developed evaluation system. It complements these systems by providing a means of gathering cumulative data over time that can be incorporated into the overall teacher appraisal as long as the necessary time lines and other relevant procedures are followed. It is independent of these systems in that it can be used as a separate assessment system for the marginally effective teacher. This is particularly true where domain scores on an appraisal instrument mask serious deficiencies in classroom performance. It also is true with regard to the probationary contract teacher where the development of appraisal-based growth and interventions plans may not be feasible because of the short time frame.

We have added a new chapter to this edition on teacher professional communication encompassing both working cooperatively with others and using electronic communication devices on and off campus. With the growing use of technology in the instructional program, administrators are increasingly confronted with the need to control inappropriate teacher communication with colleagues and students. In a final chapter we discuss how to write professional growth and teacher in need of assistance plans, providing illustrations for each.

Appendices include the new Code of Ethics and Standard Practices for Texas Educators, blank copies of the five focused observation instruments, a generic list of remediation activities, sample directives for changes in teacher behavior linked to student performance, and sample forms to be used in various stages of documentation.

As in previous editions, we hope that the Texas school community will find this fifth edition useful in fostering personnel decisions that both treat the employee fairly and are legally defensible. That ultimately is the purpose of the documentation process.

Frank Kemerer
John Crain

CHAPTER ONE: THE LEGAL FRAMEWORK

A carefully developed documentation system has become essential for conducting effective evaluations and making informed personnel decisions. The purpose of this chapter is first to examine why documentation is necessary and then to explain how significantly documentation is affected by the legal framework within which it occurs. As we will see, personnel documentation does not occur in a vacuum. Readers should be cautioned, however, that our discussion is not exhaustive. Rather, we seek to set forth the basics, referring periodically to more comprehensive sources.

WHY DOCUMENT?

In this section we describe three important reasons why effective documentation is essential for all employees.

Legal Considerations

Some years ago, the U.S. Court of Appeals for the Fifth Circuit, which has jurisdiction over Texas, disregarded the testimony offered by the employer to support the termination of a 56-year-old employee. While witnesses had testified at trial that the employee's performance was deficient, no written documentation existed to support the contention. The employee argued that he was the victim of illegal age discrimination. The appeals court concluded that "when an employer's stated motivation for an adverse employment decision involves the employee's performance, but there is no supporting documentation, a jury can reasonably infer pretext [i.e., that the adverse decision actually was based on discrimination]." The court added, "This conclusion is reasonable in light of the complete lack of documentation to support [the employer's] assertion that [the employee's] performance was unsatisfactory."[1]

During the same year as the Fifth Circuit's decision, a federal appeals court in another part of the country agreed with the trial judge that administrator testimony about alleged complaints concerning a teacher was hearsay and should be excluded because there were no signed complaint forms and because those making the complaints were not present to testify at trial.[2] Permitting testimony about the complaints would deny the teacher the opportunity of cross-examination. The teacher was 65 years old and had been employed in the district for many years. Evaluations over the years showed the teacher's performance to be satisfactory. In an apparent effort to force the teacher to retire, school administrators suddenly began visiting his class repeatedly and pointing out numerous deficiencies. A few months later, the administrators recommended nonrenewal of the teacher's contract. At trial, the jury concluded that the teacher had been forced out because of his age.

In 2001, a Texas court of appeals concluded that the absence of documentation to establish that two teachers had engaged in a sexual relationship with a student proved fatal to the school district's efforts to nonrenew the teachers' contracts.[3] The mere reliance upon widespread publicity concerning the student's allegations was insufficient. The district had to have documented that the teachers actually had engaged in the inappropriate behavior to justify contract nonrenewal for an "activity, school-connected or otherwise, that because of publicity given it, or knowledge of it among students, faculty, and community, impairs or diminishes the employee's effectiveness in the District." Otherwise, teachers would be at the mercy of unfounded rumors and would have to prove their innocence. In short, citing a reason and then not having documentation to support it is like clapping with one hand.

The absence of carefully prepared documentation also can jeopardize a district's case before the Texas Commissioner of Education. The Commissioner rejected most of the district's documentation as hearsay in a 1996 case involving the nonrenewal of a teacher for alleged failure to maintain effective working relationships with parents. The Commissioner noted that hearsay evidence must be excluded on appeal under the Texas Rules of Evidence, if objected to at the local hearing, because it is not based on personal observation or experience. The district relied in part on a petition signed by community members demanding the dismissal of the teacher for inequitable grading, irregular and improper disciplinary actions, and repeated confrontations with parents and students. However, there was no documented evidence to support the claims. The only parent who testified said his experience with the teacher was "pleasant." Further, the teacher's overall appraisal rating was "clearly outstanding," and the principal had described the teacher positively. Since the evidence did not support the proffered reason for nonrenewal, the Commissioner granted the teacher's appeal.[4]

Several years ago, the Commissioner ruled that a chronology of events assembled by a teacher's supervisor should have been excluded at the nonrenewal hearing as hearsay. Chronologies are often assembled by administrators, and they serve a very important purpose in charting events that lead to a major personnel decision. However, the chronology itself should not be relied upon to establish the basis for the decision. Rather, the events or items listed in the chronology are what are important. For example, if one of the events in the chronology states that the employee threw spaghetti at food service workers in the cafeteria, written statements to this effect from the food service workers would not be hearsay. Preferably, the written complaints should have resulted in a specific incident memorandum sent to the teacher as discussed in some detail in the next chapter. In this case, the Commissioner upheld the teacher's nonrenewal, because there was other evidence to support it and because the teacher had been given an opportunity to remediate her behavior.[5]

Documentation also can be important in protecting school administrators from personal liability in federal court. In recent years, school administrators have found themselves vulnerable to charges that they had been deliberately indifferent to students' constitutional rights to be free from sexual abuse and other bodily harm by failing to take seriously students' complaints that school employees were engaging in inappropriate behavior. The leading case in our jurisdiction is the Fifth Circuit's ruling in *Doe v. Taylor I.S.D.*[6] The case involved a student who was sexually assaulted over several years by a high school teacher. The student later sued the superintendent and the principal for ineffective supervision that resulted in repeated and continuing violation of her bodily integrity. The Fifth Circuit dismissed the case against the superintendent but sent the case against the principal back to the lower court for a trial, because there was evidence to suggest that the principal might not have investigated the matter properly. The case against the principal was eventually settled. The lesson from *Doe v. Taylor I.S.D.* is clear. If administrators have done a thorough job of investigating and documenting employee wrongdoing and have taken action to protect students, plaintiffs will have difficulty in meeting the deliberately indifferent standard. To avoid being found "deliberately indifferent" the supervisor is not necessarily obligated to arrive at the truth of an allegation of wrongdoing. The supervisor must, however, demonstrate good-faith effort to arrive at the truth. In sum, effective documentation (1) enables you as an administrator to stop employee wrongdoing, and (2) helps safeguard you from charges of deliberate indifference in a failure-to-supervise lawsuit.

Ethical Considerations

In addition to legal considerations, there are also ethical reasons why good documentation is important. Consider the Golden Rule: "Do unto others as you would have them do unto you." This maxim yields several important principles for effective personnel administration:

- Alert employees to performance deficiencies.
- If the deficiencies are remediable, provide employees with written directives for improvement and provide a reasonable time frame for improvement to occur.
- Provide feedback through periodic assessment.
- If a negative employment decision is contemplated, notify affected employees of their rights under district policy.
- Follow district policies scrupulously.

If employees facing contract nonrenewal or termination perceive that they have been treated unfairly, they may seek revenge by filing a lawsuit. For this reason, treating employees fairly, even if they are hostile, can reap dividends later by lessening the chances that they will seek to "get even." The documentation process we recommend in this handbook serves first and foremost the goal of fair treatment of school employees. Secondarily, it is meant to provide the rationale and supportive evidence to withstand legal challenges.

Political Considerations

In addition to legal and ethical concerns, remember that you are operating within a political environment. The first, and sometimes most difficult, hurdle to be cleared if an employee challenges your negative employment decision often will be the school board. It helps a school board member who is concerned about political fallout from a tough personnel decision to know that you have treated the employee fairly and that your decision is based on poor job performance. Fair treatment also will diminish the employee's ability to undermine your credibility among staff members by alleging arbitrary administrative action.

Other Benefits of a Documentation System

A carefully developed documentation system can give you the opportunity to acknowledge those employees who have remedied deficiencies or have done outstanding work. A documentation system can aid your memory by providing you with information about past employee performance. It can minimize misunderstandings between you and the employee about performance problems and reveal to you patterns of deficiencies that emerge over time. A documentation system will stimulate you to think carefully about employment decisions. Finally, a documentation system will support your successor who inherits the personnel problems that you didn't have time to remedy. However, an administrator must be careful about carrying forward documentation from one year to the next as noted a bit later in this chapter.

The remainder of this chapter examines the legal framework within which documentation occurs.

TEACHER APPRAISAL

Appraisal System Options

Procedures relating to teacher appraisal frequently change by virtue of new legislation and revised Texas Commissioner of Education rules. The discussion in this section reflects the state of appraisal law in effect as of September 2011. Under the provisions of Texas Education Code (TEC) §§ 21.351-21.353, Texas has moved away from a mandatory state-adopted appraisal system. School districts may use either the state-recommended system or their own teacher appraisal system that is developed through the district's site-based decision-making process and approved by the board of trustees. No approval from the Commissioner is required if districts choose the latter. The state-recommended system, known as Professional Development and Appraisal System (PDAS), became available in the fall of 1997. During the 2011 legislative session an effort was made to require the Commissioner to develop a new appraisal system. While unsuccessful, it is clear that the days of PDAS may be numbered.

PDAS presently consists of eight domains, each encompassing a series of indicators. The eight domains are:

Domain I	Active, Successful Student Participation in Learning
Domain II	Learner-Centered Instruction
Domain III	Evaluation and Feedback on Student Progress
Domain IV	Management of Student Discipline, Instructional Strategies, Time, and Materials
Domain V	Professional Communication
Domain VI	Professional Development
Domain VII	Compliance with Policies, Operating Procedures, and Requirements
Domain VIII	Improvement of Academic Performance of All Students

Districts deciding to develop their own appraisal system must add a student performance component. Significantly, the Commissioner's appraisal rules specify that the evaluation of the teacher on PDAS Domain VIII and the similar components of other options is to encompass improvement of academic performance of all students on the campus (19 Texas Administrative Code § 150.1002). This includes enhancing student performance, enhancing student attendance, identifying and assisting students in at-risk situations, and improving the campus performance rating. While the rules do not specifically require tying the performance of a particular teacher's students to that teacher's appraisal (they do for a district-developed appraisal system — see 19

Texas Administrative Code § 150.1009 (b)(2)(C)), it is clear that the law is moving in that direction. Note: While Commissioner rules have the force of law, periodic appraisal updates issued by the Texas Education Agency do not. Rather, updates are suggestions of what the best practice should be, and the Commissioner does not have jurisdiction over alleged violations of them.[7]

Conducting Appraisals

Whichever appraisal system is used, teachers must be appraised at least once a year. The appraisal is to include a minimum of one 45-minute observation or mutually agreed upon shorter time segments. A teacher may be appraised less frequently if the teacher agrees in writing and the teacher's most recent evaluation rated the teacher at least proficient and did not indicate any area of deficiency. A teacher who is appraised less frequently must be appraised at least once every five years.

Under PDAS, additional walk-throughs and observations may be conducted at the discretion of the appraiser. Determining the weight to be accorded an unscheduled classroom walk-through observation in reconsidering a teacher's prior rating on a formal observation is a matter for the appraiser's professional judgment. In a 1991 appeal to the Commissioner, a teacher contested the principal's refusal to change the credit for one indicator on her summative evaluation. The principal had conducted and documented numerous walk-throughs following the formal evaluation. The teacher alleged that during these walk-throughs, the principal must have noticed that the deficiency had been corrected but the principal refused to change the rating. The Commissioner upheld the principal's decision, noting that "if [the principal] determined that [the teacher's] performance did not improve sufficiently to warrant credit for the indicator, then that was her assessment, and such exercise of judgment is not arbitrary and capricious."[8]

A campus administrator who is a certified PDAS appraiser and approved by the school board conducts the teacher appraisal. An individual other than the campus administrator may act as an appraiser if the person is certified and the district lacks a sufficient number of certified appraisers. A PDAS appraiser who is a classroom teacher may conduct teacher appraisals on other campuses but not on the same school campus unless acting as a department or grade level chair with a job description that includes classroom observation responsibilities. Training requirements for appraisers are spelled out in Commissioner rules (19 Texas Administrative Code § 150.1006).

For PDAS and local systems, whether or not to give advance notice of the date and time of the appraisal is left to the discretion of the school district. A teacher must be appraised only on the basis of classroom teaching performance, not performance in directing extracurricular activities. Teachers are entitled to a copy of their completed evaluations. After receiving a written copy of the observation or evaluation, a teacher may request a second appraisal by a different appraiser or may file a written rebuttal to the evaluation (under PDAS rules as of September 2011, the rebuttal must be filed within 10 working days — 15 working days with supervisor's approval — after receiving a written observation summary, a summative appraisal report, or any other written documentation associated with the teacher's appraisal). The appraisal process must guarantee a conference between the teacher and the appraiser. Schools are authorized to send copies of a teacher's evaluations, along with any rebuttals, to a district in which the teacher has applied for employment if the new district requests such information.

The appraisal of a teacher or administrator is considered confidential (TEC § 21.355). The Texas Attorney General has construed Section 21.355 to apply to any document that evaluates the employee's performance. Further, the attorney general has construed the provision to apply only to certified teachers engaged in teaching and to certified administrators functioning in that capacity. Thus, teacher interns, teacher trainees, librarians, educational aides, and counselors are excluded (ORD-643, 1996). However, Section 21.355 was amended in 2011 to encompass both certified and non-certified persons employed in an open-enrollment charter school. The amendment also permits an open-enrollment charter school to provide a performance evaluation to a school district or open-enrollment charter school to which a teacher or administrator at the open-enrollment charter school has applied. In 2006 a Texas court of appeals construed TEC § 21.355 to apply to a letter of reprimand concerning complaints about the teacher and directing corrective action.[9]

Among the features unique to PDAS are the following:

1. The appraiser is responsible for documenting cumulative data regarding job-related teacher performance in addition to conducting the formal classroom observations and reviewing the teacher's self-report form if the appraiser believes walk-through data are necessary or will be helpful. The appraiser must verify and document data from a third-party source. If cumulative data will influence the teacher's summative annual appraisal report, the data must be shared in writing with the teacher within 10 working days of the occurrence or of the appraiser's knowledge. When the appraiser is not the teacher's principal, the principal is to be notified in writing. Chapter 4 of this handbook discusses gathering cumulative data in the classroom in a systematic way using our focused observation instruments and incorporating the data in follow-up memoranda.

2. A written summative annual appraisal report must be shared with the teacher no later than five working days before the summative conference and no later than 15 working days before the last day of instruction for students. Any documentation collected after the summative conference but before the end of the contract term during a school year may be considered as part of the appraisal of a teacher. If the documentation affects the teacher's evaluation in any domain, another summative conference must be held.

3. A teacher whose performance is less than proficient in one or more domains or is unsatisfactory in two or more domains is to be designated a "teacher in need of assistance." This requires the development of an intervention plan in consultation with the teacher. In cases where the teacher's appraiser is not the teacher's principal, the principal shall be involved in the development and assessment of the intervention plan. (Note: an intervention plan can be developed at any other time at the discretion of the appraiser when the appraiser has documentation that would potentially produce an evaluation rating of below expectations or unsatisfactory.)

4. According to rules developed by the Texas Commissioner of Education, the intervention plan is to include domains that designate the teacher as one in need of assistance, directives or recommendations for professional improvement activities, evidence to be used to determine successful completion of improvement activities, directives for changes in teacher behavior, evidence that is used to determine if teacher behavior has changed, and the time

frame for completion of the intervention plan (19 TAC § 150.1004 (b)). As we will illustrate in Chapter 6, the assessment component of improvement plans (i.e., whether or not directed changes in behavior and/or compliance with directives for professional development have occurred and have resulted in improved student performance) is critically important and is often neglected. At least one of the professional development options specified in the growth plan is not to place a significant financial burden on either the teacher or the district.

5. The Commissioner's rules specify that a teacher who has not met all requirements of the intervention plan within the specified remediation time may be considered for "separation from the assignment, campus, and/or district" (19 TAC § 150.1004 (d)).

Grievances Over Appraisals

All public employees have a right to present grievances to their employers under Ch. 617 of the Texas Government Code and under Article 1, Section 27 of the Texas Constitution. The Commissioner of Education has held that both the *process* by which an employment evaluation was conducted and the *content* of the evaluation are grievable.[10] Additionally, a school board can review the educational judgment of an appraiser but may reverse the appraiser's judgment only if the appraiser's educational judgment was "clearly erroneous or an abuse of discretion." [11] PDAS rules require the development of a grievance system for teachers to present grievances and to receive written comments in response to the written annual appraisal report. Administrators must be very careful not to retaliate against a teacher — or any employee, for that matter — who files a grievance. That point was illustrated in a decision from the Commissioner in 1992 involving Texas Teacher Appraisal System (TTAS), the predecessor to PDAS. A principal commented negatively to the teacher's prospective employer about the teacher's filing grievances over her appraisals. The Commissioner noted, "Under the Texas Teacher Appraisal System, teachers rest assured that no appraisal or evaluation of their work performance can affect their career without notice to them and an opportunity to respond." The principal had breached that assurance by providing negative employment references. The Commissioner took the stringent action of revoking the principal's mid-management certification.[12]

Does a Positive Appraisal Shield a Teacher from Contract Nonrenewal or Termination?

The Commissioner has ruled that satisfactory appraisal ratings do not insulate a teacher from having the teacher's contract nonrenewed based on deficient classroom performance, since the appraisal is not the only means of classroom evaluation. In a 2008 case, the teacher argued that because his most recent evaluation was very good, the board should not have nonrenewed his contract. But the Commissioner noted that while the board must consider relevant recent evaluations before deciding not to renew, it is not limited to them and need not consider them as the most important evidence.[13]

PDAS is very comprehensive in its coverage of job-related behavior. Domain VII of PDAS encompasses compliance with policies and with operating procedures and requirements. If this domain is central to a recommendation for contract nonrenewal or termination, there must be evidence to support a below expectations or unsatisfactory rating. If there is none, then such a rating is invalid and can't be used to support contract nonrenewal or termination. However, the improper scoring of one domain does not affect the rest of the appraisal.[14]

What About Using Teaching Deficiencies from Prior Years to Build Support for Contract Nonrenewal or Termination?

When classroom deficiencies are evident, it is important to make sure teachers are aware of them from one year to the next. This is especially true when one-year contracts are renewed. The Commissioner has observed that "When a school district with full knowledge of a teacher's actions takes no action against the teacher and decides to offer the teacher a new contract, the district has waived any right it had to take action against the teacher's contract for the events in the prior school years."[15] Such is not the case for an employee on a multiple year contract when the deficiencies have been pointed out and the employee been given a remediation plan to correct them. In this event, it may take the duration of the contract to determine whether the teacher has met the terms of the remediation plan. We will discuss remediation plans in more detail in the last chapter.

For the one-year contract teacher when a remediation plan is not established, listing items in the "Areas of Concern" on the ratings form will show that despite high appraisal scores, the teacher was on notice that deficiencies remain despite the contract renewal. Still, an administrator can't expect to utilize past deficiencies to support a future contract nonrenewal of a teacher with high appraisal ratings when no remediation effort is ever extended to a teacher to remedy the areas of concern. Both a school board and the Commissioner may find the nonrenewal unfair.

ADMINISTRATOR APPRAISAL

In response to a legislative directive set forth in TEC § 21.354, the Commissioner of Education has enacted a set of rules relating to the evaluation of school administrators. These apply to principals as well until the Commissioner completes developing rules for a separate appraisal and professional development system for them.* A school district may use either this system or one developed locally. In either case, the appraisal of a school principal must include consideration of the performance of the campus on the student achievement indicators established under TEC § 39.053 and on the campus objectives established under TEC § 11.253, including performance gains of the campus and the maintenance of those gains. The legislature appears particularly serious about administrator appraisal. School district funds can not be used to pay an administrator who has not been appraised in the preceding fifteen months.

---

* In 2011, the legislature passed a measure directing the Commissioner to do so (TEC § 21.3541). The principal appraisal system to be developed is to include school leadership standards and a set of indicators aligned with principal training, appraisal, and professional development. Districts will have a choice of using the state-developed principal appraisal system or one developed by the school district in consultation with district- and campus-level committees and adopted by the school board. Under the new system, principals must be evaluated annually.

Minimum procedures for administrator appraisal including an annual calendar that involves the administrator and appraiser in setting goals, as well as in holding formative and summative conferences. Administrator appraisers are required to provide evidence of training in appropriate evaluation skills related to locally established criteria and process. The district also may collect staff input for evaluating administrators. If so, the input must not be anonymous. This means that the appraisers need to know who made the comments, but the appraisal rules do not require that their identity must be shared with the administrator being evaluated, though this is required for teachers. Whether the identity of persons making critical comments is to be revealed to the administrator being evaluated is up to the district.[16]

The Commissioner-recommended administrator appraisal system sets forth a list of performance domains encompassing (1) instructional management; (2) school or organizational morale; (3) school or organizational improvement; (4) personnel management; (5) management of administrative, fiscal, and facilities functions; (6) student management; (7) school or community relations; (8) professional growth and development; (9) academic excellence indicators and campus performance objectives; and (10) school board relations (superintendents only). For each, a set of descriptors is set forth (19 Texas Administrative Code § 150.1021). The Commissioner has advised that all but one of these rules is recommended. The exception is the domain on student performance.[17] That is because Section 150.1021 (c) requires that the student performance domain "shall be included in the appraisal of principals and superintendents" and is to encompass for principal appraisal the improvement of student performance on the campus through such activities as comparing campus disaggregated student performance results to state accountability standards and to prior year performance. The same is required for superintendents in the context of the district as a whole.

The rules for the Commissioner-recommended appraisal process also specify that the appraisal instrument must be based on the local job description. Other components include periodic training for both principals and appraisers, an implementation process approved by the Commissioner, incorporation of student performance results on the local appraisal instrument, an intervention plan for principals whose results on the student performance domain fall below the Commissioner's standards, and limited use of student performance data for new principals (19 Texas Administrative Code § 150.1022 (g)).

In addition to appraising teachers and administrators, many districts have developed evaluation systems for other employees such as coaches, librarians, counselors, secretaries, and maintenance workers. It is important for administrators to follow the procedures for these systems because failure to do so will quickly undermine an administrator's negative employment recommendations, no matter how well intentioned.

TEXAS EMPLOYMENT LAW

Understanding the basics of employment law is critical to successful documentation, because both the amount and types of documentation are heavily influenced by it. The purpose of this section is to provide an overview of the employment provisions of the Texas Education Code and to discuss the implications for documentation. Quite obviously, employment law is comprehensive, complex, and frequently changing. Here, we sketch only the basics. For a detailed discussion, see Chapters 4 and 5 of Walsh, Kemerer & Maniotis's *Educator's Guide to Texas School Law,* 7th ed. (Austin, TX: University of Texas Press, 2010) and its 2012 Supplement.

At-Will Arrangements

At-will employment is most often used with auxiliary employees such as custodians, cafeteria workers, clerks, and secretaries. The at-will option may also be used for non-certificated teachers selected under the teaching permit option afforded by TEC § 21.055, because certification is required for employment under the contractual options discussed below that afford procedural protection.*

Frequently teachers are employed on an at-will basis to undertake supplemental duty assignments (e.g., serve as student council sponsor for a $500 stipend). "At-will" means that there is no expectation of continued employment. Either party may dissolve the employment relationship at any time. Because there is no expectation of continued employment, no constitutionally protected property right is at stake.[18] Furthermore, oral assurances of continued employment do not alter the status of an at-will arrangement.[19]

It would seem at first glance that neither due process nor documentation should be a concern for at-will arrangements. Such an assumption would be erroneous. Many districts employ auxiliary workers for some specific length of time (e.g., from one thirty-day pay period to the next). Thus, the employee may have an expectation of continued employment for the duration of the pay period. Termination during that period may require adherence to formal due process procedures and sufficient documentation to constitute good cause for discharge. Based on federal court rulings over the years, "good cause" can be loosely defined to mean clear and convincing reasons accompanied by sufficient supportive evidence to deprive a person of a constitutionally protected property right in employment. If the district waits until the end of the pay period to sever the employment relationship, no due process would be required absent local district policy creating such a requirement. In the case of professional employees, one district ran into trouble when the Commissioner of Education construed conflicting terminology in a teacher's contract in favor of the teacher's argument that the supplemental duty assignment of assistant band director was part of the contract and could not be ended without following due process procedures associated with nonrenewal and termination.[20] Had the contract been confined to teaching responsibilities and the supplemental duty assignment been a separate at-will arrangement, the conflict would not have arisen. For this reason it is important to pay attention to the terms of any written agreement with the employee, to district policies, and to district past practice before terminating at-will employees from work.

Even when there is no contractual language or district policy that would require due process before discharging an at-will employee, documentation cannot be ignored. Consider, for example, the following scenario. A supervisor tells a female custodian late on a Friday afternoon not to report to work on Monday because her employment is no longer needed. Angered by this decision and concerned that she may not be able to find employment in a tight labor market, the

---

* Teachers hired under the teaching permit option also may be employed on contracts similar to those used with other employees whose position does not require certification. As noted a bit later, these are termed "Non-Chapter 21" employees.

custodian decides to contest the termination. She files a grievance under school district policy and contacts the Equal Employment Opportunity Commission (EEOC) or the Texas Commission on Human Rights (TCHR), asserting that the termination resulted from her refusal to grant sexual favors to the supervisor. In order to establish that sexual harassment was not a factor in the decision, the supervisor must have documentation relating to poor job performance or some other reason unrelated to the allegation.

This scenario demonstrates that documentation is important even when administrators have maximum discretion in terminating an at-will arrangement. How much documentation is needed? Enough to support a job-related reason for terminating the person's employment. In the next chapter, we will illustrate how a supervisor might go about preparing the necessary documentation for doing so.

Contracts for Professional Employees

The term "teacher" in the law is broadly defined to include principals, supervisors, classroom teachers, counselors, or other full-time professional employees who are required to hold an educator certificate under Subchapter B of Chapter 21 of the Texas Education Code. The Chapter 21 contract provisions setting forth the conditions under which probationary, term, and continuing contracts operate in Texas public schools also apply to school nurses and librarians who work full time. But they do not apply to teachers holding only a teaching permit.[21] Superintendents are included within the definition of "teacher" under the term contract provisions only. Given the broad definition of "teacher," we will substitute the term "professional employee" in the following discussion. It is important to note at the onset that we are focusing our attention primarily on statutory provisions dealing with contract nonrenewal and termination. However, the actual wording of contracts cannot be ignored. In some cases, school districts have approved contract provisions that are unique to the district and sometimes unique even to the employee.

What about employees who do not fall into the "professional employee" category as we define it above? For example, surely a business manager and a director of maintenance are professional employees. Yes, they are. But the provisions of Chapter 21 dealing with probationary, term, and continuing contracts do not apply to them. We call these persons "non-Chapter 21 employees." They may have a contract of employment, but the contract is not governed by Chapter 21. This means in effect that the conditions of their employment are defined by provisions set forth in the contract. Suppose a school district wants to nonrenew or terminate the contract of a non-Chapter 21 employee. Are there any procedures that must be followed? For nonrenewal of the contract when its term is up, the provisions of the contract will answer this question. For termination of the contract during its term, the matter is more complex. Generally, unless the terms of the contract state otherwise, a public school employee has an expectation of employment until the contract ends. This expectation is termed a property right. Under the Fourteenth Amendment to the U.S. Constitution, a political entity like a school district cannot take away life, liberty, or property without due process of law. In the context of a non-Chapter 21 contract, the basics of due process require that the employee:

- Be advised of the cause or causes of the termination in sufficient detail to fairly enable the employee to show any error that may exist.
- Be advised of the names and the nature of the testimony of witnesses against the employee.

- At a reasonable time after such advice, be given a meaningful opportunity to be heard in the employee's defense.
- Be given an opportunity for a hearing before an impartial tribunal.

This is the teaching of a venerable ruling of the U.S. Court of Appeals for the Fifth Circuit, which has jurisdiction for several states, including Texas.[22] The case involved the dismissal of a teacher during the teacher's contract. Today, the teacher would be entitled to more elaborate due process procedures that are part of Chapter 21. However, the four basic due process steps set forth above still apply to non-Chapter 21 employees.

That said, we now turn our attention to those professional employees including teachers, administrators, supervisors, counselors, librarians, and nurses who are covered by Chapter 21 of the Texas Education Code in effect as of the fall of 2011.

Probationary Contract

Except for superintendents and except for experienced principals and teachers who may be employed on term contracts when new to the district, professional employees are required to serve a one-year probationary contract if employed in the district for the first time or if not employed by the district for two consecutive school years after August 28, 1967 (see Figure 1-1). The latter provision means that a professional employee who resigns before serving two consecutive years of employment and then returns to the district must be re-employed on a one-year probationary contract. In the past, there has been some confusion as to when the probationary period is over for a teacher who is hired in mid-year. The Commissioner of Education resolved the problem in 1996, deciding that the term "year" is to have the normal meaning it has in the school business, meaning a scholastic year.[23] Thus, the one-year probationary period for a teacher hired mid-year is not concluded until the end of the next school year. Persons who voluntarily accept assignments in a new professional capacity requiring a different class of certificate also now may be employed on a probationary contract. Should the person be returned to the former position, the person is to be employed on the same contractual basis as before the new assignment.

Figure 1-1 THE ONE-YEAR PROBATIONARY CONTRACT

(All Employees Who Have Not Been Employed for Two Consecutive Years Except the Superintendent, Experienced Principals and Teachers at District Discretion, and Employees Who Accept Reassignments Requiring a Different Class of Certificate)

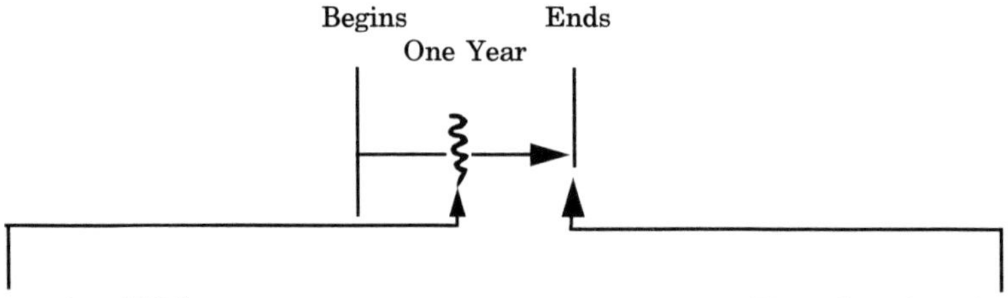

Discharge/Suspension Without Pay During Contract
- Property Right
- Good Cause
- Notice
- Hearing Before Hearing Examiner (board option for financial exigency)
- Oral Argument Before School Board
- Right to Appeal

TEC §§ 21.104 - 21.1041, 21.251 - 21.307

Termination At End Of Contract
- No Property Right
- 10-Day Notice
- Best Interest of School District
- Board Decision Final and Nonappealable

TEC § 21.103

Education Code Section 21.103 states that a probationary contract may be "terminated at the end of the contract year" if the district believes that it would be in the best interests of the district to do so. The term normally used in this situation is "nonrenewal." However, for some reason Education Code Section 21.103 uses the term "termination," and we will do so here as well. Due process is limited to providing notice of termination no later than the 10th day before the last day of instruction under the contract. The notice must be delivered personally by hand delivery to the teacher on the campus where the teacher is employed. If the teacher is not present when hand delivery is attempted, then the notice must be mailed by prepaid certified mail or delivered by express delivery service to the teacher's home address. The notice is considered timely if postmarked on or before the 10th day prior to the last day of instruction. If the board fails to give timely notice and the employee has served fewer than three years in the district, the person is to be given a probationary contract for another year in the same professional capacity.

From a documentation standpoint, an end-of-year termination of a probationary employee's contract is the easiest negative employment decision to make. During this "window of opportunity," the district only has to comply with the 10-day notice requirement. No other due process procedures are necessary. Further, the board's decision is final and nonappealable. Still, the same concerns regarding at-will employees also pertain to probationary contract employees. While the Texas Commissioner of Education declines to hear appeals from probationary contract employees whose contracts are terminated at the end of the year, the employee can always file a grievance with the district or contact the EEOC or the TCHR to contest the action as illegally motivated. In this sense, nothing is ever "final and nonappealable." Thus, if challenged, administrators should be prepared to defend their actions by having sufficient documentation to establish the legitimacy of the end-of-year termination. However, the burden is clearly on the employee to establish that the district had an impermissible motive for the action.

Terminating or suspending a probationary contract without pay *during the contract* is an entirely different matter. Doing so requires more administrative attention. Since the professional employee has a constitutionally protected property right to the salary (and to the position if the contract is worded to convey a specific job title), formal due process procedures must be followed. TEC § 21.1041 provides that a mid-year termination of a probationary teacher's contract requires a hearing before a hearing examiner as set forth in TEC §§ 21.251-21.307 in the same manner as necessary for terminating term and continuing contracts, as well as suspending professional employees without pay. The one exception is personnel reduction caused by financial exigency declared under TEC § 44.011. In this event, the school board has the option of conducting the hearing as it does with term contract nonrenewals. This in effect provides a somewhat less formal procedure than hearings before hearing examiners.

As outlined in Figure 1-1, hearings before hearing examiners assigned by the Commissioner of Education are formal affairs. The hearing must be closed unless the employee wants an open hearing, though the hearing officer may close the hearing "to preserve decorum." At the hearing the employee is entitled to have a representative of the person's choice, hear the evidence including a teacher's appraisal on which the charges are based, cross-examine adverse witnesses, and present evidence. The hearing is conducted like a trial without a jury in a state district court. Unless the employee and the district have agreed that the hearing examiner's decision will be final and nonappealable on all or some issues, the record of the hearing and the recommendation of the hearing examiner are forwarded to the school board or subcommittee of the board before which the parties later have the right to make an oral argument. The hearing officer's conclusions of law including a determination regarding good cause for contract termination or suspension without pay may be adopted, rejected, or changed by the school board or board subcommittee. The employee has a right to appeal the board's decision to the Commissioner of Education. Thereafter, either party may appeal the Commissioner's decision to state district court.

Given the formality of the termination process and the high cost involved, administrators will want to prepare carefully. The central concern is documenting "good cause" to support the decision. Good cause for terminating professional employees is defined in TEC § 21.104 to mean "failure to meet the accepted standards of conduct for the profession as generally recognized and applied in similarly situated school districts in this state."

When the behavior is remediable, the administrator first must (1) give the employee an explicit directive to change or improve his or her conduct or to cease certain behaviors, and (2) provide the employee an opportunity to comply before mid-contract termination will be justified. Isolated instances of misconduct often can and should be handled by less drastic means than termination. The legislature has enacted a mentoring program for classroom teachers who have less than two years of teaching experience in the subject or grade level to which the teacher is assigned (TEC § 21.458). If a school district decides to assign mentors, the mentors must teach in the same schools as the novice teachers, preferably teach the same subject or grade level, and meet qualifications specified by the Commissioner of Education. The qualifications include completion of an approved research-based mentor and induction training program and at least three years of teaching experience with a superior record of improving student performance. Clearly, helping novice teachers improve via mentoring is preferable to either end-of-year contract termination or mid-year contract termination. In the next chapter, we will discuss how to prepare sufficient documentation to support a mid-year termination or suspension without pay and what the implications are for appropriate supervisory style. In Chapter 6, we will elaborate on remediation requirements and when they are required. Suffice it here to say that mid-contract actions are not to be taken lightly.

Once the professional employee has served the one-year probationary contract, the district has three options regarding future employment as outlined in Figure 1-2. School district policy will delineate which of the options is to be used for its professional employees.

> *Option 1.* The district can continue to employ the person who has served fewer than five of the previous eight years of employment in public education on a probationary contract for two additional one-year periods. A fourth year of probationary status is also permissible if the district is uncertain whether to give the employee a continuing or term contract. Following the fourth year, the district either must end the employment or give the employee a term or continuing contract as provided by district policy. TEC § 21.102(c).
>
> *Option 2.* The district can offer the employee a term contract.
>
> *Option 3.* The district can offer the employee a continuing contract.

Under the first option, nonrenewal and termination procedures are the same as those previously discussed for first year probationary employees. However, the procedures are quite different for the term and continuing contract options. We will discuss each in turn.

Term Contract

If hired initially on a term contract (experienced principals and teachers only) or after completing a probationary period, a professional employee may be employed on a term contract for up to five years. Term contract employees are entitled to a copy of their contracts and a copy of the district's employment policies. Term contract employees must be evaluated at least annually. The school board is required to consider the most recent evaluations before making a decision not to renew an employee's term contract, if the evaluations are relevant to the decision. If the evaluations for the current year have not been completed, there is no requirement that they be considered. The Commissioner has ruled that a board's violation of its own policies that themselves go beyond Chapter 21 requirements in the context of contract nonrenewal is not grounds for overturning the decision. The case involved a Dallas I.S.D. school administrator who argued that her nonrenewal was invalid because the board did not consider her most recent evaluations prior to proposing nonrenewal as required by district policy. The Commissioner noted that TEC § 21.203 requires the board to consider the most recent evaluations prior to actually making a nonrenewal decision but not before proposing to do so. There was no evidence that the board failed to do so prior to making the nonrenewal decision.[24]

Current law requires school board policies to contain reasons for contract nonrenewal, and documentation for nonrenewal must support one or more of these reasons. If the reason for nonrenewal is not listed in board policies, the board's nonrenewal decision is not valid.[25] The law specifically states that the term contract does not convey property rights beyond the term of the contract. The same is true for "stopping the roll" of a multi-year term contract that is routinely extended one year every year. Stopping the routine extension does not interfere with a property right that exists during the term of the contract. However, as we will point out later, the employee can always challenge the action as legally impermissible. Thus, it is important to base such action on job-related deficiencies and, of course, follow local district policy in making such a decision.

Under TEC § 21.206-21.209, the key procedural requirements for nonrenewing term contracts include:

- Notice of the proposed nonrenewal at least 10 days before the last instructional day in the school year. The notice must be delivered in the same way as the notice of nonrenewal of probationary contracts described earlier. Failure to give timely notice will result in the employee's being employed in the same professional capacity for the following school year. The Commissioner of Education has advised in several decisions that the reasons for the proposed nonrenewal should be stated specifically so that the employee can prepare to defend against the allegations at the nonrenewal hearing.[26]

- Right to request a hearing not later than 15 days after notification of the proposed nonrenewal. The hearing is to be closed unless the employee requests an open hearing. The hearing may be before the school board or, if the board chooses, before a hearing examiner appointed by the Commissioner of Education. In districts with at least 5,000 students, the board may designate an outside Texas licensed attorney to conduct the hearing on behalf of the school board as its designee. The attorney provides the school board with the record of the hearing and the attorney's recommendation not later than 15 days after the hearing. The board conducts a follow-up hearing at which each party is allowed to make oral arguments. The board may obtain legal advice

Figure 1-2 THREE OPTIONS FOR DISTRICTS AFTER ONE-YEAR PROBATIONARY CONTRACT

Option 1: Probationary Contract Continuation

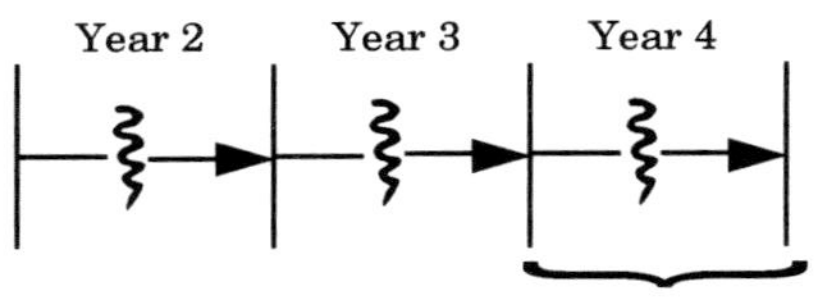

Possible at Board Discretion

Discharge and Termination Procedures Same as for First Year Probationary Contract

> **Option 1 is not available for employees who have worked in a public school for at least 5 of the previous 8 years. TEC § 21.102**

Option 2: Term Contract

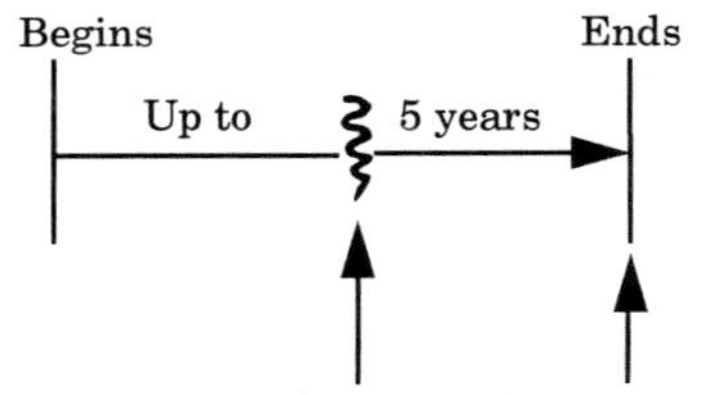

Termination/Suspension Without Pay During Contract*
- Property Right
- Good Cause
- Notice
- Hearing Before Hearing Examiner (board **option for financial exigency**)
- Oral Argument Before School Board
- Right to Appeal

TEC §§ 21.211, 21.251 - 21.307

Nonrenewal At End Of Contract*
- No Property Right (Statute)
- 10-Day Notice
- Hearing Before School Board or Board-**appointed Attorney**** **(board may opt for Commissioner-appointed hearing examiner)**
- Right to Appeal

TEC §§ 21.206 - 21.209, 21.251 - 21.307

Option 3: Continuing Contract

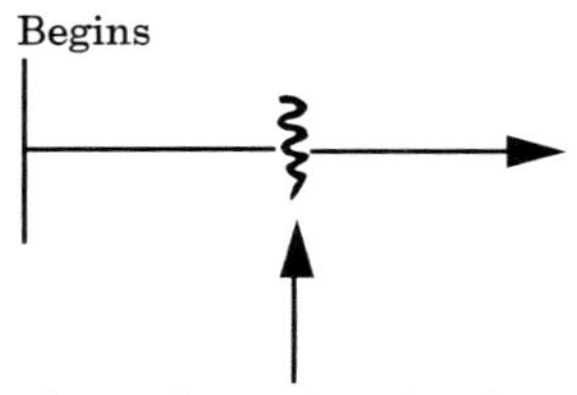

Retirement
Resignation
Death
Termination
Returned to Probationary Contract

Termination/Suspension without Pay During Contract*
- Property Right
- Good Cause**
- Notice of Reasons and Grounds
- Hearing Before Hearing Examiner (board **option for financial exigency**)
- Oral Argument Before School Board
- Right to Appeal

TEC §§ 21.156 - 21.159, 21.251 - 21.307

**At any time for good cause; at end of school year for reduction-in-force.

*In lieu of termination or nonrenewal, may return employee to a probationary contract with employee consent. TEC § 21.106

**Districts with at least 5,000 students

from another attorney at the hearing and may accept, reject, or modify the hearing attorney's recommendation.

- Right to a representative of the employee's choice.
- Right to hear evidence supporting the reason for nonrenewal, to cross-examine witnesses, to present evidence, and to receive notification of the board's decision within 15 days of the hearing.
- Right to appeal to the Commissioner of Education. The Commissioner will not substitute his judgment for the school board unless the decision was arbitrary, capricious, unlawful, or not supported by substantial evidence.

From a documentation standpoint, the task of nonrenewing a nonprobationary term contract employee requires careful preparation but is not as painstaking as necessary for a mid-contract termination where a constitutionally protected property right is at stake. If the school board opts to conduct the nonrenewal hearing rather than turn the matter over to a hearing examiner, political concerns may become prominent, because the board is a political body. Further, if the employee appeals a nonrenewal decision to the Commissioner of Education, it will be important for the school district to show that its decision was based on substantial evidence and was not arbitrary, capricious, or unlawful. In a number of decisions, the Commissioner of Education has ruled that so long as there is "some evidence" to support nonrenewal, the board's decision will not be disturbed. As the Commissioner noted as far back as 1985, substantial evidence means "more than a mere scintilla" but less than the great weight and preponderance of the evidence.[27] The preponderance of evidence standard, however, does apply to the nonrenewal hearing before the school board.[28] This is why, from a documentation standpoint, the school board hearing represents a high hurdle for school administrators. Further, as a political body, the school board will be more comfortable with a nonrenewal decision that is backed by convincing documentation. Thus, sufficient documentation must be assembled to convince the school board and others in the community that the nonrenewal is based on one or more reasons listed in school board policies and that the employee has been treated fairly. As a practical matter, we advise administrators to assemble enough documentation to convince the board that substantial evidence — taken literally — does indeed exist to support the nonrenewal recommendation.

If the Commissioner decides a teacher's contract has been improperly nonrenewed, the Commissioner has the authority under TEC § 21.304 to reinstate the teacher and order back pay and employment benefits. However, the district can avoid reinstatement by paying the teacher one year's salary.

Term contracts may be terminated at any time for good cause or for financial hard times that requires a reduction in personnel. "Good cause" in this section of the Code is not defined but left to the discretion of the school board. The Commissioner has provided some guidance by borrowing a definition used by a Texas court of appeal: "Good cause for discharging an employee is defined as the employee's failure to perform the duties in the scope of employment that a person of ordinary prudence would have done under the same or similar circumstances. An employee's act constitutes good cause for discharge if it is inconsistent with the continued existence of the employer-employee relationship."[29] Illustrations of reasons meeting the "good cause" standard from previous Texas Commissioner of Education decisions include, but are not limited to:

- Conduct potentially harmful to students such as inappropriate sexual contact and innuendo.[30]
- Assault or threats of assault.[31]
- Significant or repeated failure to follow board policy or administrative directives.*[32]
- Misappropriation of public funds. [33]
- Serious violation of the Code of Ethics and Standard Practices for Texas Educators.**[34]
- Violating the privacy rights of students under the federal Family Educational Rights and Privacy Act (FERPA).[35]
- Discovering confidential reprimands on a computer and giving students access to them.[36]

A school board may also suspend a professional employee without pay for a period not to extend beyond the school year pending discharge of the teacher or in lieu of termination. An employee who is not terminated after being suspended without pay is entitled to back pay for the period of suspension. Both procedural due process and good cause are required under state law for suspensions without pay. As noted earlier, mid-contract terminations are not to be taken lightly. The procedures are the same as those discussed above for a mid-year contract termination or suspension without pay of a probationary contract employee. Note that in the case of terminations resulting from a reduction in force, the due process procedures are streamlined by allowing the school board to conduct the hearing rather than the hearing examiner. In lieu of these actions, the school district may return a term contract employee to a probationary contract with the employee's written consent. The employee then must serve a new probationary period as though employed by the district for the first time. Note that the employee's consent must be obtained. In order for consent to be freely given, documentation of deficiencies should be thorough and fair, and should have been communicated to the employee.

As noted in TEC § 21.212, superintendents in Texas must be employed on term contracts but are not required to serve a probationary period. The term contract provisions provide that a majority of the school board may choose not to renew the term contract of a superintendent at the end of the contract period. The board must give the superintendent written notice of proposed nonrenewal and the reasons supporting it not later than 30 days before the last day of the contract term. The school board must have a policy that lists reasons for nonrenewal of the superintendent's contract. Failure to give timely notice results in the superintendent's being reemployed in the same capacity for the next school year. The superintendent has 15 days to request a nonrenewal hearing. Nonrenewal hearing procedures, as well as mid-contract termination procedures, are the same as those for other term contract employees. If financial exigency requires a reduction in personnel, the board may amend the terms of the superintendent's contract.

---

* This reason is often known as "insubordination," an emotionally-laden term that should be avoided where only minor infractions are involved. "Repeated failure to comply with administrative directives" is preferable.

** Because of its importance in setting forth reasons for nonrenewals and terminations in combination with school board policy provisions pertaining to ethical behavior such as DH and DH (Exhibit), we have included the current *Code of Ethics and Standard Practices for Texas Educators* in Appendix A.

Continuing Contract

The continuing contract has been the chosen option for employment of teachers by a number of Texas public school districts. It remains uncertain whether administrators and others classified as "teachers" also can be employed on continuing contracts. TEC § 21.155 does provide that administrators who return to teaching can be employed on continuing contracts.

As noted in Figure 1-2, a professional employee who is given a continuing contract in effect has a property right until the employee retires, resigns, dies, is terminated, or is placed back on a probationary contract. The continuing contract provides the most job security of any of the employment arrangements used in Texas public schools. Accordingly, the documentation burden on the school administrator is heavy for preparing for a negative employment decision. The Commissioner of Education has overturned terminations of continuing contract teachers in the past because the documentation has been deficient. In one case, the Commissioner cautioned administrators against "moving too fast to make a negative employment decision in the face of a *continuing contract* (emphasis in original)."[37] The teacher had been employed for 15 years in the district and had an unblemished record. Based on observations over a one-year period, a new principal sought to place the continuing contract teacher back on a probationary contract, which at the time required the same due process and documentation as terminating the teacher outright. The Commissioner upheld the teacher's appeal.

Statutory provisions unique to the continuing contract include the following:

- Termination for reduction of personnel may only be made at the end of the school year and must be based primarily on teacher appraisals and other criteria determined by the school board.
- Before a professional employee may be terminated, the employee is entitled to written notice that includes the grounds for the action.
- A professional employee who is discharged or suspended without pay for actions relating to the inability or failure to perform assigned duties is entitled upon request to a copy of each evaluation or other written memorandum relating to the fitness or conduct of the employee.

The procedures for terminating a continuing contract employee or suspending the employee without pay until the end of the school year are the same formal proceedings before a certified hearing examiner as described above for a mid-year termination of a probationary contract or a term contract. As with these contracts, if financial exigency triggers a reduction in personnel, the hearing can be conducted by the school board. Given the presence of a property right and the formality of the hearing examiner process for all but reduction in personnel actions, careful preparation once again is essential. In lieu of terminating a continuing contract employee, a school district may return the employee to a probationary contract with the employee's written consent. The employee then must serve a new probationary period as though employed by the district for the first time. The same documentation implications discussed above about returning the term contract employee to probationary contract status apply here as well.

While many districts no longer give continuing contracts, they may have a number of teachers who were given continuing contracts in the past. The district's decision to no longer give continuing contracts does not cancel previously issued continuing contracts. Thus, even though more recent employees are employed on term contracts, some veteran teachers will continue to be employed on continuing contracts. Thus, it is important for administrators to know the type of contract a particular teacher holds and the implications for both documentation and personnel decision making.

Furloughs

Normally, an educator is employed for a minimum of 10 months service constituting 187 days. In 2011, a new law went into effect permitting a district to institute a furlough program providing not more than six days reduction in service and commensurate reduction in salaries during the school year if the Commissioner of Education certifies that the district will receive less state and local funding than was provided in 2010-2011 (TEC §§ 21.4021-21.4022). The professional staff must be involved in the development of the furlough program, and a public meeting must be held at which the school board and administration discuss the district's financial situation. The board must explain how the district intends through the furlough program to limit the number of employees to be discharged or whose contracts will not be renewed. The board's decision on implementing a furlough program is final and may not be appealed. Reduction in an employee's annual salary must be equally distributed over the course of the contract. Other provisions specify that all contract personnel are subject to the same number of furlough days and that educators may not be furloughed on instructional days (a minimum of 180 days of instruction is required under TEC § 25.081 unless the Commissioner approves otherwise because of some calamity). Educators may not use personal, sick, or any other paid leave while on furlough. Furloughs do not constitute either a break in service or a day of service under the Teacher Retirement System of Texas. It is also important to note that another law added in 2011 permits reduction in classroom teacher salaries as a result of financial exigency (TEC § 21.4032). This law provides that if classroom teacher salaries are reduced from the year before, the salaries of school district administrators or other professional employees are to be reduced by an equal percentage.

CONFERENCES, GRIEVANCES, AND TAPE RECORDING

Sometimes administrators are startled to see an employee bring a lawyer or other representative to a conference. How should administrators respond? Employees are entitled to legal representation at any level when presenting a grievance.[38] However, in two decisions, the Texas Commissioner of Education has ruled that employees do not have a similar right during employer-employee conferences or during parent-teacher conferences. In the first decision, a school custodian requested that a representative from his professional association attend a meeting with his supervisor to discuss job complaints. The Commissioner concluded that the right to representation does not extend to employer-employee conferences, including those that are investigatory.[39] The second decision involved a teacher who walked out of a parent-teacher conference, maintaining that she was entitled to legal representation because of possible disciplinary action against her. The Commissioner concluded that "a teacher has no right to representation outside a formal grievance proceeding."[40]

While an employee may not have a legal right to representation, would an administrator be better off allowing the representative to be present? We believe so for most conferences, provided that the representative has been advised not to play an active role in the discussion other than to represent and advise the employee. Excluding a representative, particularly the employee's spouse, only polarizes the employer-employee relationship. Sometimes lawyers or association representatives schooled in confrontational tactics will seek to place the administrator on the defensive or to take over the meeting. If this happens, the representative should be first warned and then if the behavior continues, the meeting should be recessed or adjourned. In particularly sensitive situations, administrators may want to talk first with the school human resources director or school attorney before proceeding.

Public employees have a right to present grievances concerning wages, hours, and conditions of work to their employer. These generally are processed through a series of steps set forth in board policy beginning with informal discussion and ending with a hearing before the school board. Virtually anything is grievable, including evaluations, assignments and reassignments, and even the wording of a letter of reprimand. TEC § 11.171 requires that the school district grievance policy must permit an employee who files a grievance the right to make an audiotape of any meeting or proceeding at which the substance of the grievance is investigated or discussed. This section also specifies that an employee cannot be required to present a grievance to the employee's supervisor if the grievant believes the supervisor has violated the law in the workplace or has unlawfully harassed the employee. Such a grievance is to be presented to another supervisor.

What about audiotaping conferences that don't involve grievances? There are advantages and disadvantages to audiotaping. The advantage is that an accurate record is made of the conversation. The disadvantage is that the presence of the tape recorder tends to inhibit a frank exchange of views. It also preserves slip-of-the tongue remarks. Rather than make an issue of it, we advise administrators to let employees audiotape the conference, provided that the administrator also audiotapes it. That way, the administrator will not have to rely upon the employee's audiotape for an accurate portrayal of what was said. The administrator's audiotape will be the official record of the proceeding.

Is it permissible to videotape a teacher's performance in the classroom over the teacher's objection? Yes. A teacher in the Houston I.S.D. tried unsuccessfully to argue that her personal privacy was violated when the supervisor videotaped her class over her objection. The state appeals court observed that "Appellant has not cited any authority, and we have found none, relating to her claim of 'involuntary videotaping' of her performance as a teacher." The court went on to note that teaching in a public classroom does not fall within the zone of protected privacy, since public school teaching is by its nature open to public view.[41] Under TEC § 26.009 (b), classroom audiotaping or videotaping of students does not require parent permission if used for a purpose related to regular classroom instruction. However, we do not recommend as a matter of sound personnel practice that videotaping or audiotaping routinely be done over a teacher's objection. Videotaping can be an excellent diagnostic tool for the supervisor. To use it effectively, the supervisor should endeavor to convince the teacher of its value and solicit the teacher's cooperation. Only rarely and as a last resort should involuntary videotaping occur.

Can an employee use a tape recorded conversation against a supervisor in a hearing before the school board if the supervisor was not aware that the tape recording was taking place? In Texas, there is no legal prohibition on a person's recording his own conversation. Of course, by implication, the person also tape records the remarks of other parties to the conversation. The admissibility of tape recordings into a court proceeding in this state is governed by certain standards.[42] Whether surreptitious recordings can be introduced into a school board hearing is another matter. While the rules of evidence used in a court of law do not apply to administrative hearings conducted by school officials, the hearing officer or school board president may well conclude that such tape recordings violate principles of fairness. On the other hand, there may be some situations where a tape recording may provide critical evidence necessary to establish truth. Thus, whether or not the recordings should be made a part of the record is a matter to be determined by the hearing officer.

REASSIGNMENT AND RESIGNATION

Reassignment

Does a reassignment require documentation? From a due process standpoint, the answer is usually no. Most Texas administrator and teacher contracts contain a clause indicating that the employee may be assigned and reassigned at the discretion of the superintendent or the superintendent's designee. Further, the position of employment in most contracts is now stated generically: One is employed as a "teacher" or "administrator." Much litigation has occurred in the past regarding whether or not the employee is entitled to notice and a hearing before being reassigned. Federal court decisions have put the matter to rest. No property right is implicated when an employee is reassigned from one position to another as long as the salary associated with the position is not diminished.[43] The one exception may be the superintendent, who occupies a unique position in the district.[44] While no constitutionally recognized property right usually exists in the position to which one is assigned, an individual does possess a property right to receive the designated salary during the life of the contract.

Having said that, we must once again note some caveats. First, if there is no reassignment clause in the contract and the employee is assigned a specific job title, then the employee has a strong claim to having a property right to the position. For example, if Ima Scholar is hired to teach fifth grade at Sterling Middle School and there is no reassignment clause in her contract, then Ms. Scholar likely has a property right in the named position for the duration of the contract. This being the case, her reassignment would be no different from a mid-contract termination — she would be entitled to notice and hearing. And, as noted above, documentation becomes important to establish good cause for the change in employment status. Thus, it is important to make sure that employment positions are listed in generic terms.

Second, the law requires that term contract employees who are not nonrenewed must be employed "in the same professional capacity" in future years. The Texas Commissioner of Education has interpreted this clause to give considerable flexibility to administrators to reassign personnel to similar professional positions (hence the generic "administrator" and "teacher" employment categories spelled out in contracts). However, in a 1993 decision upholding the reassignment of a science supervisor to an assistant high school principalship, the Commissioner cautioned that "if taken to extremes, this tactic would be against public policy as expressed in the Term Contract Nonrenewal Act [this provision is now found in TEC § 21.206(b)]."[45] In 1985 the Commissioner noted that it would not be appropriate to place an administrator in a teacher's position, a counselor in the position of nurse, or a nurse in the position of librarian. "In other instances, the validity of a particular placement might not be so clear. For example, a placement might be to another position within the same professional capacity (e.g., administrator), but nevertheless be invalid (e.g., from superintendent to assistant elementary principal). Factors to be considered in determining the validity of such a placement include, but are not necessarily limited to, differences in authority, duties, and salary."[46]

Third, employees may not be reassigned for impermissible reasons. As will be explained in the final section of this chapter, impermissible reasons include illegal discrimination and retaliation for the exercise of constitutional rights.

A Case-In-Point

In *Fife v. Curlee* a secretary who was employed on an at-will basis challenged her reassignment to a job duplicating and laminating documents after she removed her daughter from public school and enrolled the child in an all-white private school. Since the U.S. Supreme Court long ago recognized the constitutional right of all parents to choose a nonpublic school for their children, the U. S. Court of Appeals for the Fifth Circuit held that the reassignment amounted to retaliation for the exercise of a constitutional right. The appeals court sent the case back to the trial court for a determination of appropriate remedies.[47]

Employees always have a right to challenge the motives behind their reassignments by pursuing a grievance or by filing employment discrimination claims and lawsuits. Thus, it behooves administrators to have sufficient documentation of job-related deficiencies to provide an acceptable explanation for a reassignment.

Resignation

The answer to every school administrator's prayer in making difficult personnel decisions is a voluntary resignation. Resignations work to everyone's benefit. For the school district, they eliminate costly due process procedures. For the employee, they help pave the way to a new position. For both the administrator and the employee, they avoid the emotional toll of an adversary proceeding.

For each of the three employment options illustrated in Figure 1-2, Texas law provides that professional employees may resign without penalty at the end of the school year by filing a written resignation with the school board or its designee no later than 45 days before the first day of instruction of the following year or at any other time with the school district's permission (TEC §§ 21.105, 21.160, and 21.210). Under these provisions, a written resignation mailed by certified or registered mail to the school board president or the board's designee at the school district's post office address is considered filed at the time of mailing. This means that it is self-executing and no acceptance is required. As the Commissioner has noted, "Because acceptance is automatic, once filed, a resignation cannot be withdrawn before acceptance."[48] Contract sanctions may be imposed by the State Board for Educator Certification for employees who do not comply with these statutory resignation provisions.

Here are some simple recommendations for handling employee resignations other than those falling within the 45-day self-executing period noted above:

- Consider having a witness present when discussing the option of resigning. A witness will help curtail employee claims later on that you threatened recrimination if the employee did not resign.
- If the employee wants to bring an attorney or other representative to the meeting, consult with the human resources director or superintendent regarding district practice. Since you are interested in treating the employee fairly, having a representative present should not compromise the value of the

meeting, provided that you make clear to the representative that he or she is there at your discretion and that his or her role is to advise and represent the employee. The representative should not be allowed to question you or attempt to take over the meeting. In particularly sensitive cases, the school attorney should be consulted.

- Advise the employee about applicable school district grievance and due process procedures. Full disclosure of the rights the employee will relinquish by resigning will help demonstrate your commitment to fair play.
- Avoid coercion in discussing resignation. In some cases, you may be acting more like a counselor than an administrator as you help the employee weigh the pros and cons of resigning. On the other hand, do not be afraid to tell the employee in a non-threatening manner that you are sincere about following through on your recommendation of contract nonrenewal or termination. If you have done a careful job of documentation, the employee will be well aware of the basis for your intentions and will know that you are serious. **NOTE**: If you are considering "sweetening the pot" by telling the employee you will not formalize your termination recommendation or will write a favorable recommendation if the employee resigns, we strongly advise that you consult the human resources director or school district attorney first for the reasons described below.
- Require that the employee submit a written resignation by a certain date. That way, you will keep your own options open. For example, if the 10-day notice of proposed nonrenewal for a term contract employee is near, you can avoid holding off past the date in hopes the employee might submit a resignation.
- Have the employee submit the resignation to a person authorized to receive it and to acknowledge its receipt. Doing so will avoid a time lag between the submission of the resignation and its official acceptance, in case the employee has second thoughts and decides to withdraw the resignation.

In addition, State Board for Educator Certification (SBEC) rules in effect in 2011 require a school superintendent or director of an open enrollment charter school, private school, regional service center, or shared services arrangement to report within seven days to TEA staff whenever a certified employee resigns or is terminated in the face of evidence of misconduct with students, illegal drug involvement, illegal use of school property or funds, alteration of a certificate, or commission of a crime on school property or at a school event (19 Tex. Admin. Code § 249.14(d)). Before accepting the employee's resignation, the school administrator must notify the employee of this requirement and of the possibility that sanctions may be taken against the employee's certificate. It should be noted that employees may be terminated for failure to disclose to SBEC or the district, open-enrollment charter school, private school, regional education service center, or shared services arrangement their conviction of a felony or misdemeanor involving moral turpitude (TEC § 22.085).

Depending upon the situation, a resignation can be the least painful way to resolve a difficult employment situation. However bullying an employee into resigning or making the job so difficult that the employee gets disgruntled and quits could work against you. The employee may decide to file a grievance or a lawsuit claiming the resignation was forced. In 1995 the Commissioner of Education was faced with appeals by a teacher and by a counselor who contended that their resignations resulted from duress, undue influence, or misrepresentation by the principal.[49] *Duress* is evident when an administrator (1) threatens to do something he has no legal right to do and (2) engages in fraud or deception that undermines the free will of the employee. *Undue influence* occurs when the employee's free will is so compromised that the employee's decision reflects the choice of the administrator who is exerting the influence. *Misrepresentation* involves a material misstatement that (1) the administrator either knew to be false or made without knowledge of its truth and (2) served as the basis for the employee's decision. Because the facts in the cases established that both the teacher and counselor had resigned of their own free will in connection with the falsification of a leave form, the Commissioner rejected their appeals. In the case involving the school counselor, the counselor contended that the principal had threatened to revoke her certificate, terminate her, or put unfavorable comments in her file if she did not resign. Based on the testimony at the hearing, however, the Commissioner chose not to believe the counselor. Had a witness been present when resignation was discussed, the matter may never have come up.[50]

At the extreme, a forced resignation may constitute "constructive discharge," rendering the employer liable for the illegal conduct leading to the discharge. A constructive discharge occurs when administrators make the job so uncomfortable that the reasonable employee has no choice but to resign.[51] While the employee's burden to prove such a case is demanding, constructive discharge cases increasingly are being litigated in federal courts. The second federal appeals court decision discussed on p. 1-1 involving the 65-year-old teacher whose classroom was visited repeatedly by administrators is a good example of a constructive discharge case.

As we noted earlier, an offer of resignation becomes official when it is submitted to the person or persons designated in district policy to receive it and that person acknowledges its acceptance. Normally, this is the superintendent and/or the human resources director. Occasionally, an employee will have second thoughts after submitting a resignation and will attempt to rescind it. Such was the case with a special education teacher in the San Benito Consolidated Independent School District in 1994.[52] After her hand-delivered resignation was forwarded to the superintendent, the superintendent sent the teacher a letter accepting the resignation. The next day, the teacher hand-delivered a letter to the superintendent rescinding the resignation. But it was too late. The so-called "mailbox rule" had gone into effect. Under the "mailbox rule," the superintendent's acceptance of the teacher's resignation became effective as soon as he deposited the acceptance letter in the mailbox. When the superintendent accepted the resignation by sending his letter of acknowledgement, a new agreement between the teacher and the district to sever the employment relation came into existence. Until this time, the teacher was free to revoke her resignation decision. In Texas, the "mailbox rule" does not apply unless the party submitting the resignation expressly or impliedly authorizes the use of the postal system for its acceptance. The teacher had not used the mail system to send her letter of resignation or her subsequent revocation. However, she had acknowledged that the mail system was a proper form for communication, because in her resignation letter she had implicitly authorized the superintendent to communicate through the mails by requesting that he forward her final check to her home address.

In a 2005 decision, the Commissioner elaborated on the mailbox rule.[53] The school district argued that the Commissioner didn't have jurisdiction over the case, because the teacher had not filed an appeal within the requisite 20 days after receiving notice of contract nonrenewal from the district. The district asserted that the time line began when the notification was mailed on May 5, 2005. However, the teacher didn't receive the notice until May 18. If the notice is considered given on May 5 when mailed, the teacher had exceeded the 20 days by not filing her appeal until June 2. The Commissioner noted an exception to the mailbox rule in the Texas Rule of Civil Procedure. If notice is not received within three days of deposit in the mail, then a court may extend the time line. In this case, because the notification was not received within three days of mailing, the time line for the teacher to file her appeal should have been extended to June 7, 20 days after she actually received the notice on May 18. Because the teacher filed her appeal on June 2, the time line to appeal was met. In making this decision, the Commissioner assumed that the Texas Rule of Civil Procedure mailbox rules apply to nonrenewal appeals filed before his office. This decision illustrates how tricky the procedures involving resignations are. For this reason, school administrators once again are advised to work closely with the school district's human resources office.

In another decision, the Commissioner ruled in favor of a teacher who resigned, then withdrew the offer of resignation before receiving notice of its acceptance.[54] The superintendent's designee dated the acceptance letter several days after receiving the teacher's hand-delivered letter of resignation. However, the teacher didn't receive that letter until after she formally rescinded her resignation. The envelope containing the acceptance letter had a postage meter marking showing that it was mailed after the teacher had submitted her rescission. What mattered in this case was not the date on the acceptance letter but the postage meter date on the envelope containing it. The Commissioner ordered the district to pay the teacher the compensation she should have received for the school year.

A WORD ABOUT EMPLOYEE REFERENCES

Administrators are often uncertain how to respond to inquiries about former employees. They are concerned that a frank reply in writing or over the telephone might subject them to a defamation lawsuit. The law conveys a qualified privilege to employers with respect to employee decision making. Article 5206 of Texas Civil Statutes states that "Any written statement of cause of discharge, if true, when made by such agent, company or corporation, shall never be used as the cause of an action for libel, either civil or criminal, against the agent, company or corporation furnishing same." TEC §22.0511(a) shields school professional employees from liability from damage suits in most situations. Section 101.051 of the Texas Civil Practices and Remedies Code does the same for school districts. In 1991 a Texas appeals court upheld the grant of immunity for a school administrator under TEC § 22.0511(a) [then codified at TEC § 21.912(b)], noting that "a letter of reference written by a professional supervisor of a public school merely expressing his professional *opinion* on an employee's work performance under his supervision is an act within the scope of the employee's duties with the school district and is, consequently, not subject to libel action by virtue of section 21.912(b) unless such statements are false statement of *fact* or are libelous *per se*."[55] In 1999, the Texas Legislature added a provision to the Labor Code shielding employers from civil liability or damages for providing job performance information to prospective employers about current or former employees, unless at the time of disclosure the employer knew the information to be false or made the disclosure with malice or with reckless disregard of its truth or falsity (Texas Labor Code § 103.004). Job performance information can encompass attendance, attitudes, effort, knowledge, behaviors, and skills.

Of course, a former employee can always file a defamation lawsuit against an administrator, in which case the latter will be able to assert the various immunity defenses in court. The best protection against defamation lawsuits in the context of employment references is (1) to stick to the truth and (2) to secure the employee's permission to release the information before the employee leaves the district by signing a reference release form. An employee who authorizes a former employer to release employment information to prospective employers is less likely to file a lawsuit later on.

AVOIDING IMPERMISSIBLE REASONS FOR EMPLOYMENT DECISIONS

On several occasions we have mentioned the importance of basing employment decisions on reasons that are legitimately related to the interests of the school district and to job-related behavior. For the most part, these reasons will be found in board policies. School administrators must avoid basing negative employment decisions on impermissible reasons. Impermissible reasons generally fall into two categories: (1) retaliation for the exercise of constitutional rights and (2) illegal discrimination. We briefly discuss both in turn. A detailed discussion can be found in Walsh, Kemerer & Maniotis's *The Educator's Guide to Texas School Law,* 7th ed. and its 2012 Supplement.

Constitutionally protected conduct encompasses a number of activities including, but not limited to:

- Speaking on matters of public concern[56]
- Sending a child to a private school[57]
- Participating in the activities of a political party[58]
- Participating in unions and professional associations[59]
- Having a child out of wedlock[60]

Employees often allege that one or more of these rights are implicated in negative employment decisions. Administrators should be careful that the documentation about the employee does not support such allegations.

Free Speech

The most prevalent constitutional challenge to a nonrenewal or termination is retaliation for the exercise of free speech. Public employees, including those who are employed at-will, enjoy broad protection for expression in their role as citizens on matters of public interest, so long as (1) the statements are not made recklessly or with knowledge of their falsity, and (2) the statements do not impede either the school's functioning or the employee's performance. Comments made in the employee's role as a citizen that concern the community interest are constitutionally protected under the First Amendment to the U.S. Constitution. These might include a speech made to the PTA about deficiencies in the bilingual education program, a presentation to the school board about alleged discriminatory hiring practices by principals, or statements on a radio talk show about a lack of student discipline at the high school. However, if the employee makes the same comments while on the job, there is no constitutional protection.[61] Thus, a school human resources director who speaks out to the superintendent's cabinet about discriminatory hiring practices of a school principal may not be entitled to constitutional protection. Employee expression that relates to the employee's own working conditions also may not be constitutionally protected.[62] We will explore communication issues in more detail in Chapter 5 in conjunction with discussing new issues emerging with PDAS Domain V on professional communication.

Unfortunately, it is often difficult to distinguish an employee's expression as a citizen on matters of public concern from expression as an employee concerning working conditions. Most educators, school board members, and citizens do not understand the difference. Consequently, any employment decision even partially related to free speech is likely to trigger an outcry about censorship and curtailment of protected rights. For this reason, it is usually best to try to avoid First Amendment issues altogether in documentation.

If a disgruntled employee produces evidence that the negative employment decision was made at least partially in retaliation for the exercise of protected rights, will the school likely lose? Not necessarily. Under a 1977 U.S. Supreme Court decision, if the administration *can document other legitimate reasons justifying the employment decision that are unrelated to the employee's exercise of the constitutional right,* then the fact that a constitutional right was substantially implicated may not make any difference.[63]

Academic Freedom

A final consideration involving protected rights of expression concerns a teacher's right to academic freedom in the classroom. How much academic freedom does a public school teacher have in that setting? Despite frequent assertions to the contrary, the law protects that right only minimally. In 1980, the Fifth Circuit held that teachers do have a right to lead classroom discussion on controversial topics and cannot be penalized for doing so unless the teacher's effectiveness to teach has been undermined.[64] However, this precedent would not support a teacher who deviates from the established curriculum.[65]

While classroom discussion is protected under the rubric of academic freedom, other teacher activities are not. Included among them are the awarding of grades, the use of teaching techniques not approved by the school board, and the use of profanity for motivational purposes.[66]

Federal Civil Rights

Employment decisions that violate the nation's civil rights laws are also impermissible. Here in capsule form are the civil rights laws most prominently related to employment:

> *Race.* 42 U.S.C. Section 1981 accords all persons the right to make and enforce contracts free from racial discrimination. The statute also prohibits discrimination occurring during the contract term. Penalties include both injunctive relief and compensatory damages.
>
> *Race, Religion, Sex.* Title VII of the 1964 Civil Rights Act prohibits discrimination on the basis of race, color, religion, sex, or national origin in all aspects of public and private employment. In addition to equitable relief such as back pay and reinstatement, the law allows monetary damages for intentional discrimination.
>
> *Disabilities.* The Americans with Disabilities Act of 1990 (ADA) accords persons with disabilities meaningful access to the programs of a public or private entity. In conjunction with Section 504 of the Rehabilitation Act of 1973, the ADA prohibits employment discrimination against persons with disabilities and requires employers to make reasonable accommodation for persons with disabilities, once it is determined the person can perform the job. Penalties are

similar to those for Title VII.

Age. The Age Discrimination in Employment Act (ADEA) prohibits discrimination in employment against employees age 40 and over unless there is a bona fide occupational qualification reasonably necessary to carry out job responsibilities (e.g., airline pilots). Penalties are similar to those for Title VII.

Administrators need to be sensitive to the protections given employees under these and other federal statutes and should avoid inadvertently documenting behavior that is protected by statutory provisions. Thus, for example, it would not be appropriate to document that a teacher's age was a major reason for removing the teacher as the cheerleader sponsor. Employees who advocate on behalf of other employees whose rights have been violated under these laws also are likely to be protected from retaliation.[67]

Texas Law

Finally, some employee activities are protected under Texas law and cannot serve as the basis for a negative employment decision. As we discussed earlier, public employees have the right to file a grievance and to be free from retaliation for doing so. Three other important activities protected by state law are (1) refusal to undertake an illegal act, (2) the reporting of suspected wrongdoing ("whistle-blowing"), and (3) the filing of workers' compensation claims. The first situation might occur when an employee refuses to undertake repairs to the superintendent's house or refuses to bury toxic chemicals on the school premises. The Texas Supreme Court has ruled that such refusal cannot be the basis for a termination.[68]

The Texas Whistleblower Act protects an employee from adverse employment action for reporting in good faith a violation or suspected violation of law to appropriate law enforcement personnel or to someone within the school district that the employee believes is responsible for enforcing the law allegedly violated (Texas Government Code § 554.002). School administrators must avoid the temptation to label these employees "malcontents" or "disloyal team players" or to retaliate against them because of the report.

One important provision of the workers' compensation statute prohibits employers from retaliating against an employee who files a compensation claim. Thus, school administrators must exercise great caution in making negative employment decisions about employees who do so.

SUMMARY

In this chapter, we have sketched the major features of the legal framework within which documentation takes place. It should be clear that documentation is significantly influenced by federal and state statutes, Texas Commissioner of Education decisions, and court rulings. When all is said and done, the best advice is to know employment law and to follow the Golden Rule. That advice, coupled with common sense, will go a long way to assure that your employment decisions are fair and will be upheld if challenged. Now we turn in the next chapter to examine the basic principles of documentation and how they apply in the context of both professional and auxiliary school personnel.

REFERENCES

1. *Lloyd v. Georgia Gulf Corp.*, 961 F.2d 1190 (5th Cir. 1992).
2. *Lee v. Rapid City Area School District No. 51-4,* 981 F.2d 316 (8th Cir. 1992).
3. *Peaster I.S.D. v. Glodfelty,* 63 S.W.3d 1(Tex. App. - Fort Worth, 2001).
4. *Dunlap v. Breckenridge I.S.D.*, Dkt. No. 34-R1-692 (Comm'r Educ. 1996). In reaching the decision, the Commissioner referenced a well-known prior decision in which he had noted that adverse community or parental "perceptions" is an illegal reason for contract nonrenewal when the employee has excellent evaluations. Noting that when the evidence at the local hearing does not support the specific reason given the teacher for the nonrenewal, the Commissioner may substitute his judgment for that the school board and decide in favor of the teacher. *Seifert v. Lingleville I.S.D.*, Dkt. No. 174-R1a-782 (Comm'r Educ. 1983). Later, the Texas Supreme Court affirmed the Commissioner's conclusion but on the grounds that "community feeling of incompetence" was not one of the reasons listed in the district's policies for contract nonrenewal. Since the law requires that districts must provide employees with the reasons for the proposed contract nonrenewal, Seifert had not received fair notice. The high court avoided considering whether "community feeling of incompetence" might be a valid reason to support contract nonrenewal. *Seifert v. Lingleville I.S.D.*, 692 S.W.2d 461 (Tex. 1985).
5. *Carnot v. North East I.S.D.*, Dkt. No. 066-R1-605 (Comm'r Educ. 2005).
6. *Doe v. Taylor I.S.D.*, 15 F.3d 443 (5th Cir. 1994) (en banc), *cert. denied sub nom Caplinger v. Doe,* 113 U.S. 980 (1993). The Fifth Circuit held that schoolchildren have a liberty right in their bodily integrity that is protected by the due process clause of the 14th Amendment and that physical sexual abuse by a school employee violates that right. The court also held that school officials can be liable for supervisory failures that result in the molestation of a student if those failures manifest deliberate indifference to the student's constitutional rights. In order for supervisory school officials to be held liable for a subordinate's violation of an elementary or secondary school student's constitutional right to bodily integrity in sexual abuse cases, it must be established that:

   1. The school official learned of facts or a pattern of inappropriate sexual behavior by a subordinate pointing plainly toward the conclusion that the subordinate was sexually abusing the student,

   2. The school official demonstrated deliberate indifference toward the constitutional rights of the student by failing to take action that was obviously necessary to prevent or stop the abuse, and

   3. Such failure caused a constitutional injury to the child.
7. *Solis v. Pasadena Independent School District,* Dkt. No. 003-R10-900 (Comm'r Educ. 2002).
8. *Webster v. Alief I.S.D.*, Dkt. No. 288-R3-789 (Comm'r Educ. 1991).
9. *Abbott v. North East I.S.D.*, 212 S.W.2d 364 (Tex. App. – Austin, 2006).
10. See, for example, *Etzel v. Galveston I.S.D.,* Dkt. No. 231-R9-885 (Comm'r Educ. 1987); *Falvey v. Alief I.S.D.*, Dkt. No. 113-R3-1185 (Comm'r Educ. 1987).
11. *Navarro v. Ysleta I.S.D.*, Dkt. No. 007-R8-988 (Comm'r Educ. 1994). In this case, the Commissioner originally had issued a decision that a school board is not the appropriate body to second-guess the conclusions of a trained appraiser. The decision was appealed to a state district court judge in Austin who ruled that the school may do so if the appraiser's decision was "clearly erroneous or an abuse of discretion." The judge sent the case back to the Commissioner for reconsideration. Using this standard, the Commissioner ruled that the Ysleta school board had no basis for overruling the assistant principal's denial of credit to a teacher on an evaluation. The Commissioner granted the assistant principal's appeal.
12. *Sitzler v. Babers,* Dkt. No. 092-PPC-1191 (Comm'r Educ. 1992). In 1996 the Commissioner overturned the decision of a school board to nonrenew the contract of a probationary teacher who complained through memos and the school's grievance system about various working conditions. The school board president had sent a letter to the teacher in which he indicated that her filing a number of grievances was a factor in the nonrenewal decision. The Commissioner concluded that the school board failed to produce evidence to rebut the teacher's claim of retaliation for filing grievances. *Ostroff v. Manor I.S.D.,* Dkt. No. 320-R2-694 (Comm'r Educ. 1996).
13. *Anderson v. Tyler I.S.D.*, Dkt. No. 048-R1-0508 (Comm'r Educ. 2008). The Commissioner also has observed that while third-party documentation cannot be used in the appraisal process if it has not been shared with the teacher in a timely manner, the appraisal rules do not prohibit the use of such documentation for other purposes. *Taylor v. Wichita Falls I.S.D.,* Dkt. No. 069-R10-601 (Comm'r Educ. 2002).
14. *Garza v. McAllen I.S.D.*, Dkt. No. 018-R10-1106 (Comm'r Educ. 2009).
15. *Goodfriend v. Houston I.S.D.,* Dkt. No. 079-R2-703 (Comm'r Educ. 2003).
16. *Hall v. North East I.S.D.*, Dkt. No. 019-R10-1106 (Comm'r Educ. 2008).
17. *Hall v. North East I.S.D.*, DKt. No. 019-R10-1106 Comm'r Educ. 2008).
18. *Federal Express v. Dutschmann,* 846 S.W.2d 282 (Tex. 1993); *Cook v. Dayton I.S.D.*, Dkt. No. 133-R8-189 (Comm'r Educ. 1993); *Strother v. Columbia-Brazoria I.S.D.,* 839 F.Supp. 459 (S.D. Tex. 1993), aff'd without opinion, 32 F.3d 565 (5th Cir. 1994).
19. *Montgomery County Hospital District v. Brown,* 965 S.W.2d 501 (Tex. 1998). In *Brown* the Texas Supreme

Court ruled that at-will status cannot be altered by oral assurances of discharge for good cause only, absent a definite stated intent to be bound not to terminate the employee except under specific circumstances and absent an agreement on what would encompass good reason or good cause for termination.
20. *Salinas v. Roma I.S.D.,* Dkt. No. 058-R3-1196 (Comm'r Educ. 1997).
21. *Houston v. Nelson,* 147 S.W.3d 589 (Tex. App. – Corpus Christi-Edinburg, 2004).
22. *Ferguson v. Thomas,* 430 F.2d 852 (5th Cir. 1970).
23. *Young v. Lipan I.S.D.,* Dkt. No. 102-R1-496 (Comm'r Educ. 1996).
24. *Strickland v. Dallas I.S.D.,* Dkt. No. 075-R1-0808 (Comm'r Educ. 2008).
25. *King v. Big Sandy I.S.D.,* Dkt. No. 006-R1-501 (Comm'r Educ. 2001).
26. *Lowry v. Brookesmith I.S.D.,* Dkt. No. 054-R1-0509 (Comm'r Educ. 2009). In a 1998 decision the Commissioner commented that a notice of proposed nonrenewal worded to say "Deficiencies as pointed out in observation reports, appraisals or evaluations, supplemental memoranda, or other communications" is too broad to be very meaningful. *Kopycinski v. Fort Bend I.S.D.,* Dkt. No. 111-R1-598 (Comm'r Educ. 1998).
27. *Heger v. Frisco I.S.D.,* Dkt. No. 120-R1a-584 (1985).
28. *Rodgers v. Edinburg Consolidated I.S.D.,* Dkt. No. 171-R1-898 (Comm'r Educ. 1998). See also *Whitaker v. Moses,* 40 S.W.3d 176 (Tex. App. - Texarkana 2001).
29. *Tave v. Dallas I.S.D.,* 067-R2-501 (Comm'r Educ. 2001).
30. *Taplin v. Fort Worth I.S.D.,* Dkt. No. 276-R2-887 (Comm'r Educ. 1989); *Brown v. Crosby I.S.D.,* Dkt. No. 181-R2-781 (Comm'r Educ. 1983).
31. *Martinez v. Crosbyton I.S.D.,* Dkt. No. 079-R2-284 (Comm'r Educ. 1985); *Mitchell v. Pewitt I.S.D.,* Dkt. No. 186-R2-785 (Comm'r Educ. 1987).
32. *Jones v. Northside I.S.D.,* Dkt. No. 015-R2-1084 (Comm'r Educ. 1987).
33. *Brosette v. Wilmer-Hutchins I.S.D.,* Dkt. No. 190-R2-782 (Comm'r Educ. 1984).
34. *Green v. Irving I.S.D.,* Dkt. No. 042-R2-1086 (Comm'r Educ. 1988).
35. *McGilvray v. Boyd I.S.D.,* Dkt. No. 185-R2-597 (Comm'r Educ. 1996).
36. *Tave v. Dallas I.S.D.,* Dkt. No. 067-R2-501 (Comm'r Educ. 2001).
37. *Tyler v. Galveston I.S.D.,* Dkt. No. 132-R1b-783 (Comm'r Educ. 1984). See also *Richter v. Northside I.S.D.,* Dkt. No. 215-R3-885 (Comm'r Educ. 1986) and *McRuiz v. Cleburne I.S.D.,* Dkt. No. 047-R2-1087 (Comm'r Educ. 1990).
38. *Lubbock Professional Firefighters v. City of Lubbock,* 742 S.W.2d 413 (Tex. App. - Amarillo 1987).
39. *Arce v. Ysleta I.S.D.,* Dkt. No. 317-R8-692 (Comm'r Educ. 1994).
40. *Thrower v. Arlington I.S.D.,* Dkt. No. 190-R10-790 (Comm'r Educ. 1991).
41. *Roberts v. Houston I.S.D.,* 788 S.W.2d 107 (Tex. App. – Houston [1st Dist.] 1990, writ denied).
42. *Seymour v. Gillespie,* 608 S.W.2d 897 (Tex. 1990).
43. A leading case is *Jett v. Dallas I.S.D.,* 789 F.2d 748 (5th Cir.), *aff'd in part,* 109 S.Ct. 2702 (1989). Further, it is not necessary to advance reasons for the reassignment unless required by district policy or requested to do so during an appeal process. *Schneider et al. v. San Antonio I.S.D.,* Dkt. No. 356-R10-794 (Comm'r Educ. 1997).
44. *Briggs v. Crystal City I.S.D.,* 486 S.W.2d 829 (Tex. Civ. App. - Beaumont 1972, *writ ref'd n.r.e.*).
45. *Carpenter v. Wichita Falls I.S.D.,* Dtk. No. 247-R3-491 (Comm'r Educ. 1993).
46. *Barich v. San Felipe-Del Rio I.S.D.,* Dkt. No. 117-R1a-484 (Comm'r Educ. 1985). See also *Young v. Leggett I.S.D.,* Dkt. No. 175-R3-898 (Comm'r Educ. 1999) and *Ramos v. El Paso I.S.D.,* Dkt. No. 002-R10-900 (Comm'r Educ. 2002).
47. *Fyfe v. Curlee,* 902 F.2d 401 (5th Cir. 1990).
48. *Fantroy v. Dallas I.S.D.,* Dkt. No. 034-R8-0206 (Comm'r Educ. 2009).
49. *Lazenby v. Spring Branch I.S.D.,* Dkt. No. 144-R8-193 (Comm'r Educ. 1995); *Hysell v. Spring Branch I.S.D.,* Dkt. No. 113-R8-1292 (Comm'r Educ. 1995).
50. *Hysell v. Spring Branch I.S.D.,* Dkt. No. 113-R8-1292 (Comm'r Educ. 1995).
51. *Woods v. Sheldon I.S.D.,* 232 Fed.Appx. 385 (5th Cir. 2007). In this unreported ruling, the Fifth Circuit identified six possible bases for a constructive discharge claim related to forced resignation, retirement, or employment on less favorable terms: (1) a demotion; (2) a salary reduction; (3) a reduction in job responsibilities; (4) reassignment to menial work; (5) reassignment to work under a younger supervisor; or (6) badgering, harassment, or humiliation by the employer. An unreported ruling means that it has no value as judicial precedent but is instructive. In the documentation context, the lesson from this ruling is to have job-related deficiencies clearly documented and revealed to the employee so that any negative decision is based on them.
52. *Cantu v. Central Education Agency,* 884 S.W.2d 565 (Tex. App.- Austin 1994).
53. *Carnot v. North East I.S.D.,* Dkt. No. 066-R1-605 (Comm'r Educ. 2005).
54. *Chilton v. Alvin I.S.D.,* Dkt. No. 031-R10-0107 (Comm'r Educ. 2009).
55. *Hammond v. Katy I.S.D.,* 821 S.W.2d 174 (Tex. App. - Houston [14th Dist.] 1991).
56. *Pickering v. Board of Education,* 391 U.S. 563 (1968).

57. *Pierce v. Society of Sisters,* 268 U.S. 510 (1925).
58. *Alaniz v. San Isidro I.S.D.,* 742 F.2d 207 (5th Cir. 1984).
59. *Professional Association of College Administrators v. El Paso Community College.* 730 F.2d 258 (5th Cir. 1984).
60. *Avery v. Homewood City Board of Education,* 674 F.2d 337 (5th Cir. 1982)
61. *Garcetti v. Ceballos,* 126 S.Ct. 1951 (2006). The U.S. Supreme Court did recognize in this 5-to-4 ruling that speech related to scholarship or teaching made on the job may be constitutionally protected. However, it is likely that the majority was referring to academic freedom at the postsecondary level, because academic freedom for public school teachers enjoys little constitutional protection. The majority also recognized that a public employer cannot make job descriptions so broad that everything employees say falls within official duties.
62. *Connick v. Myers,* 461 U.S. 138 (1983). It is important to note that under Article I, § 8 of the Texas Constitution, free speech rights appear to be broader than under the U. S. Constitution. The Texas Supreme Court ruled as much in *Davenport v. Garcia,* 834 S.W.2d 4 (Tex. 1992). That ruling convinced a state district court in an appeal from a decision by the Texas Commissioner of Education to conclude that under Article I, § 8, even if speech is not on a topic of public concern, such speech is protected if it was invited, solicited, or encouraged by a governmental employer. Upon rehearing, the Commissioner applied this rule of law to the termination action involving an at-will employee and concluded that because the employee's speech was not solicited, his job was appropriately terminated. *Rymkus v. Spring Branch I.S.D.,* Dkt. No. 058-R8-1091 (Comm'r Educ. 1996).
63. *Mt. Healthy City School District v. Doyle,* 429 U.S. 274, (1977).
64. *Kingsville I.S.D. v. Cooper,* 611 F.2d 1109 (5th Cir. 1980). In *Whalen v. Rock Springs I.S.D.,* the Texas Commissioner of Education found that a teacher who had led a graphic and prolonged classroom discussion on sexual topics and techniques in a science class had abused the right and thus the teacher's contract was appropriately terminated. Dkt. No. 065-R1b-284 (Comm'r Educ. 1985).
65. In *Kirkland v. Northside I.S.D.,* 890 F.2d 794 (5th Cir. 1989), the Fifth Circuit refused to extend academic freedom to encompass a teacher's selection of an unapproved supplemental reading list. In several decisions, the Texas Commissioner of Education has ruled against teachers who cited academic freedom in deviating from the established curriculum. One decision involved the nonrenewal of a teacher who used sexually explicit plays in her drama class and had students read portions of books dealing with sexually explicit language, despite directives to the contrary from the principal. The Commissioner noted that when classroom expression is related to the school curriculum, "a district may impose restrictions on the expression so long as they are reasonably related to legitimate pedagogical concerns." The Commissioner noted that instructing students "is part of the school's curriculum and therefore constitute matters of private concern." *Hammonds v. Mt. Pleasant I.S.D.,* Dkt. No. 322-R1-793 (Comm'r Educ. 1995). This decision appears at odds with the Fifth Circuit's decision in *Kingsville I.S.D. v. Cooper.*
66. *Hillis v. Stephen F. Austin State University,* 665 F.2d 547 (5th Cir. 1982) (no academic freedom right to award a grade); *Kirkland v. Northside I.S.D.,* 890 F.2d 794 (5th Cir. 1989) (no academic freedom right to select an unapproved supplemental reading list); *Martin v. Parrish,* 805 F.2d 583 (5th Cir. 1986) (no academic freedom right to use profanity in the classroom as a motivational technique).
67. *Jackson v. Birmingham Board of Education,* 544 U.S. 167 (2005).
68. *Sabine Pilots Services, Inc. v. Hauck,* 687 S.W.2d 733 (Tex. 1985).

CHAPTER TWO: PRINCIPLES OF DOCUMENTATION

WHEN TO DOCUMENT

Surprising though it may seem, not every employee deficiency should be formally documented. Not only is documentation time-consuming, it also has a tendency to polarize the supervisor-employee relationship. Consider the teacher who learns for the first time from an e-mail message that he has failed to follow the principal's directive regarding returning parent phone calls. The principal requests that the teacher follow administrative directives in the future or face a formal reprimand. No doubt the teacher will be angry and defensive. These feelings will affect his working relationship with the principal. For this reason, we advise administrators to use simple oral directives, accompanied by notes to the file, when relatively minor problems with an employee's performance first arise.

Example

> One of your teachers is late to school one day for no apparent reason. The most appropriate strategy is to talk with the teacher informally about the tardiness and the inconvenience it caused. No doubt the teacher will offer an explanation for the incident and probably will try to assure you that it will never happen again.
>
> A few weeks later, the teacher is late to school again. As before, talk informally with the teacher about the tardiness. This time, be a little more direct. Warn the teacher that if it happens a third time, you will issue a memorandum, with a copy to the personnel file.
>
> When the tardiness occurs a third time, you should begin formal written documentation.

There is a down side to oral directives. Their informality limits their usefulness later in a nonrenewal or termination proceeding. The employee is likely to challenge your recollection of the conversation. At the extreme, your testimony may be dismissed as hearsay. Keeping a record of the dates and times you talked with the employee about specific deficiencies has two advantages: (1) it will help bolster your credibility on the witness stand, and (2) it preserves details to include in a memorandum if the deficiency persists. Still, be aware that oral directives have limited value in defending a negative employment recommendation.

Despite these drawbacks, we still believe that the necessity of maintaining a good working relationship with employees justifies relying on informal oral directives when relatively minor problems first surface. Sometimes formal documentation in this context can work to your disadvantage. A Dallas school attorney provides an illustration from one of his first teacher nonrenewal cases. The principal assured the attorney that he had built up a large folder of documentation that more than justified contract nonrenewal. When the attorney opened the folder, the first memorandum caught his attention. "You failed to greet me this morning when we passed in the hall," it read. As the attorney thumbed through the other memoranda, he discovered similar trivialities weakly linked to job performance such as needing to smile more, asking too many questions at faculty meetings, and wearing dresses that were out of style. Despite the attorney's best efforts at the nonrenewal hearing, the school board voted to reject the proposed nonrenewal. Afterward, several board members told the attorney that they could not go on record to end the teacher's employment in the district based on documentation that merely established the existence of a personality conflict between the principal and the teacher.

The lesson is clear. Employ formal documentation when:

- District policy requires it.
- A pattern of behavior needs to be changed.
- A serious incident has occurred.

Remember that the *quality* of what you write is more important than the *quantity* of accumulated paper.

TYPES OF DOCUMENTATION

Much has been written about the various types of written documentation. We have chosen to focus on four. Each is briefly described here.

Notes to the File Accompanying Oral Directives

Notes to the file are memory-joggers. Their purpose is to assist you in recalling specific dates and facts for use in later conversations with employees or in drafting formal memoranda. They also are useful in establishing a pattern of misbehavior that later can be formally documented in written memoranda. Once incorporated in the latter or following a lengthy period without further incident (e.g., the remainder of the year) they can be destroyed.

Notes to the file should be kept systematically. Many school administrators keep a file or loose-leaf notebook for this purpose with a sheet of paper for each employee. Other administrators maintain a spiral notebook and keep running records of conversations, conferences, and telephone calls. Spiral notebooks have the advantage of demonstrating that the notes to the file were sequential and contemporaneous with the event. This can be used to defend against the accusation that these notes were created after the fact. A few administrators keep a file for each employee on their computer. Wherever kept, employees or their representatives have access to this information under the Texas Public Information Act.[1] Thus, it is important to keep notes to the file factual and unemotional. Write notes to the file in such a way that you would not be embarrassed if they were circulated to the entire teaching staff, surfaced in a due process hearing, or were reported in the newspaper.

With regard to the tardy teacher described in the previous example, here is how a note to the file should and should not be written:

DON'T WRITE IT LIKE THIS!

> 9/14/11 Mrs. Jones was late to school again today. Her excuse this time was that her alarm clock did not go off. Likely story! She is getting to be a real pain in the ass. If she is late to school one more time, I am going to show her who is boss.

WRITE IT LIKE THIS!

> 9/14/11 Spoke with Mrs. Jones at noon in the cafeteria about her being fifteen minutes late to school today. She said her alarm clock did not go off and assured me she would not be late again. This is the second time within the past 10 days she has been tardy.

Would it be a good idea to send a copy to the teacher? Our answer is no, unless school policy is otherwise. If you send the note to the teacher, it no longer is a note to the file. It now is a specific incident memorandum, as discussed below. Notes to the file are for your use. They are not part of the formal written documentation process. However, the employee should be notified verbally of the deficiency that made the note to the file necessary. And, if the employee insists on seeing your note to the file, go ahead and show it. As previously noted, under the Texas Public Information Act, any file or note that administrators make in their capacity as employee supervisors has to be made available to the employee or the employee's representative if requested. Some information should not be released (e.g., student personally identifiable information, matters relating to child abuse or neglect, and matters involved in pending litigation). We strongly endorse a very simple maxim in personnel decision making involving both professional and auxiliary personnel:

NO SECRETS, NO SURPRISES

The purpose of documentation is not to entrap. The purpose is to assure that personnel decisions are fair. Thus *employees always should be informed of their deficiencies, even if minor.* In the case of the tardy teacher, first tell the teacher about the problem. Then make a note to the file about the time and content of the discussion. If the incident is not repeated, then you can discard the note at the end of the year and the matter will be closed.

Can a verbal warning or directive serve as cumulative data for purposes of complying with PDAS's 10-day rule? No. The rules state that "any documentation that will influence the teacher's summative annual appraisal report must be shared in writing with the teacher within 10 working days of the appraiser's knowledge of the occurrence" (19 Texas Administrative Code § 150.1003). So if an administrator wants to include the subject of the oral directive as cumulative data, the administrator must communicate with the teacher in writing. We believe that formalizing the documentation process in this way defeats the purpose of using oral directives. Their informality preserves the employer-employee relationship. However, if several oral directives are not effective in changing teacher behavior, then it is time to formalize the documentation process by communicating with the teaching in writing. Information preserved in the notes to the file can be incorporated in the written communication. The written communication signifies that the administrator has concluded that failure to correct the behavior may affect the teacher's summative appraisal. We address writing this form of documentation in the section on writing a specific incident memorandum below.

Performance Appraisal

The second type of documentation we address relates to performance appraisal processes mandated by state law or district policy. These processes have their own documentation formats and procedures. The specific incident memorandum discussed in the next section is particularly useful for the informal "walk-through" phase of teacher appraisal. In Chapters 4, we will describe how classroom documentation using focused observation instruments can be used most effectively to improve the performance of the marginally effective teacher or to support contract nonrenewal or termination in conjunction with the writing of a specific incident memorandum.

Specific Incident Memorandum

A specific incident memorandum applies to a specific episode or pattern of employee wrongdoing sufficiently serious that a written record must be made. Sometimes the term "letter of reprimand" is used, but this carries a negative connotation and should be avoided. The specific incident memorandum usually will include directives for future on-the-job behavior and may include a remediation component. With the remediation component added, this type of written documentation is sometimes called a "corrective memorandum." In the context of instruction, the term "instructional memorandum" is often used. Regardless of the label, these memoranda will have similar purposes and characteristics.

Follow these essential elements in writing specific incident memoranda:

- ***Letterhead Stationery***

  Use letterhead stationery to convey the importance of the memorandum. Letterhead stationery is preferable to electronic communication because it sets up the opportunity for face-to-face meeting for delivery and because it is less likely to be forwarded to third parties in an altered form.

- ***Date***

  Include the date the memorandum was written.

- ***Nature of the Allegation and Follow-Up Investigation***

  Describe both the nature of the allegation and the investigation you conducted if one was necessary, the dates and times of specific incidents, and the dates when you spoke with the employee about the matter.

- ***Findings of Fact***

  Set forth your findings of fact in objective terms resulting from your investigation, classroom visitations, conferences, etc.

- ***Conclusions***

  State your conclusions regarding what happened and which laws, policies, administrative directives, or ethical provisions were violated.

- ***Specific Directives***

  Issue specific directives regarding expected future conduct. Include any remedial activities the employee is to undertake.

- ***Opportunity to Respond***

  Offer the employee an opportunity to respond within a specified time period.

- ***Dated Signature of the Employee***

  Require the dated signature of the employee or if the employee refuses to sign, have a third party witness that the employee has received the memorandum.

We will illustrate later in this chapter how these guidelines can be used to write specific incident memoranda to both classified and professional employees.

Last Chance Memorandum

A last chance memorandum pulls together the record of previous deficiencies discussed with the employee as recorded in formal performance appraisals, notes to the file, and specific incident memoranda. Last chance memoranda can include data from prior years if relevant to establishing a continuing pattern of deficiency.[2] However, as noted in the previous chapter, administrators need to be very cautious in using data from prior years. While there is no provision in the Education Code that says that contract nonrenewal or termination can only be based on matters occurring during the present school year, the Commission of Education has cautioned that a school district should issue a proposed termination or nonrenewal within a reasonable amount of time from when the district is fully aware of the teacher's actions. If this doesn't occur, then the district may have waived the right to take employment action.

Clearly, it is not appropriate to include previous incidents that have been corrected. Assume, for example, that a teacher had several instances of arriving late to school during the teacher's first year of employment and was issued a written directive to arrive on time or face possible termination of the teacher's probationary contract at the end of the year. For the next two years, the teacher never was late. Then the teacher failed to attend a scheduled in-service without a valid excuse. Citing the prior lateness episode in documentation would not be appropriate, because it has no relationship to the current incident and, indeed, never recurred after the directive had been issued. In effect, the teacher complied with the lateness directive, and the matter should remain closed.

The last chance memorandum puts the employee on notice that you are prepared to recommend contract nonrenewal or termination unless significant improvement is forthcoming. An example of such a memorandum is given later in this chapter and, with regard to classroom teaching deficiencies, at the end of Chapter 6.

WRITING A SPECIFIC INCIDENT MEMORANDUM

Examples of Ineffective Memoranda

Consider the following two written communications, the first to a classified employee and the second in the form of an e-mail to a middle school English teacher.

WRITTEN MEMO TO ARNEY ARTISAN

TO: Arney Artisan, Head Custodian, Normal Curve Middle School

FROM: Wendell Wheelturner, Director of Maintenance, NCISD

I understand that you told other employees that you think my reqeust that all classified staff wear identification badges is stupid. I further understand that you say you will not wear one because everyone in your building knows who you are. As the oldest member of our staff, I expect you to set a good example for others. If you refuse to wear a badge, it will be considered insubordination. You know what that means.

E-MAIL TO BOB INSTRUCTOR

To: Bob Instructor

From: Angie O'Plasty

Date: November 11, 2011 5:17 PM

Subject: Faculty Meeting

You seem incapable of understanding a very simpel directive: attend faculty meetigs. As I told you before, claiming you have papers to grade before a weekend trip and saying up didn't find the discussion relevant to your needs is hardly reasons not to be there. Today, you simply didn't show up at all. I have one word for you: BE THERE OR FIND ANOTHER JOB. I am forwarding this e-mail to the superintedant

Angie O'Plasty, Principal

In both of these instances, the supervising administrators are clearly upset. Both have a right to be if the alleged incidents occurred. Employees cannot be allowed to willfully disregard job requirements, including administrative directives. But both Mr. Wheelturner and Ms. O'Plasty have committed some major errors in handling these matters. First, both have neglected to follow a cardinal rule in documentation: ***Investigate First***. Can Wendell be sure that the rumors he has heard about Arney are true? Can Angie be certain that Bob purposely played hooky from the faculty meeting? What is necessary in both instances is some spadework before reaching conclusions and writing memos.

Before continuing, let us pause a moment to consider some suggestions about conducting investigations.

How To Conduct An Investigation

Conducting investigations often requires considerable time and effort. *However, if your investigation is poorly done, the quality of your documentation may be seriously, if not fatally, compromised.* Of course, the scope of your investigation will be determined by the seriousness and complexity of the alleged incident. Here are some pointers on conducting investigations.

- *Do not delay beginning an investigation into either alleged wrongdoing or ineffectiveness.* Decide whether an investigation is warranted after receiving a complaint. Generally, an investigation should be conducted when an allegation, if proven true, would violate board policy. As we noted in Chapter 1, matters involving employee free speech or private conduct off campus often are beyond the legitimate interests of the school. Some administrators assume that if persons who witness events are unwilling to prepare a statement or step forward to testify, nothing can be done. While it is true that employees have a right to confront witnesses against them at a due process hearing and therefore witness statements are essential, nothing precludes an administrator from beginning an investigation. Don't dismiss rumors or anonymous tips. Look for strong, independent corroborating evidence. In some instances such as allegations involving sexual harassment or abuse, administrators who fail to initiate an investigation risk exposing both the school district and themselves to liability.

- *Decide whether the matter is sufficiently serious that the human resources director, school attorney, or outside investigator should be involved.* In matters involving allegations of employee sexual harassment or abuse of students, alert the district's Title IX coordinator and, depending upon the circumstances, campus security. When matters are potentially serious, the school attorney will need to be involved and actually may direct the investigation. This is most likely to be true when complaints also have been filed with law enforcement or outside administrative agencies. In such cases, it will be necessary to contact them to coordinate efforts and to assert the school district's obligations, such as maintaining confidentiality of records, safeguarding privacy rights of students, and protecting the professional reputation of employees. Together with the human resources director, superintendent, and/or school attorney, consider whether the matter is sufficiently serious that suspending the employee with pay is warranted.

- *If students are victims of alleged employee wrongdoing, notify their parents at the earliest opportunity.* Under Texas law, parents are considered "full partners" in the education of their children. They have a right under TEC § 26.004 and § 26.008 to see all the documents relating to their children except those involving child abuse.[3] Include parents in interviews and allow them to bring legal counsel, if desired. Remember that you would rather have parents as partners with you in your investigation than for them to learn about allegations of employee wrongdoing involving their child later on. It is the latter situation that triggers lawsuits from angry parents. When the student reaches adulthood at the age of 18 and is no longer subject to the compulsory school law, the parents generally do not have to be informed or involved in the investigation. However, there may be situations where it would be prudent and wise to involve the parents (e.g., the student is cognitively impaired or otherwise in need of legal assistance). For this reason, the school's human resources director, Title IX coordinator, or other appropriate official should be consulted before a decision is made not to involve the parents of older students in an investigation.

- *If a complaint has been registered against an employee, ask complainants separately to fill out and sign a complaint form, describing the nature of the wrongdoing and identifying other witnesses.*[4] (See Appendix D for a sample complaint form.) Follow up with an interview to ascertain the credibility of the allegation. Do not promise confidentiality, because the accused may have the right to confront accusers if formal action is taken.

- *Interview student and employee witnesses separately, have each complete a witness statement form.* Follow a set of questions prepared in advance targeted toward what you want to learn. Have witnesses complete a written statement of what they observed and secure a signature. Do not reference witness statements in memoranda unless you have secured a completed witness statement form. When students are witnesses, it would be wise to alert their parents ahead of time that you are going to ask them to complete a witness statement form and secure their consent. (See Appendix D for a sample witness statement form.) Again, do not promise confidentiality. Make sure that your investigatory procedure is in accord with district policy and practice. Consult district officials if in doubt.
- *Interview the accused, following the same procedures used when interviewing witnesses.* Do not assume guilt. Treat the accused in the same manner you treat complainants and witnesses. Do not encourage resignations or make settlement offers unless the accused asks about them. Consult the human resources director or school attorney before taking any final action on either matter. Do not release complaint statements to the accused that contain personally identifiable information about students. However, the attorney general has advised that letters sent to a school board complaining about a teacher are to be made available to the teacher with this information redacted (ORD-332, 1982).
- *With few exceptions, do not disclose personally identifiable information about students or families.* Because this information is protected from disclosure by the Family Educational Rights and Privacy Act (FERPA), obtain written authorization from parents before releasing a student's name and any written statement. In the absence of such authorization, remove personally identifiable student information from witness statements and other documentary evidence. Statements from students in their own handwriting should not be disclosed because the handwriting may be personally identifiable. Note that under TEC § 26.009 (a)(2), parent permission is necessary before audiotaping or videotaping a student. Further, § 552.135 of the Texas Government Code includes students within the protection of the "informer's privilege." That provision excludes from public disclosure the name or statement of an informer who reports to the school district or regulatory agency an alleged violation of a law or regulation absent the informer's consent or complicity in the alleged wrongdoing. Sometimes, teachers ask to see a letter of complaint submitted by a parent. While the teacher has a broad right of access to information in the teacher's personnel file, FERPA gives parents the right to request that personally identifiable information (e.g., names, phone numbers, addresses) about themselves and their children not be released. While teachers do have access to personally identifiable information about students when there is a "legitimate educational interest,"* the teacher would not be authorized to see the letter under this provision. The attorney general has advised that letters sent to a school board complaining about a teacher are to be made available to the teacher, provided the names of the students and parents are deleted (ORD-332, 1982).

---

* You will note that the memoranda contained in Chapter 4 do contain the names of students. These memoranda reflect deficiencies in teacher classroom performance with regard to meeting the educational needs of students in the teacher's classroom. Because both the teacher and the principal need to know the identity of students who are not being taught effectively, student personally identifiable information is included, because it constitutes a legitimate educational interest under FERPA. Later, this student personally identifiable information will be deleted if the memoranda are used for other purposes (e.g., to support nonrenewal of a teacher contract in a hearing before the school board).

- *Work closely with the school district's officer of public information when requests for information about an investigation arise from third parties under the Texas Public Information Act (TPIA).* This law presumes that information must be disclosed unless it is specifically exempted from disclosure under either federal or state law. As already noted, personally identifiable information about students and families is exempted from disclosure. Under Section 552.101 of the Texas Government Code, information that is considered to be confidential by constitutional, statutory, or judicial law does not have to be disclosed. Section 552.102 provides that information in an employee's file does not need to be disclosed if it constitutes a clearly unwarranted invasion of personal privacy (however, with few exceptions, it does have to be disclosed to the employee or the employee's representative, if requested). Courts have interpreted these two provisions to mean that information does not have to be disclosed to third parties if it would be highly objectionable to a reasonable person and if there is no legitimate public interest in disclosure. Applying these principles, the Texas attorney general has advised that a school district had to release the documents in an investigatory file pertaining to sexual harassment in the absence of a summary report but must withhold the identities of victims and witnesses. OR2000-1233 (2000). The attorney general has advised that records and documents resulting from the investigation of sexual harassment allegations against a principal must be released, with the deletion of identifies of victims and witnesses but including references to the principal's name, because of the public's interest in sexual harassment in the workplace. OR2003-5194, OR2003-4773 (2003). In another decision, the attorney general advised that information regarding the alleged improper conduct by a coach towards a student was not so embarrassing that it would be offensive to a reasonable person. Further, the public interest in knowing about the possible misconduct by the coach outweighed the coach's privacy interests. Therefore, the information had to be disclosed with some personally identifiable information redacted. OR2000-1319 (2000). Texas Government Code § 552.152 specifies that informaton was added to TPIA specifying that information relating to an employee or officer of a governmental entity is exempt from disclosure if disclosure would subject the employee or officer to substantial threat of physical harm. In sum, what must and must not be disclosed is complex and highly dependent upon the facts of a given situation. For these reasons, we recommend that you seek assistance from district's officer for public information before releasing information.

- *If complaints also have been filed with the police or outside administrative agencies, contact them before beginning your investigation in order to coordinate efforts and to assert the school district's obligations.* Remember that the district has interests of its own such as maintaining confidentiality of records, safeguarding privacy rights of students, and protecting the professional reputation of employees.

- *Be cautious in communicating with the news media because student and family privacy rights and employee constitutional rights may be involved.* Use prepared statements, preferably handled by the district communications office. Remember that nothing is ever "off the record."

- *When the investigation is over, retain the investigatory file for possible use later on.* Where these files are stored varies. In some districts, they are kept by the school attorney. In others, they are kept in the human resources office or superintendent's office. In any case, they should not be inserted in the employee's file because of (1) the possibility of reprisal by the employee, (2) the difficulty of excising all personally identifiable information under FERPA, and (3) the potential damage that could accrue to the employee from portions of the investigatory file that are false or misleading. What should be kept in the employee's file is the specific incident memorandum that results from the investigation.

A careful investigation is essential to providing a firm foundation for effective documentation. What's more, it will demonstrate to all that you have not been careless, negligent, or callously indifferent to allegations of serious employee wrongdoing. As noted in Chapter 1, failure to take allegations seriously, especially in the context of student sexual harassment and abuse, can lead to potentially serious litigation involving both the school district and school administrators.

In the case of the incident involving Arney Artisan reflected in the memoranda above, an investigation will confirm whether Mr. Wheelturner's concerns are true. If after conferring with the employee the facts remain unchanged, the way is clear for issuing Mr. Artisan a specific incident memorandum, following the guidelines set out in the previous section. With regard to Bob's being absent from the faculty meeting, a simple conversation with him will reveal the circumstances.

Beyond the failure of the maintenance director and the principal to investigate before they wrote, what is wrong with the two memoranda as they are? Among other things, Mr. Wheelturner's memo was not written on letterhead stationery and did not include a date. While Ms. O'Plasty's e-mail was sent via the school's computer system and thus included a date, it, like Wheelturner's, was poorly written. Both contain insensitive and inflammatory language that will make the employee angry (e.g., "expect you to set an example," "insubordination," "be there or find another job"). Both contain spelling and grammatical errors (e.g., "reqeust," "simpel," "meetigs," "superintedant," the verb "is" instead of "are"). And in both instances the administrators imply possible job action if matters don't improve. The problem is that administrators normally *recommend* termination or contract nonrenewal. The authority to take either action usually resides with the school board.

Not only will these two memoranda likely set up an adversarial relationship with the employees, they may prove embarrassing to the administrators who sent them. The memo to Arney refers to him as "the oldest member of our staff" and could prompt an allegation of age discrimination if Arney's employment is later terminated. For this reason, it is preferable to rely on *job-related deficiencies* whenever possible. Since Ms. O'Plasty has sent a copy of her memorandum to the superintendent, the superintendent may be as concerned with Ms. O'Pasty's actions as with those attributed to Bob Instructor!

There is another potential problem. Both Arney and Bob may decide to share their communiques with colleagues — in the case of the e-mail that Bob received, perhaps with the spelling, grammatical, and typing errors highlighted. The documents may well be circulated within the building and perhaps throughout the school district, especially if an aggressive employee association is present. What better way to recruit members than to produce written evidence of arbitrary and abusive administrative action! And Bob's e-mail may end up on the Internet!

Lessons To Be Learned

What can we learn from these examples?

- **Investigate, confer, write — in that order.**
- **Avoid acting when angry.**
- **Avoid sexist, racist, and inflammatory language that will provoke an employee to seek vengeance.**
- **Spell out acronyms (e.g., IEP, FAPE, TXDOT, TPRI) so that those who may review the memorandum in a grievance or nonrenewal hearing will understand the thrust of what is being said.**
- **Assume your memoranda and e-mail messages will be widely distributed and read.**
- **Avoid using e-mail for formal documentation, given the ability of recipients both to change the content of e-mails and disseminate them widely.**
- **Have someone edit what you write.**

In addition to these lessons, it is also important to treat all employees alike. Don't play favorites. Treat the employees you like in the same way that you treat those you don't like. And *keep it simple*!

Examples of Well Written Specific Incident Memoranda

On the next two pages are much better written memoranda to Arney Artisan and Bob Instructor. Notice how the format of each reflects the essential elements of a specific incident memorandum (the essential elements are listed on the left side of the sample memoranda for illustrative purposes; you would not include them in the actual memorandum).

With regard to the memorandum on the next page to Arney Artisan, note that it is possible that a written memorandum would not be necessary in this situation. An oral directive might suffice. However, that determination cannot be made until Wendell has completed his investigation and conducted his conference with Arney. When you read the memorandum on the next page, note also that Wendell begins his memo by stating "It was reported to me." He does not begin by stating "This concerns your failure to wear the identification badge." It is very important to begin your memo with an *allegation* rather than a factual statement unless you are the source of concern. Doing so sets up the investigation necessary to establish the truth or falsity of the allegation. Phrasing the first sentence in terms of an allegation avoids the assertion later on that you already had reached your conclusion of noncompliance and the rest of the memo is of no consequence. Here, we will assume that in this instance, Arney meant what he said: Give me a specific directive if we are to wear identification badges. Wendell chose to do so in a written memorandum. If Arney then fails to comply, it will be easy to show failure to follow an administrative directive. And that would be grounds for terminating Arney's contract, if he has one. Even if he does not, the memorandum will safeguard Wendell from an allegation that the termination was illegally motivated.

Comments regarding the memorandum to Bob Instructor are set forth on the page following that memorandum.

ESSENTIAL ELEMENTS	
Letterhead Stationery	**NORMAL CURVE INDEPENDENT SCHOOL DISTRICT** 555 Intelligence Street Normal Curve, Texas 70000
Date	October 17, 2011 TO: Arney Artisan, Head Custodian, Normal Curve Middle School FROM Wendell Wheelturner, Director of Maintenance, NCISD RE: Our October 14 Conference
Nature of Allegation and Investigation	It was reported to me on Tuesday, October 11, that you voiced strong public criticism regarding my request that all classified staff members wear identification badges. You indicated that, given your long tenure as head custodian at Normal Curve Middle School, everyone knows who you are and, as result, you do not feel it necessary to wear the badge. I spoke with Hugh Mongus, the school principal, who confirmed that you did express these comments to him. He also said that you advised the other custodians in the building that they did not have to wear badges. None has done so.
Findings of Fact and Conclusions	At our conference last Tuesday, you confirmed making the statements. You also said you would not wear the badge unless I specifically directed you to do so. I explained again my rationale for wearing badges and pointed out that your refusal constitutes failure to follow an administrative directive. While you have been employed at the middle school for a long time, neither you nor members of your staff are known to new
Specific Directive	students and to most of those who visit the building. For this reason, you and members of the custodial staff must wear the badges at all times during working hours.
	Thank you for your cooperation in this matter. Copy: Personnel File
Opportunity to Respond	I have received a copy of this memorandum. I understand that my signature does not necessarily indicate that I agree with its contents. I further understand that I have a right to respond within 10 working days if I disagree.
Dated Signature	/s/________________________ Date ____________ Arney Artisan

ESSENTIAL ELEMENTS

Letterhead Stationery

ALAMO MIDDLE SCHOOL

NORMAL CURVE INDEPENDENT SCHOOL DISTRICT

555 Intelligence Street
Normal Curve, Texas 70000

Date

November 17, 2011

TO: Bob Instructor
FROM: Angie O'Plasty, Principal
RE: November 14 Conference

Nature of Allegation and Investigation

During the past semester, you have failed to attend the regularly scheduled weekly faculty meetings in timely fashion. Specifically:

Findings of Fact

- You were 25 minutes late to the faculty meeting on Friday, September 16. When I spoke with you about this after the meeting, you indicated that you had papers to grade in your room and had simply lost track of time.
- You left 15 minutes early at the Friday, October 14 faculty meeting. You responded to my e-mail the following Monday indicating that you found the discussion not relevant to your grade level. I advised you that this is not a valid excuse to leave a faculty meeting and that you must make sure that any need to arrive late or leave early is approved by me ahead of time. You said you would follow this request. Copies of the e-mails are attached.
- You did not attend the faculty meeting on Friday, November 11, nor did you explain the need for your absence before the meeting. At our conference on Tuesday, November 15, you explained that you thought the meeting had been cancelled, though you could point to no communication from my office to this effect.

Conclusions

Your failure to attend the weekly faculty meetings in timely fashion is a violation of the job expectations for Alamo Middle School. This is clearly indicated both in the faculty information packet that I distributed at our first meeting on Friday, August 26, and in my oral and e-mail comments to you on September 16 and October 17. Further, your noncompliance does not meet the expectations of Domain VII of our district's appraisal system regarding complying with district policies and operating procedures.

Specific Directive

In the future, I expect you to attend all scheduled faculty meetings. If you find that you will be late, leave early, or not be in attendance at all, you must convey the reasons to me in writing prior to the meeting. I reserve the right to approve or disapprove them.

Att.
Copy: Personnel File

Opportunity to Respond

I have received a copy of this memorandum. I understand that my signature does not necessarily indicate that I agree with its contents. I further understand that I have a right to respond within 10 working days if I disagree.

Dated Signature

/s/______________________________ Date____________________
Bob Instructor

Notice that while Angie used e-mails to follow up her informal discussions with Bob, she uses letterhead stationery for the formal specific incident memorandum. Notice as well how the communication corresponds to the characteristics of an effective specific incident memorandum. Here, an investigation was not necessary, because Angie directly observed Bob's attendance problems at faculty meetings. However, she did fail to confer with Bob before she sent the last e-mail. When the facts are in dispute, it will be necessary to state the nature of the investigation that the administrator conducted (who was interviewed, what documents were examined, etc.) and the findings from it. *The findings of fact must always be stated in objective terms.* It is critically important to avoid subjective wording that may be used to accuse the administrator of bias. Follow the ***Sgt. Joe Friday Rule*** based on the 1950s TV series "Dragnet": *"Just the facts, ma'am, just the facts."*

Notice how Angie anchors her conclusions based on the findings of fact in the published expectations of employment at Alamo Middle School. This is the "law of the district" and avoids accusations that Angie is merely substituting her way of doing things for Bob's. Sometimes it is difficult to arrive at a conclusion, because the facts might conflict. However, as the "trier of fact," the administrator will have to decide whether district policy and/or administrative directives have been violated. This is what a jury does once a case has been submitted to it.

The importance of the opportunity to respond cannot be overemphasized. If Bob's response reveals new information that Angie did not consider, then she will have the opportunity to reopen the investigation. Based on the new information, she may decide that she should be more accommodating. For example, suppose Bob sends Angie a response e-mail that he must meet with her as soon as possible after he received her memorandum. At the meeting, Bob breaks down in her office, telling her that he is under treatment for leukemia and doesn't want anyone to know about it. His treatments are on Friday, and this is accounts for his behavior. He gives the name of his doctor to verify that this is the case. On the other hand, if Bob's response offers nothing new, then Angie should acknowledge this fact in a brief reply e-mail or memo and place both Bob's response and her reply in his personnel file. There is no need for her to become Bob's permanent adversary pen pal.

Suppose Bob does not reply within the specified time frame. If there is no response, then it can be assumed that Bob accepts the contents of the letter. It will not be very convincing for Bob or his representative to claim months later when a notice of contract nonrenewal is issued that the letter was a tissue of lies. If so, why hadn't he taken advantage of the opportunity to respond?

Finally, always check to make sure that your personnel decisions are in accord with district policy. In relatively serious matters, it is wise to have a representative from human resources participate in the investigation and memo writing. If litigation is possible, the school attorney may also become involved.

WRITING LAST CHANCE MEMORANDA

The Scenario

Melba Toast is serving her fourth year on a term contract in Piney Woods Independent School District. She teaches fifth grade. During a staff development program on August 22, she expresses great resentment toward a new discipline plan the principal has proposed for the building.

She asserts that the plan is far too punitive and is unworkable. She takes particular offense at a provision that provides for all-day in-school suspension for troublesome students, contending that the suspension period is too long. She states that any teacher who complies with the plan is no better than a child abuser. "I will not carry out the plan," she states defiantly.

Later that day, the principal, Paula Leader, holds a conference with Melba to talk over the discipline plan and to explain her disapproval of the outburst at the faculty meeting. The principal tells Melba that she, Paula, is the disciplinary leader for the school and that Melba must follow the proposed plan as a condition of employment. The teacher listens but says she has no intention to do so. Paula follows up the conference with a specific incident memorandum in which she reviews the substance of their discussion and directs Melba to follow the discipline plan despite her reservations.

The principal implements the plan when school begins. Melba promptly files a grievance against her. On October 11, Melba confronts Paula in the hallway. Visibly upset, the teacher tells the principal that she does not want her to discipline her students when they are sent to the office by other teachers. Melba is upset because the principal has disciplined one of her students for fighting on the playground. The principal explains again that she has the final authority regarding disciplinary matters at the school. Melba responds angrily, "You are incredibly ignorant about child development. Don't expect me to comply with your stupid militaristic discipline ideas." Melba's comments were overheard by several other teachers and students.

The Memorandum

Here is the last chance memorandum that Paula sent to Melba in October. The numbers in parentheses correspond with the observations in the Commentary section following the memorandum.

Hidden Trail Middle School
Piney Woods Independent School District
123 Woods Path
Piney Woods, TX 71234

October 17, 2011

TO: Melba Toast
FROM: Paula Leader
RE: Follow-up To Our Conference of October 12

This memorandum is a follow-up to our October 12 conference during which I expressed my concerns regarding your continuing antagonism toward me and toward my disciplinary policies.

As you will recall, we first talked on the afternoon of August 22, following the morning staff development program on the new student **(1)** discipline plan. You criticized the plan at the meeting, labeling teachers who comply "no better than child abusers." A number of teachers at the meeting were offended by this remark, as was I. You also stated "I will not carry out the plan."

During our conference, I expressed concern over the unprofessional nature of your outburst and reminded you that I am responsible for **(2)** student discipline in this building. Both at the meeting and in my August 24 follow-up memorandum, I directed you to follow the discipline plan whether you agree with it or not. Subsequently, you filed a grievance against me over implementation of the plan.

Our October 12 conference resulted from the hallway encounter the previous day when you stopped me to say that you did not want me to discipline any of your homeroom students when they are sent to the office by other teachers. Your comment apparently was triggered by my disciplining one of the students from your classroom for fighting on the playground during lunch. I reminded you that I have the final authority for discipline in this building. You responded by labeling me in front of other teachers and students as "ignorant" and my discipline approach as "stupid."

As I explained, you have a right to express your views about school-wide matters such as the student discipline plan. At the same time, you have a responsibility to do so in a professional manner. Such was not the case at the August faculty meeting, nor during our hallway encounter on October 12. You also have a right to file a grievance over the issue. But failure to implement the discipline program constitutes failure to follow an administrative directive. **(3)**

Your criticizing me in offensive terms before other teachers and students is contrary to District Policy DOAD, which lists as one of the reasons for contract nonrenewal "Failure to meet the District's standards of professional conduct." **(4)**

I direct you to express your opposition to school programs and activities in more moderate terms and to refrain from using intemperate language in your public comments about me or your colleagues. If you have a personal concern you wish to address to me, please make an appointment to talk with me in my office and not in the hallways or other public areas of the school. With regard to student discipline, I direct you to implement the new plan consistently and cooperatively. It is imperative that you do so. I also remind you of my policy that any teacher may send a discipline problem to the office for appropriate action regardless of whether that student is assigned to that teacher. If you fail to comply with these directives, I will have no choice but to recommend nonrenewal or termination of your contract. **(5)**

I hope that we can put these unpleasant episodes behind us and work together for the mutual benefit of our students even when we disagree. I welcome your comments and criticisms so long as they are voiced in a professional manner. I look forward to an early and equitable resolution of your grievance. **(6)**

If you disagree with the contents of this memorandum, please respond to me in writing within 10 working days. I will be pleased to talk with you further about this matter if you wish.

(7)

Copy:
Personnel File Dr. Paul Peopleprocessor, Director of Human Relations

I have received a copy of this memorandum. I understand that my signature does not necessarily indicate that I agree with its contents. I further understand that I have a right to respond within 10 working days if I disagree.

/s/______________________________ ______________________________

Melba Toast Date

Commentary

(1) Notice how promptly Paula acted on these incidents. Following each incident (August 22 and October 11), she met with Melba a short time thereafter. She wrote the memorandum within five days of her second conference with Melba. It is clear that Paula considers this a serious matter. The principal carefully spells out exactly what happened at the August 22 faculty meeting, during the October 11 confrontation in the hallway, and during her conferences with the teacher. She relies on information contained in her notes to the file, from her conferences, and from her first memorandum. She presents this information in a very objective and non-judgmental manner. Her doing so will go a long way to convince a school board member, hearing officer, or media reporter that she acted professionally. If these statements go unchallenged by Melba, they will convey an appearance of accuracy, thus easing the burden on the school lawyer to establish the facts by calling forth witnesses at a hearing.

(2) Note that this memorandum follows up on a specific incident memorandum issued on August 24 that directed Melba to follow the terms of the new student discipline plan. Melba's apparent failure to do so constitutes repeated failure to follow administrative directives, a reason contained in the district's board policies for contract nonrenewal.

(3) Note how Paula recognizes Melba's statutory right to file a grievance. Arguable, it might be better for Paula to leave any mention of the grievance out of the memo. Doing so will curtail a challenge later on from the teacher's attorney that Paula targeted Melba over the grievance filing.

(4) Paula is specific regarding the board policy implicated by the name-calling. As we noted in Chapter 1, the U.S. Supreme Court has ruled that complaints over working conditions are not constitutionally protected. Certainly name-calling of the type Melba employed in the hallway within earshot of others is unprofessional. If it is clear that Paula remained calm in the face of the epithets and did not encourage them, Melba will be on the defensive in challenging the appropriateness of Paula's directive.

(5) Paula is quite specific in her directives. Melba is clearly on notice of what the principal's expectations are for future employment behavior.

(6) Note how Paula closes out her memo on a positive note. The impartial reader likely will conclude that the principal is acting professionally and has no personal animosity toward the teacher.

(7) Paula has given Melba 10 working days to respond. If the teacher does respond, the two have another opportunity to meet again, particularly if Melba brings new information to light. Another meeting is preferable to an exchange of claims and counter-claims. If no reconciliation is possible, then the two memos will appear together in the personnel file along with a brief recognition memo from Paula indicating that Melba's communique was received and noted. As we pointed out with the specific incident memorandum, if new information is received that requires a change in Paula's conclusions and directives, better to make the changes now than to dig in her heels and lose later either at the grievance or contract nonrenewal hearing stage. If Melba does not respond, then the facts set forth in Paula's memo will convey an appearance of accuracy.

It is important to recognize that contract termination requires considerable supporting evidence. It is early in the school year, and Paula does not yet have sufficient evidence to support outright termination. In addition, remediation usually is required before terminating an employee's contract. Here, Paula has given Melba the opportunity to improve. If Melba does not, Paula will be in a strong position to justify contract nonrenewal and, depending upon the circumstances, even outright termination of Melba's contract.

Suppose Melba follows the directives explicitly and no further incidents occur during the school year. The next year, she asks Paula to remove the memorandum from the personnel file, asserting that the incident is closed and should not taint her employment relationship with the district. Should Paula do so? Many school lawyers believe it is better to leave the memorandum in the folder for possible use later on should the employee repeat the misbehavior. In such a case, the memorandum may become necessary to establish a pattern of failing to follow directives by the employee. Rather than remove the memorandum, administrators are better advised to place a second memorandum in the folder indicating that the directives outlined in the first memorandum have been followed.

SUMMARY

Here is a summary of the main points discussed in this chapter.

- Use oral directives to deal with minor employment problems, confining written documentation to more serious matters.
- Notes to the file are useful as memory-joggers but have limited value for other purposes.
- Keep employees informed of job-related deficiencies. Follow the maxim "No secrets, no surprises."
- Follow the essential elements of a specific incident memorandum to enhance your chances of changing employee behavior, having your employment recommendations upheld if challenged, and being consistent with all employees.
- Whenever possible, employ remediation efforts before planning a negative employment action.
- Use a last chance memorandum to put the employee on notice that unless substantial improvement in performance occurs, you will recommend contract nonrenewal or termination. By its nature, a last chance memorandum must be carefully developed, usually in consultation with the human resources director or school attorney. Last chance memoranda should be used only when circumstances warrant.

In short, effective documentation takes time. *Do not be in a rush!*

ENDNOTES

1. Texas Attorney General Opinion ORD-327, 1983. The thrust of this opinion is that employees have the right of access to notes to the file made by their superiors if the latter make such notes for use in the evaluation process.
2. *Dominguez v. United I.S.D.*, Dkt. No. 169-R1-690 (Comm'r Educ. 1991). In 2001 the Commissioner of Education upheld the contract termination of a teacher who was given a directive in 1991 not to be alone with students following an unconfirmed allegation from a second grader that the teacher had sexually assaulted her. Nearly 10 years later, a parent complained that the teacher had driven her son home after school without parental permission. Further, the teacher was alone with students in an unused classroom during the summer school. The Commissioner observed that despite the passage of time, the teacher's actions constituted repeated failure to follow directives. *Allen v. Houston I.S.D.*, Dkt. No. 014-R2-1001 (Comm'r Educ. 2001).
3. *Lett v. Klein I.S.D.*, 917 S. W.2d 455 (Tex. App. -Houston [14th Dist.] 1996) (parent has access under the Texas Public Information Act to documents, memoranda, investigative notes, and statements prepared by school personnel relating to his child in connection with a low conduct grade in choir class). School counselors can withhold records only if the counselor is a licensed professional under Health and Safety Code § 611.001(2) and determines that release "would be harmful to the patient's physical, mental,or emotional health." Otherwise, all records must be released to the parent with few exceptions. Atty. Gen. Op. JC-0538 (2002).
4. Some years ago, the Commissioner of Education issued an instructive decision with regard to obtaining statements from non-English speaking complainants. The case involved the termination of an at-will bus driver, a member of the Texas State Teachers Association (TSTA), over her criticism of a directive that bus drivers work an additional fifteen minutes before and after bus runs without pay. The Commissioner concluded that the bus driver had abused her rights of free speech and upheld the termination. However, he found the case a "close call," in part because of the manner in which complaint statements had been obtained. The statements presented to support the supervisor's termination decision were all written by someone other than the person testifying. This was apparently done because the complainants were Spanish-speaking employees. The Commissioner advised that "a better practice would be for employees to first write their complaints in their native language and then have a disinterested person translate the complaint into English. This would obviate confusion as to the true meaning of the complainant and would provide evidentiary assurance in the record that the allegations were of that person's own doing – not someone else whose motives might be suspect." *Huerta v. Rio Hondo I.S.D.*, Dkt. No. 253-R8-593 (Comm'r Educ. 1995).

CHAPTER THREE: THE MARGINALLY EFFECTIVE TEACHER

In a time of increased accountability for student achievement, many educators are concerned about the teacher who is marginally effective. The marginally effective teacher may be the teacher who is effective in some ways, but ineffective in others. This may also be the teacher who performs well when being observed by a supervisor, but chooses not be effective the rest of the time. The supervisory strategies used with this teacher are often different from those used with the teacher who is consistently ineffective or willfully fails to follow recommendations or directives for improvement. With the marginally effective teacher, your main goal as instructional leader is to assist the teacher to improve. Failing that, your goal is to use the accumulated documentation to support a recommendation of contract nonrenewal or termination.

You may be wondering why a handbook on documentation includes the topic of supervision. First, when you are working with a marginally effective teacher, it is extremely important to know which goal you wish to attain: helping the teacher improve or preparing for contract nonrenewal or termination. This distinction is vital because some developmental supervision practices — constant encouragement or positive reinforcement for changes that are made, for example — can be counterproductive if your goal is termination or nonrenewal. Conversely, some tactics that are useful in a nonrenewal or termination proceeding (frequent written documentation or a professional growth plan, for instance) are counterproductive if you believe the teacher can and will improve.

There is a second reason we address supervision here. When your goal is nonrenewal or termination, you must use a directive style of supervision. Although many educators prefer to see themselves in a "helping" role and want to be collaborative or nondirective in all their professional relationships, a strong message of this chapter is: "Know what goal you are trying to accomplish and make sure you use the correct supervision style in accomplishing that goal!" Regardless of the desired outcome — teacher growth and improvement, contract nonrenewal, or contract termination — the principles of good supervision generally apply. Good supervision tools are essential to effective classroom observation and documentation.

IDENTIFYING THE MARGINALLY EFFECTIVE TEACHER

The *ineffective* teacher attracts a great deal of attention and is the target of intense supervision, while the *marginally effective* teacher typically is ignored as not "bad enough" to warrant much time and effort either for improvement or for termination. However, when you as a supervisor inevitably ask, "Would I choose to put my child in this teacher's class?" the honest answer must be no. Once a supervisor identifies the marginally effective teacher, the next step is to determine *why* the teacher's effectiveness is marginal. The 2002 Association for Supervision and Curriculum Development (ASCD) handbook entitled *Leadership for Learning* provides some useful insight into some of the reasons for weak teacher performance. According to its author, Carl Glickman, two factors lie at the heart of poor classroom performance. One factor concerns the level teacher's level of abstraction--the ability to identify classroom problems and generate solutions. The other factor is related to the teacher's level of commitment--the willingness to accept responsibility for student learning and to place students first in the adult decision-making. These two factors are discussed in the following sections.

Abstract Thinking and Problem-Solving in the Classroom

In an effective classroom a teacher must identify problems, generate solutions, act on those solutions, and monitor and adjust to the ever-changing classroom environment. A marginally effective teacher is one who may not even recognize a problem when it arises. Once the teacher knows about it, he* may have no idea how to solve it.

Sometimes it is hard for him to imagine making changes. He may be unaware of the relationship between his actions in the classroom and the success of his students. When students fail to learn, he is likely to believe that they are at fault. This teacher is often involved in many projects and activities, but rarely completes one before moving on to the next. Glickman describes a teacher with these characteristics as having a "low level of abstraction." A high abstractor, on the other hand, typically can diagnose problems and can generate alternatives for solving them. He understands the relationship between his actions and his students' success. If one strategy does not work, he looks in his "tool kit" and chooses another strategy. He takes responsibility for instruction and its impact on his students.

If one of the teachers you supervise is performing poorly because of a low level of abstraction, you first must address the *cause* of his ineffectiveness. Below are five possible causes and some strategies for supervision.

Lack of Experience

Beginning teachers, in particular, often expend all of their physical and emotional energy just to get through each lesson. Each lesson is planned and taught for the first time – a frustration that veteran educators may well have forgotten! While a new teacher may be aware of instructional or management problems, he lacks sufficient experience from which to draw possible solutions--his tool kit is still relatively small. At other times he may not even be aware that problems exist; to him, everything is operating just as it should.

Many districts have found it desirable to orient the new teacher to the school and district and to follow up with a high-quality first year induction program with a good mentor teacher.

Lack of Knowledge

For this discussion, we'll assume that the teacher is knowledgeable about the subject he is teaching. Chapter 4 addresses supervision and documentation strategies to use when he is not.

Most teachers plan their daily lessons within an instructional comfort zone that is defined by what they know how to do and what they are comfortable doing--their tool kit of instructional strategies is small. They may not teach well because they simply do not know or understand in-

---

** We interchange "he" and "she" when referencing teachers in this chapter* structional strategies that lie beyond their current practices. This lack of knowledge may increase when teachers are faced with students from different cultural, social, ethnic and/or economic backgrounds than students they have taught in the past. While effective in one teaching context, past teaching practices may not work with the current student population. Rather than admit that their reliance on traditional teaching practices is at fault, these teachers may blame students (or their parents, or society, etc.) for their ineffectiveness.

Many teachers respond predictably to problems that arise in the classroom. For example, a beginning teacher may have a limited repertoire of skills for classroom management or for delivery of instruction. A more experienced teacher who finds the students in his classroom culturally, economically, or ethnically different from those he is used to teach may become frustrated when the strategies he considers "tried-and-true" no longer work. The teacher in need of assistance is often a teacher who has failed to learn and/or implement new instructional strategies, as in the case of the ten-year veteran who has had the same year of teaching experience ten times. This teacher may face mounting classroom problems when his limited teaching practices prove ineffective.

Difficulty Solving Problems

Sometimes a teacher in need of assistance recognizes the problems in his classroom but does not understand how to solve them. Even when problems and solutions are identified, he may adopt a "just show me what you want me to do" attitude rather than taking the initiative to transform possible solutions into concrete action. When this teacher says, "I'm doing everything I know how to do," he is probably telling the truth!

Lack of Awareness

An effective teacher with a high level of abstraction is able to analyze instructional decisions that are made before and during a lesson and routinely questions his instructional choices: Why did I choose this demonstration technique? Why did I use these materials? Were my materials effective? Could I have used better examples? What strategies did I plan to make certain that students were actively participating in the learning process? He makes conscious decisions both in planning the lesson and in implementing moment-to-moment adjustments during instruction, and he reflects upon the thought processes that guide his instructional practices.

On the other hand, the teacher who is in need of assistance because of a low level of abstraction may be operating more from habit or from intuition than from conscious decision-making, and he may fail to see the connection between what he does and what his students do or do not do. He may be unaware that few students are participating, that many students do not understand the instruction, or that several students have disengaged from the lesson. Teachers with low levels of abstraction may fail to recognize that the true measure of good teaching is the level of student engagement and success it evokes. As one teacher told co-author John Crain, "I think you should really observe me teach without any students in the room. Then you could see what my teaching is really like." This is a truly low abstractor!

Personal Problems

A teacher experiencing a serious crisis in his life outside the classroom may find himself emotionally and psychologically drained. If his problems diminish his classroom performance, his students may suffer. Marital difficulties or problems with family members, illness or injury, or financial woes may so occupy his attention that he is unable to devote much time and energy to the task of teaching, leaving him little to give once he arrives at school.

The supervisor must be sensitive to the teacher's problems while remaining attentive to the needs of his students. If his problems persist, it may become necessary to consider whether his problems are impairing his long-term classroom effectiveness and whether the problems are temporary or even remediable.

Level of Commitment

Suppose one of the teachers you supervise can think abstractly and has no difficulty solving classroom problems, and yet she is still only marginally effective. In this case, you will need to consider her general attitude toward the teaching profession and toward her specific instructional responsibilities – in other words, how high is her level of commitment?

A low level of commitment may be caused by a deliberate "why bother" attitude or it may be a result of circumstances beyond the teacher's immediate control. A teacher whose level of commitment is low may see no need to change, claiming that everything is "just fine." On the other hand, she may be the teacher who talks positively about changes but fails to follow through with effective action. Another manifestation of low commitment is the egocentric "what's in it for me?" attitude. The self-centered teacher fails to take action or make changes unless she can see some benefit for herself. Contrast this type of teacher with the highly motivated and committed teacher who is concerned about her students, her school, and the profession in general; who sees problems, chooses among alternative solutions, and follows through with decisions; or who continually seeks improvement and strives to make teaching and learning more interesting and exciting for her students.

In the preceding section, we noted that supervision of the teacher in need of assistance because of a low level of abstraction requires assistance that extends beyond identifying classroom problems and their symptoms. The same is true when you supervise a teacher who lacks commitment. In order to make informed decisions regarding remediation, the supervisor must identify and address the causes of low levels of commitment. As with the abstraction issue, the following is not an exhaustive list of causes, but it does provide a beginning point for supervision.

Burnout

The education literature is full of reports about teacher burnout. Some teachers have become frustrated because students today are very different from students they taught in the past. These teachers are often less effective in working with increasingly diverse student populations. While once quite effective, these teachers may simply have stopped trying. Others are disillusioned by what they perceive as administrative and bureaucratic structures that limit or interfere with their classroom autonomy. They may also have had one of more experiences in which they perceive that trust within the organization has been violated. In addition, misunderstandings and misinterpretations of the district's teacher evaluation system or the State of Texas Assessment of Academic Readiness (STAAR) may contribute to teacher frustration and burnout.

Self-Centeredness

Beginning teachers, in particular, may lack sufficient commitment, because they are struggling to establish themselves professionally and to balance the demands of their personal and professional lives. It is difficult to make a commitment to be innovative and creative when just attending to the basics is overwhelming.

An experienced but ineffective teacher may be quite satisfied with the status quo and see little reason to change. Perhaps the teacher has good ideas but is unwilling to commit the necessary time and energy to carry them out. Her "What's in it for me? Why should I work harder and change what I do?" attitude may suggest that she is more concerned with her own interests than with the needs of her students.

Unwillingness to Change and Fear of Change

Closely related to self-centeredness is the issue of change. Some teachers may simply be unwilling to change. They may realize that their old ways of teaching are not effective, but they are unwilling to commit the time and energy needed to learn and apply new pedagogy. Their old methodologies may not be very good, but they are very good at them! Change sometimes involves learning about and acting on new insights into the teaching-and-learning process: new curriculum and assessment standards, learning styles, differentiated instruction, brain research, inductive/inquiry lessons, integration of technology and electronic communication devices, and learning characteristics of children living in a culture of generational poverty. Some teachers may want society and students to change so that the old ways of doing business in the classroom can be perpetuated. They complain that poor parenting and social problems are the cause of low student achievement and resist pressure to adapt their teaching practices to include methods that are more effective for contemporary student populations. Other teachers may, understandably, simply fear change. Changing approaches to the design and delivery of instruction requires more risk than many are willing to accept, and there is comfort and safety in the old ways of doing things.

Personal Problems

While personal problems may hinder a teacher's ability to think abstractly and solve classroom problems, as discussed previously, they also may interfere with her commitment to her duties. The same marital or family difficulties, health problems, or financial stresses may occupy so much attention and energy that she is unable to devote significant time and energy to her professional obligations. It is difficult for the teacher to be highly motivated and committed to the job when her attention is absorbed by personal issues.

THE ISSUES INVOLVED IN SUPERVISION

In instructional supervision, there are at least three issues that will form the essential elements for a productive conference with the teacher: diagnosis, prescription, and time lines.

Diagnosis

The diagnosis responds to the question "What is effective and what is ineffective--what is working and what is not working?" The diagnosis may address issues related to the level of student participation and success, depth and complexity of the learning, connectivity of the learning to other disciplines and/or the world beyond the classroom, or the degree to which the classroom environment was supportive of student learning.

Prescription

Depending on the diagnosis, the prescription sets a direction for improving or maintaining teaching behavior. The prescription responds to the question "What must (or could) change?" Teachers with high levels of abstraction of commitment may generate their own prescription, but teachers with low abstraction and/or low commitment will need help in identifying areas for change and the direction in which changes must take place.

The following examples illustrate the language and the relationship between the diagnosis and the prescription:

DIAGNOSIS	PRESCRIPTION
The level of active, successful student participation does not meet the expectation of the district.	Plan and implement instruction in such a way that most students are actively, successfully participating in the teaching/learning process.
Monitoring and managing student behavior does not meet the expectation of the the district.	Monitor all students and intervene to stop or redirect behavior that is inappropriate or disruptive in such a way that this behavior stops.

Time Lines

Time lines establish checkpoints at which teaching behaviors will change and/or at which professional growth activities will be completed. When considering improvements in instructional behaviors, a common question is, "How much time is reasonable for change/improvement to occur?" The answer may be somewhat ambiguous because the length of time that is reasonable depends on a number of variables, including the teacher's contract, length of service, previous evaluations, seriousness of the behavior, and the complexity of the needed changes in the teacher's behavior, as well as district policies.

Longer Time to Improve		Shorter Time to Improve
• Term or continuing contract	vs.	Probationary contract
• Multiple years of experience	vs.	New to teaching
• History of good evaluations	vs.	No evaluations or consistently weak evaluations
• Minor/remediable problem	vs.	Serious/irremedial problem
• Complex changes in teacher behavior	vs.	Simple changes in teacher behavior

When the desired changes in behavior are complex (e.g., designing student-centered, inductive/inquiry lessons instead of teacher-centered, deductive lessons), it is reasonable to expect an extended period of time for those changes to occur. However, if the desired changes in behavior are rather simple (e.g., post rules for student behavior in the classroom), it is reasonable to expect changes within a much shorter time frame.

There may be some behaviors that are not remediable and will require no time for improvement. Assaulting a student would probably be considered irremediable behavior. The issue of remediation is addressed in more detail in Chapter 6.

MATCHING SUPERVISORY STYLE WITH TEACHER LEVEL OF DEVELOPMENT

Who Controls These Three Issues?

In the supervisor/teacher relationship, it is critical that you consciously understand who the decision-maker will be: who will decide what is effective/ineffective (the Diagnosis), who will decide what (if anything) will change (the Prescription), and by when will changes occur (the Time Lines)? Will you be the decision-maker? Will the teacher be the decision-maker? Will you and the teacher share decision-making?

Supervisory goals are generally focused on assisting teachers in improving their instructional practices and professional habits, and a central concern of administrators is how to match their supervisory style to individual needs of the teachers they support. In this handbook we consider three supervisory styles: collaborative, nondirective and directive. Each of these styles requires a different level of supervisory control of the three decisions. When the collaborative style is employed, the supervisor and teacher share control of diagnosis, prescription, and time lines. A nondirective approach places the teacher in control of these three issues. And a supervisor implementing the directive supervisory style retains control over all three supervisory issues. Each of these supervisory styles supports improved instructional practice when properly implemented and appropriately applied.

The modified version of Carl Glickman's paradigm shown in the figure below and the discussion which follows suggest ways that you may achieve this match by using what you know about the teacher's level of abstraction and level of commitment. (**Note:** While the paradigm is Professor Glickman's, the interpretations and applications are those of the authors.)

Figure 3-1*

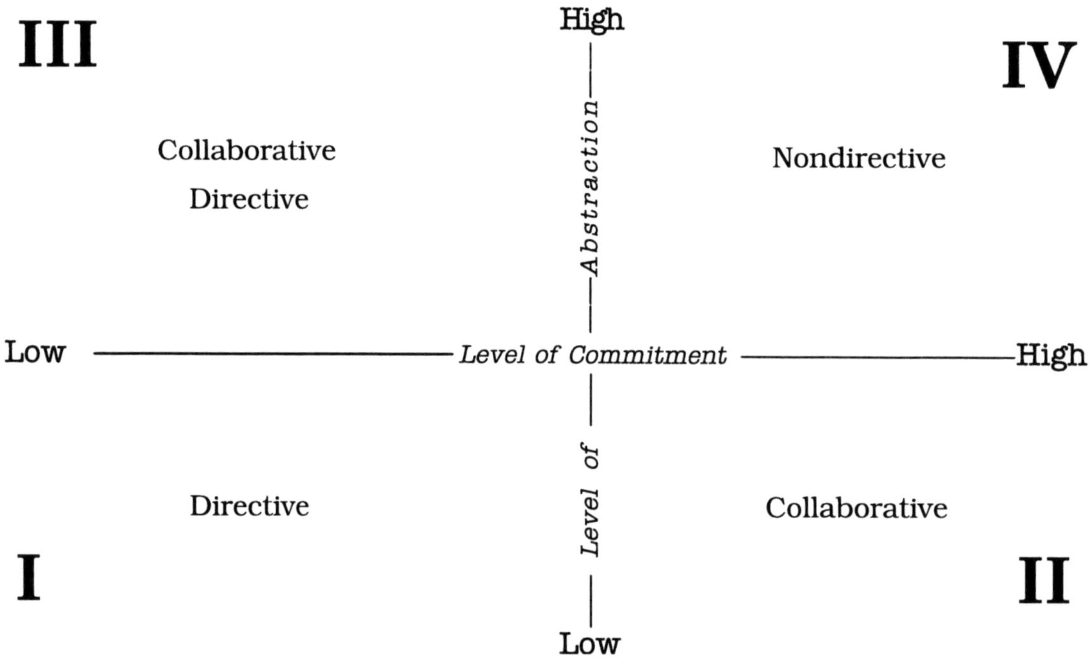

* Adapted from Carl D. Glickman, *Leadership For Learning: How to Help Teachers Succeed.* (Alexandria, VA: Association for Supervision and Curriculum Development), p. 88. Copyright © 2002 ISED, Inc. Reprinted by permission. All rights reserved.

Since we are focusing on the teacher in need of assistance, we concentrate our examples of appropriate supervision styles for teachers in Quadrants I through III. The Quadrant IV teacher is, in general, the effective teacher.

Quadrant I

Abstraction Level: Low
Commitment Level: Low

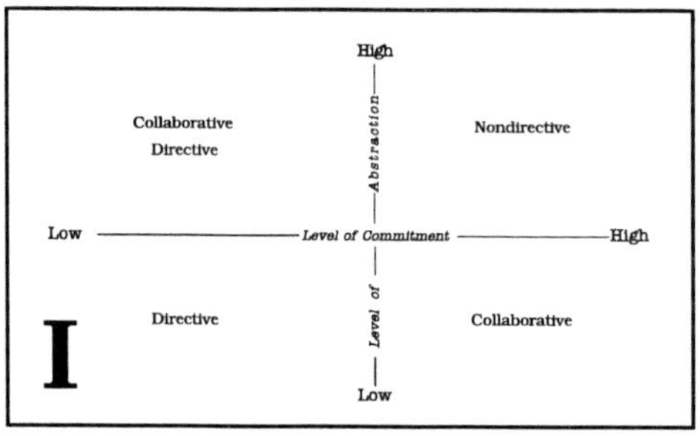

A directive style probably is most appropriate for the Quadrant I teacher. Remember, this teacher has a low level of abstraction and a low level of commitment--she has a small tool kit and may be unaware of problems, and she has a low commitment to changing/improving anything in her classroom. Consider the following scenario:

> In the post-observation conference, you tell the teacher that you observed four students passing notes. Then she responds, "Which students? When were they passing notes?" Later in the conference, you tell her that during the 45 minutes of observation three of the 28 students participated in the lesson in ways other than passive listening and note-taking. The teacher responds, "Is that a problem?" Toward the end of the conference, you ask her what changes she would make if she were to teach the same lesson again tomorrow. She replies: "I'd probably do it pretty much the same way. These remedial-level kids aren't going to do anything no matter what I do."

This teacher needs a directive style of supervision if any changes are going to occur. Her inability to see the problems in her classroom demonstrates her low level of abstraction, and even when problems are identified, she does not understand how to solve them. The directive supervisory style will be the most effective approach in this situation, and the supervisor must control the issues of diagnosis and prescription.

In addition, the post-observation conference revealed that this teacher thinks the students are the problem and that not much change will take place as a result of her initiative. Clearly, her level of commitment is low; therefore, you also must control the prescription and time lines for her improvement

QUADRANT I
Directive Supervision
Supervisor Controls

- Diagnosis
- Prescription
- Time Lines

Since this will be a directive conference, you will talk about your diagnosis, prescription, and time lines, and when you are finished, you will invite the teacher to say whatever she likes. You are the decision-maker; you will not be negotiating, arguing, attempting to convince, or attempting to reach consensus. That is what directive supervision is all about.

Quadrant II

Abstraction Level: Low
Commitment Level: High

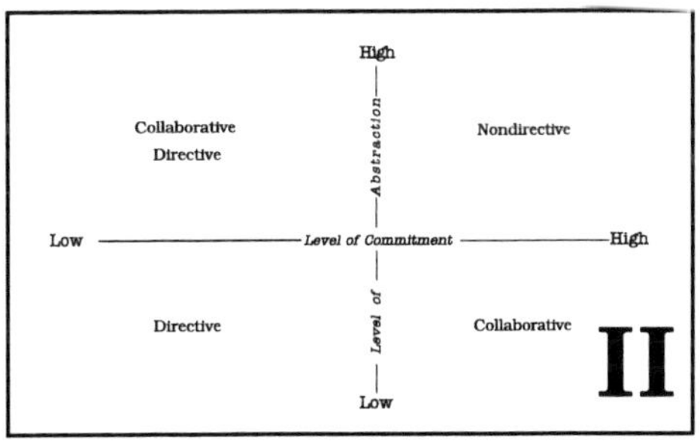

A collaborative style is most appropriate for the Quadrant II teacher. Recall from our previous discussion that many beginning teachers are in this quadrant. The following scenario illustrates how to work with a teacher who has a high level of commitment but whose low level of abstraction hinders his effectiveness.

> In the post-observation conference, you share with the teacher some of the data you gathered during the observation. You tell him that when students were successful in responding to questions, he simply called on the next student and that when students were unsuccessful he provided no prompting or corrective feedback. The teacher is surprised. "I really thought I was using more positive reinforcement with the kids. I really enjoy them, and I want them to feel good when they are successful. I know I'm not very good at giving corrective feedback and prompting. I'm always so afraid I'll make them feel dumb or embarrass them if I try to help them get the right answer." When he asks you what he can do to improve both situations, you offer a number of alternatives. He replies, "I'd really like to attend the workshop on instructional strategies for low-achieving students and to observe Mr. Jones. He's really good at helping his kids without making them feel bad." He then asks if you can come back to observe immediately after he attends the workshop and observes Mr. Jones to see if he has improved. You suggest that maybe two weeks after the workshop and the observation of Mr. Jones' class would be a better time for you to revisit his classroom. This will give the teacher time to practice what he has learned.

QUADRANT II

Collaborative Supervision

Supervisor and Teacher Share Control

- Diagnosis
- Prescription
- Time Lines

This teacher is aware of some problems but not of others. In discussing the problems, he indicates that he is not quite sure how to solve them. This indicates a low level of abstraction. If the goal is to help the teacher improve, you need to share control of the diagnosis and prescription by presenting the objective data from the observation and offering a range of suggestions from which the teacher may choose or advise him to meet with an effective teacher in his area of instruction. Fortunately, this teacher has a high level of commitment. He wants to be better at both positive reinforcement and corrective feedback and even suggests one strategy for improvement. He asks you to return to the classroom to see if he has improved. You share control of the diagnosis and prescription. Because of his low level of abstraction, he needs assistance in identifying the problems and their solutions. You also share control of the time line; because he has *high* commitment, he may be inclined to over commit to both the complexity and the speed of change.

You may find yourself supervising a Quadrant II teacher who wants to improve and who has a high level of commitment but whose level of abstraction is so low that improvement within a reasonable period of time is unlikely. In this instance, you may want to consider shifting your supervisory style from collaborative to directive.

Quadrant III

Abstraction Level: High
Commitment Level: Low

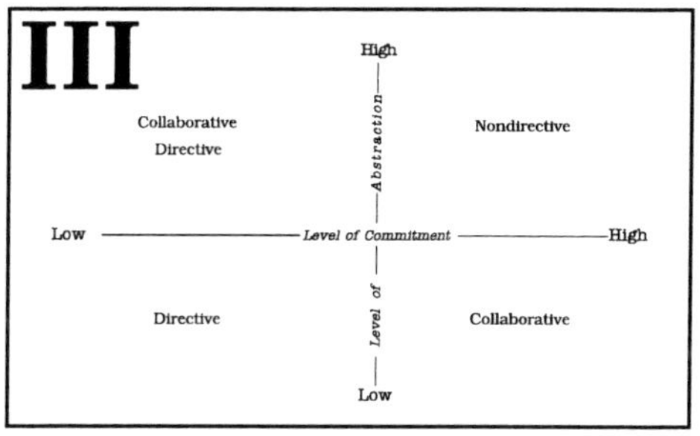

This area of supervision may be very complex. Because of the teacher's high level of abstraction, she is certainly capable of sharing control (collaborative style of supervision) of the diagnosis and prescription. Because she is low in commitment, you may learn early in the supervisory relationship that she is unwilling to accept responsibility for the ineffectiveness of her instruction. If your goal is to help the Quadrant III teacher improve, a collaborative style probably will be your first choice. If you discover that she is unwilling to change instructional strategies, then a directive style may be more appropriate for diagnosis, prescription; and time lines. Here's a possible scenario.

> In the post-observation conference, you tell the teacher that when you were observing her lesson, she put the term "existentialism" on the board and proceeded to talk about Jean-Paul Sartre and how he influenced a whole generation of American writers. When students were asked what Sartre's influence was on three short stories they recently had read, none of the six students called on was able to give a correct answer. When she assigned a three-paragraph in-class essay on Sartre's influence on the stories, at least nine students just sat at their desks looking at blank paper. At least six others had their hands up constantly. The teacher replied, "I know they had no idea what to do. I probably should have identified the four or five characteristics of existentialism and given them some examples before asking questions and making the writing assignment. I know from Madeline Hunter's work that abstract concepts are made more understandable and concrete for students if the critical attributes can be identified and elaborated. I will certainly need to do that in the future." Two weeks later, you observe the teacher teaching a lesson on Romanticism in American literature. She teaches this lesson in exactly the same way as she taught the lesson on existentialism and with the same effect on students.

QUADRANT III

Collaborative Supervision for Diagnosis and Prescription

Supervisor and Teacher Share Control

- Diagnosis
- Prescription

Directive Supervision for Standards and Time Lines

Supervisor Controls

- Time Lines

This teacher has a high level of abstraction. She knows the problem, how to address the problem, what the options are, and the research literature. She has the ability to share control of diagnosis and prescription issues with the supervisor. In this instance, she does so accurately. However, this teacher's lack of commitment becomes apparent when her teaching style remains the same even after the need for change was discussed in the post-observation conference. The supervisor, therefore, must control the time line by reminding this teacher what she committed to do and setting a deadline for doing it.

If the supervisor determines that the teacher is unwilling to change and/or if the teacher blames the students for the problems and for her lack of effectiveness, the supervisor should choose a directive style of supervision for all three issues: diagnosis, prescription, and time lines.

Quadrant IV

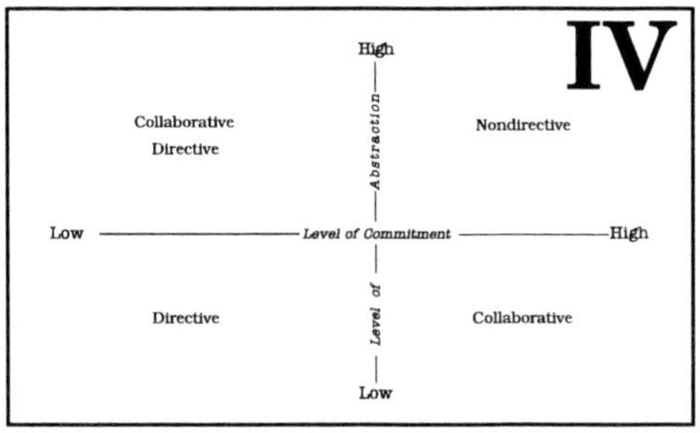

Abstraction Level: High
Commitment Level: High

It is unlikely that you will ever need to use a directive approach with a Quadrant IV teacher. This teacher has a high level of abstraction and a high level of commitment. Consider the following scenario:

> In the post-observation conference, you ask the teacher to reflect on the mathematics lesson you observed. The teacher tells you that he is generally pleased with the way the lesson went. "The students were all engaged and almost all of them participated when I was demonstrating the algorithm on the overhead. I know that's sometimes hard for them to do." When you ask the teacher what strategies he most commonly plans to maximize the level of engagement and participation, he says, "Well, I think there are several things I consider. I try to apply the concepts we study to things that are relevant to them. In this lesson, I used data from the sale of rap and pop music. There's usually more motivation to be engaged when the mathematical questions are interesting and relevant." You ask the teacher what he considering doing in future lessons to maintain a high level of participation. The teacher replies, "I really want to move away from so much traditional paper/pencil assessment of their learning. I've been reading about problem-based learning in the math journals. That approach calls on students to produce products or performances that demonstrate that they understand and can apply the math. I'd really like to learn more about that and begin to try it out—maybe some time next semester."

A nondirective style clearly will be most appropriate because his high levels of abstraction and commitment make him effective. He recognizes what works in his class and can articulate the strategies he implements. He reads the literature in his field and is familiar with other options available to him. He is quite capable of controlling his own diagnosis and prescription. Since it reasonably can be anticipated that this teacher will take action to repeat effective behaviors and work to improve ineffective behaviors, the supervisor also should allow him to control the time lines.

Note: On rare occasions, you may encounter a teacher who is truly a Quadrant IV on almost every issue; however, there is one particular issue on which the teacher behaves as a Quadrant III. For example, the teacher is very effective and earns ratings of exceeds expectations on almost every domain of his appraisal. However, the teacher is highly resistive of the state-mandated Response to Intervention (RtI). The teacher makes comments such as "I know that some of these students need extra help and support, but a lot of them kids don't need separate interventions; they just need to keep up with the regular class work. It's a waste of time to design all these so-called interventions for some of these kids." He is a great teacher, but on the single issue of RtI, he disagrees with the state's requirements. You will initially attempt to use a collaborative style of supervision to persuade him of the validity of the campus RtI plan. If you are not successful, you will need to shift to a directive style and take control of the decisions on this issue. Since RtI is a state mandate, neither you nor the teacher really have any choice!

QUADRANT IV
Nondirective Supervision
Teacher Controls
- Diagnosis
- Prescription
- Time Lines

STRATEGIES FOR COLLABORATION

As indicated above, the collaborative supervisory style is often appropriate in cases involving teachers in Quadrant II. The steps listed below are part of an overall strategy of collaborative supervision.

1. You may choose to conduct pre-observation conferences to discuss the teacher's plans for the lesson and agree on what the teacher will do and what you will see/hear (e.g., the learning objective, instructional strategies, classroom management practices, techniques of presentation of subject matter, learning climate, evidence of successful student performance).
2. Conduct classroom observations, collect data, analyze the data, and make your own preliminary judgments about the practices that are effective in terms of successful student behavior/performance and those that are not. Some observations may be announced; others may be unannounced "walk-through" observations.
3. After each observation, conduct a post-observation conference. In the conference, provide feedback on the issues discussed in the pre-observation conference and/or ask questions that encourage the teacher to analyze the lesson and the data. Remember that this is a collaborative conference, so you will be sharing control of the issues: diagnosis, prescription, and time lines. You

are sharing control of decision-making; you will be negotiating, arguing, attempting to convince, or attempting to reach consensus.

4. Diagnosis: This is a shared decision. Determine through questioning what she believes was or was not effective. Ask questions and provide data from the observation that prompt the teacher to identify teaching practices or lesson designs that were or were not effective.

5. Prescription: This is a shared decision. Ask the teacher about what changes in teaching practices or lesson design could/should occur. Offer choices (not suggestions or directives) for alternative strategies and offer choices for professional development activities to help the teacher to bring about the changes.

6. Time lines: This is a shared decision. Set reasonable time frames for changes in behavior and for completion of professional growth activities in consultation with the teacher.

7. Consider writing a specific incident memorandum following each conference. How to write effective specific incident memoranda related to instruction is addressed in detail in the next chapter. If you are truly being collaborative, if your goal is growth and improvement, and if you believe that the teacher can (level of abstraction) and will (level of commitment) improve, you may decide to be more informal and limit yourself to verbal suggestions. [Note: If your goal is to recommend termination or nonrenewal, you must write a memorandum to document that the teacher received notice of unsatisfactory job performance. (See Chapters 2 and 4.)]

8. Continue to observe the teacher in the classroom, focusing on the specific changes in behavior that you and the teacher agreed to, as well gathering evidence of successful student performance. (See Chapters 2 and 4.)

9. If you do not see adequate growth and improvement, consider collaboratively creating a professional improvement plan to formalize your shared analysis of deficiencies (diagnosis), for changes in a classroom behavior (prescription), your shared expectations for student performance, and time lines for successful implementation of the standards. (See Chapter 6.)

STRATEGIES FOR DIRECTIVE SUPERVISION

As indicated above, the directive supervisory style is often appropriate for cases involving marginally effective or ineffective teachers. Typically, these are the teachers in Quadrant I and Quadrant III. The steps listed below are part of an overall strategy of directive supervision.

1. You may choose to conduct pre-observation conferences to discuss the teacher's plans for the lesson and what you will expect to see (e.g., instructional strategies, classroom management practices, techniques of presentation of subject matter, learning climate, evidence of successful student performance).

2. Conduct frequent classroom observations, collect data, and analyze the data to determine which practices are effective and which are not in terms of successful student behavior/performance. Some observations may be announced; others may be unannounced "walk-through" observations.

3. After each observation, conduct a post-observation conference to provide feedback on the issues discussed in the pre-observation conference. Remember that this is a directive conference, so you will be in control (not shared control) of the issues — you will be the decision-maker for diagnosis, prescription, and time lines. Additionally, remember that if your goal is contract nonrenewal or termination, focus only on the observation data that show a need for improvement and your directives for improvement.
4. Diagnosis: You have control of this issue. Be very specific about what was or was not effective.
5. Prescription: You have control of this issue. Be very specific about what additional changes must occur. Suggest or require professional development activities to help bring about the needed changes.
6. Time lines: You have control of this issue. Set reasonable time frames for changes in behavior and for completion of professional growth activities.
7. Write a specific incident memorandum following each conference. (See Chapters 2 and 4.)
8. Continue to observe the teacher in the classroom, focusing on the specific changes in behavior that you directed and on evidence of successful student performance. (See Chapters 6.)
9. At some point in the supervision process, write a professional improvement plan to formalize your judgments regarding deficiencies (diagnosis), your directives for changes in a classroom behavior (prescription), your expectations for student performance, and time lines for successful implementation of the standards. (See Chapter 6.)

Note: The teacher's failure to follow directives to change instructional behavior may become the basis for decisions to nonrenew or terminate the teaching contract.

FOCUSING ON INSTRUCTION IN THE CLASSROOM

It should be clear from our discussion so far that the supervisor responsible for marginally effective teachers will be spending considerable time in their classrooms. A teacher who resents your increased attention may accuse you of harassment, claiming that she is the subject of "arbitrary and capricious treatment." Why else would you be spending so much time in her classroom in comparison with the time spent in the classrooms of other teachers? Claims of harassment are unlikely to be given much credence when the rationale for stepped-up classroom visitations is objectively clear. There are a number of tactics you can use to forestall allegations of harassment and arbitrary and capricious treatment. Begin by making certain that you do, in fact, have objective reasons for visiting the teacher's classroom more frequently. The following list includes sample reasons for spending more time in a classroom. Whether they apply in a given school will depend on your district's policies.

- Deficiencies apparent in previous classroom observations.
- Need to monitor compliance with directives and/or the requirements of a professional growth plan.
- Failure rates that exceed the norm for your campus.
- Complaints from parents, students, or other staff members.
- Low student performance indicated by the results of STAAR or AP tests.
- Uniform treatment of an entire "class" of teachers (e.g., all probationary contract teachers, all teachers in their first year of assignment to your campus); if your campus plan has targeted raising math scores, the "class" of teacher may be all math teachers.

  Note that these issues are <u>not</u> reasons for nonrenewal or termination. They are reasons for being in the teacher's classroom more frequently.

Explain to the teacher in need of assistance that your purpose is to help, not hurt. Comments such as these might be useful:

> As you know, Ms. Jones, my formal observations have revealed some significant deficiencies in your classroom performance. I am going to devote as much of my time as possible to helping you improve. I will be visiting your classes periodically to see how our professional growth plan is working and to learn what else we might do. Please don't be upset by my visits. My purpose is to help you overcome these problems so that you can realize your full potential as a teacher on this campus.

It is true, of course, that you may eventually conclude that Ms. Jones will never be an effective teacher. Because of low abstraction and/or commitment levels, some marginally effective teachers cannot and/or will not respond favorably to guidance and principles of good developmental supervision. In these instances, it may become necessary for you as the supervisor to adopt a directive style of supervision that does not include encouragement to improve, because your goal is now to assemble sufficient evidence of ineffective teaching to suggest a recommendation for contract nonrenewal or termination.

SUMMARY

In this chapter we have addressed the sources of weak instructional behaviors – low levels of abstraction and commitment – and discussed the supervisory issues and approaches that affect and support instructional improvement and professional growth in teachers in need of assistance. In Chapter 6 we will address the development of professional growth plans that clearly communicate directives for change and classroom observation and documentation techniques designed to facilitate better instructional behaviors and improved student outcomes.

CHAPTER FOUR: DOCUMENTING INSTRUCTION

As noted in the Preface, the classroom data-gathering and documentation process described in this chapter both complements, and may be independent of, the appraisal process using the Professional Development and Appraisal System (PDAS), or a locally developed instrument. It complements these systems in that it provides a means of gathering cumulative data over time that can be incorporated into the overall teacher appraisal so long as the necessary time lines and other relevant procedures of the district's appraisal system are followed.

The classroom documentation process described in this chapter also can be used as an independent assessment system for the marginally effective teacher, dependent upon local policy. As we saw in Chapter 1, the Texas Commissioner of Education has issued decisions indicating that satisfactory ratings on an overall appraisal system do not necessarily insulate a teacher from contract nonrenewal or termination. This is particularly true where overall domain scores on an appraisal instrument mask serious deficiencies in classroom performance. It also is true with regard to the probationary contract teacher where the development of appraisal-based growth plans may not be feasible. It is important to emphasize that we are focusing in this chapter on the marginally effective teacher who needs considerable supervisory attention, not on the effective teacher. Our assumption is that your time is valuable and that you can realistically concentrate only on one or two marginally effective teachers at a time.

Should you document a teacher's classroom behavior before or after you develop a Teacher in Need of Improvement Plan (TINA). The answer is both. Before a TINA is developed, classroom observation and instructional documentation can assist you both in justifying the need for a TINA and in objectively verifying what specific directives it should contain. After the TINA is developed, it is essential that you document your "walk-through" and more formal observations to establish the extent of compliance with TINA directives and to demonstrate a pattern of behavior over time. You may later need to incorporate the information into a summary memorandum indicating that contract nonrenewal or termination is imminent.

In Chapter 2, principal Paula Leader documented the out-of-classroom behavior of Melba Toast, a teacher on her faculty, who disparaged Paula's leadership in a public and unprofessional manner. Melba's conduct went well beyond complaining and criticizing. She flatly refused to implement Paula's discipline policy in the classroom. The refusal, along with the unprofessional manner in which she addressed Ms. Leader, was the focus of the last chance memorandum that Paula wrote.

Your memorandum may, however, have an altogether different focus. Suppose that a teacher on your staff — we will call him Bill Laze — is marginally effective or ineffective because of his poor teaching. You have worked with Mr. Laze over a period of time, and you are beginning to believe that he cannot (level of abstraction) and/or will not (level of commitment) improve. Your task now is to document one or more of Mr. Laze's instructional practices from information you gather during classroom observations. Specific guidelines you can follow for gathering informa-

---

* While the terminology may differ in the appraisal system a school district is using, we will use the term "Teacher in Need of Assistance Plan" to refer to the formal improvement document resulting from low appraisal scores.

tion during a classroom observation and for applying the principles of documentation provided in Chapter 2 are presented here.

METHODS OF GATHERING DATA IN CLASSROOM OBSERVATION

Before you can document inadequacies in the teaching/learning process, you first must go into the classroom to observe and collect data. Your ability to write effective documentation related to instruction is directly related to your ability to gather objective information in the teacher's classroom. There are several effective ways to do this. Your choice of methods depends both on why you are observing and on how many different decisions you need to make following an observation. There are four primary methods of gathering and recording information during an observation: scripting, writing an anecdotal record, electronic recording, and using focused observation instruments.

Scripting

A script is a word-for-word transcript of what the teacher and students say. Imagine that you have come to Mr. Laze's classroom to observe and you choose to employ the scripting technique. Here is an excerpt from your script notes:

> **Mr. L.: OK. Open your books to page 87. Today we're going to be talking about the South after the Civil War, Reconstruction. You were supposed to read this chapter as part of last night's assignment. You need to be sure and take notes, because some of this is not in your chapter. Paul, why is this period called "Reconstruction"?**
>
> **Paul: I don't know.**
>
> **Mr. L.: OK. Steve, do you know?**
>
> **Steve: Because the North rebuilt the Southern cities it had destroyed.**
>
> **Mr. L.: No, not exactly. Susie, do you know?**

Scripting is useful when you are conducting a lengthy classroom observation after which you will go back to your office and make many decisions about the lesson (how to rate criteria and domains on PDAS, for example). Scripting is a good option when you need detailed documentation of everything that was said during the lesson.

An advantage of the detailed word-for-word account of the lesson obtained by scripting is that it helps you to determine precisely why certain aspects of a lesson were significant. For example, the details you recorded can tell why the lesson was extremely successful or was not at all successful.

The disadvantages of scripting are obvious. You are so busy writing (with your head down, most likely) that you may miss important non-verbal student and teacher behavior. You also might find that completeness and accuracy are very difficult to attain.

Anecdotal Record

Writing an anecdotal record differs from scripting in that the observer takes descriptive notes about what is observed rather than trying to record each word. The exchange in the example above would appear this way if written as an anecdotal record:

```
Mr. Laze told students to open books and to take notes. Called on
Paul and Steve. Neither knew the answer. No corrective feedback.
```

Like scripting, the anecdotal record is useful when you are conducting a lengthy classroom observation upon which many decisions will be based and for which you will need information about every aspect of the lesson. It is appropriate to use anecdotal records rather than scripting when you do not need a verbatim record of the teacher monologue and student/teacher interaction.

Taking notes for the anecdotal record is faster and easier than scripting, allows the observer to note non-verbal teacher and student behaviors, and provides a great deal of information about many different aspects of the teaching/learning process. On the other hand, it does not provide details about what was said by teachers or by students.

Electronic Recording

You may choose to record a lesson with audio or video equipment when the observation will be lengthy, when it will form the basis for many decisions, and when you need incontrovertible evidence of what was said or done during the lesson. You may also choose to record electronically when you decide that your skills at scripting or note-taking are not good enough to give you the information you need.

An obvious advantage of electronic recording is that you have a word-for-word record of the lesson with detailed verbal (and with video, nonverbal) information for use in analyzing the lesson and its effectiveness. You also have incontrovertible proof of what occurred in the classroom.

There are several disadvantages of electronic recording. To begin with, the video or audio recording equipment often available in schools may be of poor quality. Audio recording omits critical non-verbal behaviors while video recording sees only what the camera beholds (and the camera is often pointed at the wrong place). Another very important drawback to electronic recording is that the disruption created by the equipment in the classroom is greater than that created by the observer alone. Moreover, the presence of the equipment may aggravate the teacher's anxiety and resistance.

Focused Observation Instruments

Suppose you want to visit Mr. Laze's class specifically to observe one aspect of instruction — student participation, for example. When you are concerned only with one or two issues during a classroom visit, you should use a focused observation instrument such as a check list, graph, or short question-answer list for gathering information. In the case of student participation, for example, a seating chart and key similar to the one shown in Figure 4-1 will prove helpful. The chart will make it easy to document the interchange between the teacher and students.

Figure 4-1

Sam	Susie	Bill	Paul	Andrew
	✓ ?		✓ –	

Steve	Bob	Sarah	Sean	Aaron
✓ –		✓ +		

Key:	
✓ +	student participated successfully
✓ –	student participated unsuccessfully
✓ ?	student participated; success unknown/unclear

Focused observation instruments that target only a particular aspect of instruction are easy to use because they do not require a great deal of writing. Not burdened by taking notes, you are free to detect non-verbal behaviors and can gain a great deal of information about the issue or issues you came to observe. Recognize, however, that focused observation instruments should not be used for routine appraisals or for gathering data upon which many decisions will be made, because they do not address all aspects of the lesson.

GATHERING DATA IN THE MARGINAL TEACHER'S CLASSROOM

In Chapter 3 we described the marginally effective teacher and made a series of recommendations for appropriate supervision practices. Recall that the marginally effective teacher is one who has some competence but who also has one or more deficiencies in instructional practice. More importantly, these deficiencies impede his or her performance, as evidenced in student misbehavior, lack of success, or other factors.

Suppose that you have decided that you no longer can ignore Mr. Laze's inadequacies. The action that you take as his supervisor may assist him to improve. Or, despite your best efforts, Mr. Laze may not improve beyond his marginal effectiveness, and you may eventually recommend a negative employment decision.

If you know what specific changes he should make, you are well on your way to writing a TINA. If you do not, you should conduct some informal observations to give you more focus. In either case, your best approach is to conduct a series of fifteen to thirty minute observations in his classroom and direct your data collection efforts to his weak instructional areas. Deficiencies are likely to be attributed to one or more of the following concerns:

1. Active, Successful Student Participation in the Learning Process
   - Students are actively engaged in learning.
   - Students are successful in learning.
   - Student behaviors indicate learning is at a high cognitive level (e.g., critical thinking, creative thinking, problem solving, etc.).

- Students are self-directed/self-initiated as appropriate to the lesson.
- Students are connecting learning to work and life applications, both within the discipline and with other disciplines.

2. Learner-Centered Instruction
   - Objective and goals include basic knowledge/skills and central themes and concepts of the discipline.
   - Instructional content is learner-centered (e.g., related to the interests and various characteristics of students).
   - Instructional strategies promote critical thinking and problem solving.
   - Instructional strategies include motivational techniques to successfully engage students in the learning process.
   - Instructional strategies are aligned with objectives, activities, student characteristics, prior learning, and work applications, both within the discipline and with other disciplines.
   - The teacher varies activities appropriately and maintains appropriate pace and sequencing of instruction.
   - The teacher emphasizes the value and importance of the activity/content.
   - The teacher uses appropriate questioning and inquiry techniques to challenge students.
   - The teacher makes appropriate use of available technology as a part of the instructional process.

3. Evaluation and Feedback on Student Progress
   - Academic progress of students is monitored and assessed.
   - Assessment and feedback are aligned with goals and objectives and instructional strategies.
   - Assessment strategies are appropriate to the varied characteristics of students.
   - Student learning is reinforced.
   - Students receive specific, constructive feedback.
   - The teacher provides opportunities for re-learning and re-evaluation of material.

4. Management of Student Discipline, Instructional Strategies, Time, and Materials
   - The teacher effectively implements the discipline management procedures approved for the campus.
   - The teacher establishes a classroom environment that promotes and encourages self-discipline and self-directed learning.
   - The teacher interacts with students in an equitable manner, including fair application of rules.
   - The teacher specifies expectations for desired behavior.
   - The teacher intervenes and re-directs off-task, inappropriate, or disruptive behavior.

- The teacher reinforces desired behavior when appropriate.
- The instructional materials selected by the teacher are equitable and acknowledge the varied characteristics of all students.
- The teacher effectively and efficiently manages time and materials.

5. Learning Environment
   - The teacher uses strategies to motivate students for learning.
   - The teacher establishes and maintains a positive learning environment.

Notice that these concerns are arranged into five groups. The first group relates to active, successful student participation in the learning process. The focus is on student behavior/performance. Are students successfully engaged in critical thinking and problem solving? Are students successfully making connections within the discipline, to other disciplines, to the world of work, and/or to other issues beyond the classroom? Are students responding to and participating in instruction because the teacher has selected instructional strategies, activities, and materials that motivate the students, or are students participating only because of manipulation/coercion by the teacher?

The second group concerns how the teacher is teaching. Here again, there is an emphasis on successful student engagement in critical thinking and problem solving as well as student motivation and self-direction. In addition, this group deals with alignment among objectives, activities, materials, and the needs/characteristics of students.

The third group relates to evaluation and feedback on student progress. Are all students being monitored and assessed? Are assessment strategies aligned with the objectives and with the varied needs/characteristics of students? Do students receive appropriate reinforcement and corrective feedback on their learning?

Group four deals with management of instruction, student behavior, time and materials.

Finally, group five addresses the learning environment in the classroom.

The five focused observation instruments illustrated in this chapter are designed to gather information in the classroom when students and teachers are engaged in teaching/learning and are of significant value when making teacher evaluation and contract renewal decisions based on Domains I-IV of the Professional Development and Appraisal system (PDAS). There are four other domains that focus on issues that, generally, do not lend themselves to focused observation instruments as the primary data-collection method.

Domain V deals with Professional Communication. Some data may come from classroom observation using Focused Observation Instrument # 5: Learning Environment or Focused Observation Instrument # 3: Evaluation and Feedback on Student Progress.

- Criterion 1: The teacher uses appropriate and accurate verbal and non-verbal communication with students.
- Criterion 3: The teacher encourages and supports students who are having difficulty.
- Criterion 6: The teacher's interactions are supportive, courteous, and respectful with <u>students</u>, parents, community members, and other professionals (emphasis added).

Other issues within this domain will require gathering information outside the classroom and will be specifically addressed in Chapter 5.

Domain VI assesses Professional Development. There are four questions that are the focus of this domain. As the teacher has made choices for professional development, do these choices positively correlate with the:

- Goals of the campus and district?
- Assigned subject content and the varied needs of students?
- Teacher's prior performance appraisal?
- Teacher collaboration with colleagues on improving student performance?

If you have concerns in this domain, you will need to carefully compare the teacher's professional development activities with the campus and district improvement plans, with the content area(s) to which the teacher is assigned, with the unique needs and characteristics of the teacher's students, and the with the extent to which the teacher works with others to improve student performance. This information will come from a variety of documents, reports, student demographic data, student performance data, and observation as the teacher works with other professionals.

Domain VII addresses Compliance with Policies, Operating Procedures, and Requirements.

This domain addresses:

- Compliance with all policies, operating procedures, and legal requirements.
- Compliance with written directives.
- Contributions to a safe, orderly, and stimulating learning environment outside the classroom (emphasis added)

Information about non-compliance with policies, procedures, and legal requirements generally will come from your observations outside the classroom. Documentation may be much like the memorandum from Angie O'Plasty to Bob Instructor or the memorandum from Wendell Wheelturner to Arney Artisan in Chapter 2. Non-compliance with written directives is a clear, objective, and legal reason for a negative employment decision. Writing these directives and then documenting "failure to comply" is discussed in Chapter 6. Along with judgments concerning the teacher's contributions to the school's overall learning environment, these issues will require investigation and data collection outside the classroom.

Finally, Domain VIII attempts to address the Improvement of Academic Performance for All Students on the Campus (based on indicators included in the Academic Excellence Indicator System – AEIS). Ironically, the language of this domain to date does not embrace the idea of whether or not students actually improve their academic performance. Instead, the state's language takes the approach of describing whether or not the teacher does things that might/could/should lead to an increase in student performance but avoids any language that says students improve on any of the indicators of the Academic Excellence Indicator System (AEIS). This domain asks whether or not the teacher:

- Aligns instruction to Texas Essential Knowledge Skills (TEKS)/state assessment objectives.
- Analyzes and acts on state assessment data.
- Adjusts the sequence of instruction to incorporate TEKS/State Assessment Objectives.
- Selects/adapts instructional materials/activities correlated with TEKS/State Assessment Objectives.
- Provides feedback to students regarding their progress in learning TEKS/ State Assessment Objectives.
- Monitors attendance and contacts parents, counselors, and others when there is a serious problem.
- Identifies and assesses the needs of at-risk students
- Meets with students who are failing or in danger of failing and develops a plan for intervention.
- Modifies and adapts materials/instruction for at-risk students.

In order to gather information about these issues, classroom observation using focused observation instruments #1 (Active, Successful Student Participation in Learning), #2 (Learner-Centered Instruction), and #3 (Evaluation and Feedback on Student Progress) may yield data on how the teacher aligns TEKS/state assessment objectives with instruction, materials, activities, feedback, adjustments of materials/activities, etc. The teacher's logs, notes, RtI plans, e-mails, etc.,may provide information on student and parent conferences as well as planned interventions for at-risk students.

> Note: The Professional Development and Appraisal System (PDAS) is the recommended appraisal process and language for the State of Texas as well as the board-adopted process and language for most school districts. Therefore, PDAS language carries behind it the force of law. PDAS, as well as the focused observation instruments in this handbook, are based on effective teaching practices research such as:
>
> Burbules, N. C., & Bruce, B. C. (2001). Theory and research on teaching as dialogue. In V. Richardson (Ed.), Handbook of research on teaching (4th ed., pp. 1102-1121). Washington, DC: American Educational Research Association.
>
> Marzano, R.J., Pickering, D.J., & Pollock, J.E. (2001). Classroom instruction that works: Research based strategies for increasing student achievement. Alexandria, VA: Association for Supervision and Curriculum Development.

Let's turn now to examine how our focused observation instruments can be used to gather data during classroom walk-throughs in Domains I-IV, the areas directly dealing with classroom teaching/learning. Below, we present five different models of focused observation instruments we have developed to document Mr. Laze's instruction relative to the five groups of deficiency concerns shown above. Each of the five models employs a distinct style of recording information during an observation and of making judgments about that information once the observation is over.

First, review the following script of the words and events that transpired in Mr. Laze's classroom during a brief unscheduled observation. As you read it over, you will recognize shortcomings in several areas. The focused observation instruments presented later in this chapter will serve to classify these shortcomings and allow you as the observer to narrow your focus.

You will undoubtedly note that the transcript as written is detailed and fairly complete--the result of nonstop note-taking in the classroom itself or of a long series of write, rewind, write, rewind, write, etc., from a recorded source, which may take much longer than the original 25-minute observation. The focused observation instruments that follow are designed to minimize the time spent recording data by sharpening the observer's focus.

Class: 9th grade History

Teacher: Mr. Bill Laze

Date: October 10, 2011

Time: 8:30-8:55

Number of students: 30

(Students are entering room. Bell rings. Four students enter after the tardy bell. Mr. L. is talking to 2 students at desk. Mr. L. does not say anything to 4 students who enter late.)

Mr. L: OK. Get out homework papers. We are going to check homework.

(Mr. L. walks around and checks to see if students have completed homework, making marks in the grade book. Two students have nothing on their desks.)

Mr. L: Put your homework back in notebooks. We'll go over it later in the period if we have time. OK. Open books to page 87. Today we're going to be talking about the South after the Civil War, Reconstruction. You were supposed to read this chapter as part of last night's assignment. You need to be sure and take notes, because some of this is not in your chapter. Paul, why is this period called Reconstruction?

Paul: I don't know.

Mr. L: OK, Steve, do you know?

Steve: Because the North rebuilt the Southern cities it had destroyed.

Mr. L: No, not exactly. Susie, do you know?

Susie: I'm not sure, but I think it was because the Radical Republicans believed that the Southern leadership had violated the Constitution and needed to be re-educated and required to sign some kind of pledge of loyalty to the United States. Also because they were rebuilding, you know, the farms and factories.

Mr. L: That's a good answer. Did everybody get that?

(Mr. L. is standing behind lectern, lecturing about Reconstruction in Texas. Tells students who the leaders were, what the dates were, and three significant things the Radical Republicans did: "disenfranchised" Southern leaders, established the Freedman's Bureau, imposed heavy taxes on Southern landowners.)

Mr. L: Now, Audrey, why did they disenfranchise the Southerners?

Audrey: I don't know.

Mr. L: Why not? Didn't you read the assignment? Aaron?

Aaron: What's "disenfranchise"? (Student mispronounces word.)

Mr. L: Look it up. Susie, can you bail him out?

Susie: They disenfranchised them so that the Yankees could control who got elected to public office.

Mr. L: Right again, Susie. You guys better be paying attention and taking notes because this stuff is going to be on the test Friday. All right Aaron, I'm going to give you another chance. What was the difference between Federal fiscal policy in Texas and fiscal policy in other Southern states?

Aaron: Well, they were less physical in Texas than in other Southern states. I mean, they didn't push the Texans around like they did the ones in Mississippi and Georgia.

Mr. L: Not hardly, Aaron. Does anybody know? (Aaron closes his book and puts down his pen. Pause. No hands are raised. Mr. L. is still standing at lectern.) Didn't anybody read the assignment? (Susie raises her hand.)

Susie: The tax burden in Texas was much lower than it was in the other Southern states and, because of that, fewer Texans lost their land and fewer carpetbaggers moved in to buy it at tax sales.

Mr. L: I'm glad one person read the assignment, Susie. (Mr. L. begins to discuss military policy in Texas during Reconstruction. Six students are taking notes. All others are not taking notes. Mr. L. continues to stand at lectern. Nothing has been written on board. Lecture on military policy in Texas continues. Three students in the back – Aaron, Paul, Betsy – are whispering. Mr. L. still at lectern talking about military policy in Texas.) And why were former Southern troops asigned the job of fighting Indians on the frontier? Matt?

Matt: I'm sorry, what?

Mr. L: You sure are. Paul?

Paul: Why were Southerners what?

Mr. L: Assigned to fight Indians on the frontier.

Paul: Because they were suspicious of their loyalty and didn't trust them to serve in other places, like outside the South.

Mr. L: Right, Paul. See what happens when you pay attention?

(Observation ends at 8:55. Mr. L. is still at lectern discussing the composition of the Texas legislature during Reconstruction. Angel is helping Jason sort papers. Marsha and Reggie are talking. Two students are watching me.)

DOCUMENTING INSTRUCTION USING A FOCUSED OBSERVATION INSTRUMENT

Documenting Mr. Laze's instruction can be simplified by focusing on a single area of deficiency and by using a focused observation instrument. If you decide before entering Mr. Laze's classroom which of the five areas (Active, Successful Student Participation in the Learning Process; Learner-Centered Instruction; Evaluation and Feedback on Student Progress; Management of Student Discipline, Instructional Strategies, Time, and Materials; Learning Environment) you want to document, you can select the appropriate instrument and use it to gather information during the classroom observation. You will be saved the trouble of scripting, and the teacher will be spared the trauma of electronic recording. Your documentation will be specific and relevant to the issue you want to address. When you encounter a teacher like Mr. Laze with many instructional problems, it may be best initially to focus on the area where the teacher has the most potential for positive change. Doing so will give you the best chance to effectuate at least some improvement and at the same time not demoralize the teacher. On the other hand, it may be that you have been in Mr. Laze's classroom several times and have already had numerous conversations with him about deficiencies in his instruction. To date, you have seen no improvement. If that is the case, your goal may be to prepare for a recommendation of contract nonrenewal. You will then be in his classroom to gather information to document his deficiencies and to support your nonrenewal goal.

Documentation of Instructional Strategy Concerns

Gathering and Recording Data

Let us suppose now that your area of concern for this observation is teacher-student interaction and that you choose to use an instrument that gives you information about one or more of the following instructional issues: (1) the frequency of student participation, (2) the success of students during the lesson, and (3) the quality of learning as determined by cognitive complexity and connections to issues beyond the classroom.

What follows is a model focused observation instrument designed specifically to allow you to collect the type of data you want. It has been filled in with data from Mr. Laze's class on Reconstruction in Texas. A blank copy of this instrument is contained in Appendix B and also is available on the optional CD for easy downloading and use. Notice that there are numbers in parentheses on the forms. These numbers correspond with comments which pertain to each part of the instrument and follow in the commentary section.

FOCUSED OBSERVATION INSTRUMENT #1
Active, Successful Student Participation in Learning
- ✔ Active Student Engagement/Participation
- ✔ Student Success
- ✔ Cognitive Level/Complexity of Instruction
- ✔ Students Connecting Learning

Name of Teacher: Bill Laze **Date of Observation:** 10/11/11

Subject/Grade Level: American History/9th **Time of Observation: Begin:** 8:30

Specific Content/Activity: **End:** 8:55 **(1)**

Civil War/Reconstruction in Texas **Number of Students in Class:** 30

Learning Objective: none

Record the names (descriptions, seat assignment) of students who participated in ways other than passive listening. Record the question/prompt from the teacher. Circle the + beside the name(s) of students whose participation was successful. Circle the – beside the name(s) of students whose participation was not successful. Record the teacher's response to the student's response/performance/demonstration.

STUDENT	QUESTION	SUCCESSFUL/ UNSUCCESSFUL	TEACHER RESPONSE TO STUDENT
1. Paul	"Why is this period called Reconstruction?"	+ (–) ?	"OK. Steve, do you know?" **(2)**
2. Steve	(same question)	+ (–) ?	"No, not exactly. Susie, do you know?"
3. Susie	(same question)	(+) – ?	"That's a good answer. Did everybody get that?"
4. Audrey	"Why did they disenfranchise the Southerners?"	+ (–) ?	"Didn't you read the assignment?" (calls on Aaron)
5. Aaron	(same question)	+ (–) ?	(student asks for definition of disenfranchisement) "Look it up." (calls on Susie)
6. Susie	(same question)	(+) – ?	"Right again, Susie. You guys better be paying attention because this stuff is going to be on the test." (calls on Aaron: "I'm going to give you another chance.")
7. Aaron	"What was the difference between Federal fiscal policy in Texas and fiscal policy in other Southern states?"	+ (–) ?	"Not hardly, Aaron."
8. (to class)	"Does anybody know?"	+ (–) ?	(Aaron closes book and puts pen down)
9. Susie	(same question)	(+) – ?	"I'm glad someone read the assignment, Susie." (Mr. L. continues to lecture)
10. Matt	"Why were former Southern troops assigned the job of fighting Indians on the frontier?"	+ (–) ?	(following Mr. L.'s question, Matt asks, "I'm sorry, what?") "You sure are." Mr. L. then calls on Paul)
11. Paul	(same question to Paul)	(+) – ?	"Right, Paul. See what happens when you pay attention?"
12.		+ – ?	
13.			

Instructional Strategies Used to Promote Participation

Check any techniques that the teacher used to promote active, successful student participation. Checking the technique does not necessarily mean that the technique was used effectively — it simply means that the technique was used. Make any specific notes that will help you remember what the teacher did/failed to do.

√ Used random calling Called on 6 students **(3)**

_____ Sent students to board/chart/map

_____ Instructional activities allowed/encouraged students to interact with each other

_____ Provided application/lab activity

_____ Varied activities

_____ Made lesson relevant/interesting to student experience

√ Positively reinforced student participation and/or success Reinforced Susie's responses

_____ Corrected incorrect responses/performances in a way that preserved student dignity

_____ Encouraged slow/reluctant students

_____ Instructional activities provided for students to produce products

_____ Instructional strategies provided for students to make connections of new learning (e.g., prior/future learning within the discipline, other disciplines, world beyond the classroom)

_____ Provided opportunities for students to interact with each other

√ Provided opportunities for students to volunteer, offer feedback, make independent choices
One whole group question: "Does anybody know?"

_____ Other technique

_____ Other technique

Summary of Data and Judgments on Use of Instructional Strategies

In the space below, summarize the data from the previous two pages and make judgments about the quality of instructional strategies.

Active, Successful Student Participation **(4)**

1. How many students participated? 6 of 30 participated.
2. How many students were successful? 2 of 6 who participated.
3. How many students were unsuccessful? 4 of 6 who participated.

What was the learning objective?

No learning objective; statement of activity: "Today we're going to be talking about the South after the Civil War, Reconstruction."

What instructional activities, strategies, and resources were used in teaching this lesson?

Teacher lecture and question/answer Textbook

Teacher stood behind lecture throughout the lesson

Based on the data, which statements best describe what you observed? **(5)**

Proficient	**Below Expectations or Unsatisfactory**
____ Most students were engaged and successful	✓ Few/no students were engaged and successful
____ Student engagement/participation was self-directed/self-motivated	✓ Student engagement/participation was externally manipulated by teacher
____ Instructional activities were aligned with instructional objectives	____ Instructional activities were not aligned with instructional objectives
____ Most students were successful in learning at the application level or higher on Bloom's Taxonomy of Cognitive Learning	✓ Few/no students were successful in learning at the application level or higher on Bloom's Taxonomy of Cognitive Learning
____ Most students successfully produced products which represented complex learning	✓ Few/no students successfully produced products which represented complex learning
____ Most students successfully connected new learning with the discipline, with other disciplines, and/or with the world beyond the classroom	✓ Few/no students successfully connected new learning within the discipline, with other disciplines, and/or with the world beyond the classroom
____ Instructional strategies reflected the unique needs/characteristics of students	____ Instructional strategies do not reflect the unique needs/characteristics of students
____ Other judgment	✓ Other judgments Feedback to student not courteous/respectful
____ Other judgment	____ Other judgment

Commentary

(1) The first section of the instrument provides essential information that you will need when you are ready to write your memorandum to Mr. Laze (e.g., date and time of the observation, length of the observation, etc.).

(2) In this section, you record each teacher/student interaction as it occurs. Paul's response was incorrect, and Mr. Laze called on Steve. When Steve answered incorrectly, Mr. Laze called on Susie. Susie's response was correct, and Mr. Laze told her that she had a "good answer." When Audrey did not know an answer, Mr. Laze asked, "Why not? Didn't you read the assignment?" Note: All information is presented in objective, non-judgmental terms. Never write judgmental or editorial comments. When Mr. Laze responds to Audrey, "Why not? Didn't you read the assignment?" write down his *exact words* rather than the inappropriate judgment "put-down comment by teacher." In recording observation data and writing documentation, *stick to the facts.*

(3) This section of the instrument is completed in the classroom during "downtime," that is, when there are few teacher/student interactions and when you have time to consider other things going on in the classroom. The form indicates by check mark notations that the teacher used random calling and called on six students. Use of positive reinforcement also is checked, with the added note that Susie's response was reinforced. Providing student opportunities to volunteer is also checked because the teacher asked the whole class "Does anybody know?" Note that checking a technique does not necessarily mean that the technique was used effectively; it simply means that the technique was used. You may *later* make the judgment whether or not these techniques were effective. During the observation, however, record only that these techniques were used.

(4)-(5) The final part of the focused observation instrument should be completed back in your office. It consists of a summary of the data and preliminary judgments from the previous two sections of the instrument. Remember that the preceding data were factual and objective — no judgments were made about the quality or effectiveness of the teaching behaviors. In completing this section, you may both summarize the data and make preliminary judgments about the teacher's performance. In the case of Mr. Laze, the summary reveals the following:

- Six of the 30 students participated.
- Two of the six who participated were successful.
- Three of the four correct responses came from Susie. The observer is concerned with how many *students* gave correct responses, not with how many responses were correct.
- None of the questions connected the new learning to other disciplines or to issues beyond the classroom.
- During this observation, no students produced products that represented complex learning.
- Note that on the issue of alignment of the lesson with instructional objectives, neither paired statement was checked. Since there was no learning objective, it is not possible to know whether or not there was alignment. Unlike a PDAS observation, you are not obligated to make a

judgment on every issue; check only those judgments that you can defend by using the data from the previous two pages. Note also that the space "Other Judgments" is checked with the notation that "Feedback to students was not courteous/respectful." Even though this focused observation instrument did not include learning environment, you have data that reflect a deficiency in this area.

(5) The sections labeled "Proficient" and "Below Expectations/Unsatisfactory" provide a contrast of judgments based on the data from the observation. The issue of whether or not the instructional strategies reflected the unique needs/characteristics of the students is a difficult question. You probably know nothing about the unique needs/characteristics of any of these 30 students. While students were generally unsuccessful, there are myriad explanations for this other than whether or not the strategies reflected the unique needs/characteristics of the students. Any time you make a negative judgment, anticipate that you may later be asked to provide objective evidence to support your judgment. In this case, since you don't know about the unique needs or characteristics of the students in the scenario, you should not check this item. On your own campus, you would probably have information about these students (the number/names of students who are gifted, special education, 504, ESL, etc.). In that case you would be able to make a judgment regarding the appropriateness of the instructional strategies.

Formal Documentation

After the observation, you will schedule a conference with the teacher. Recall the three sequential steps: observe, talk, write. If this is a Quadrant II teacher and your goal is growth and improvement, you will use a collaborative style of supervision. If you goal or nonrenewal/termination, you will use a directive style.

After the conference with the teacher, you are now ready to write a memorandum to communicate the information and judgments to Mr. Laze and to preserve the information if it is needed later to develop a Teacher in Need of Assistance Plan or, if one has already been developed, to show noncompliance. In the case of Mr. Laze, no assistance plan has been developed. To be consistent with terminology introduced in Chapter 2, we are calling this instructional memorandum a "specific incident memorandum," since it has many of the same characteristics.

Directives for professional development activities and changes in behavior are essential in a Teacher in Need of Assistance Plan but not necessarily in a specific incident memorandum. You may choose, however, to include them in the memorandum if you believe that teacher deficiencies can be remedied without the necessity of a formal intervention plan. Examples of where directives for changes in behavior have been included are found in the memorandum on the next two pages to Mr. Laze regarding his instructional strategies. We have included a professional development activity in the memorandum on page 4-27 to Mr. Ziebarth, a science teacher who has made errors in teaching the physics of simple machines.

The following is a checklist for the components of a specific incident memorandum related to instruction.

Checklist for Instructional Documentation

___ Use district or campus letterhead paper.

___ Include date memorandum was written.

___ Include date and time of the classroom observation (important in demonstrating that you have not singled out one time of the day or one group of students).

___ Include number of students in the class (especially critical when dealing with issues such as active participation and student success).

___ Set forth your findings of fact resulting from the data gathered during the classroom observation. These should be written in objective, factual language — no judgments.

___ State your conclusions or judgments regarding what happened. Anchor them, whenever possible, in the district or campus criteria for effective instruction. For example, "These data indicate that your teaching did not meet district expectations for evaluating and providing feedback on student progress during instruction."

___ If you choose, include any directives regarding expected future conduct and remedial activities that the employee is required to undertake. (See guidelines for writing instructional directives in Chapter 6.)

___ Give the employee an opportunity to respond.

___ Require the dated signature of the employee or a third party witness.

Using the data from the structured observation instrument, our specific incident memorandum might look like the following. Note that for illustrative purposes, we have included on the left side of the memorandum the components of a specific incident memorandum related to instruction. You would not include these in the actual memorandum you send to the teacher.

ESSENTIAL ELEMENTS	
Letterhead	**Bestever ISD** **1234 Sunny Lane** **Bestever, TX 70000**
	TO: Mr. Bill Laze
	FROM: Dr. Great Principal
Date	**DATE:** October 14, 2011
	SUBJECT: Classroom Observation on October 10 and Conference on October 12
Nature of Allegation and Investigation	This memorandum will formally communicate information gathered during my observation of October 10, 2011, and discussed with you in our conference on October 12, 2011. I observed from 8:30 to 8:55 while you were conducting a lesson on Civil War and Reconstruction in Texas with a group of 30 ninth graders.
	The observation revealed the following information.
Findings of Fact	1. Six of 30 students participated (Paul, Steve, Susie, Audrey, Aaron, and Matt). Two of the six who participated were successful(Paul and Susie). 2. When students were not successful, you responded • (to Paul) "OK, Steve do you know?" • (to Steve) "No, not exactly. Susie, do you know?" • (to Audrey) "Why not? Didn't you read the assignment?"(then called on Aaron) • (to Aaron) (Student asked for definition of disenfranchisement) You said, "Look it up." • (to Aaron) "Not hardly, Aaron. Does anybody know?" (Aaron closed his book and put down his pen) • (to Matt) (Following your question, Matt asked, "I'm sorry, what?") "You sure are." 3. None of the questions or activities resulted in students making any connections between the new learning and prior learning, other disciplines, or issues in the world beyond the classroom.
Expectations/Basis of Authority	The Bestever I.S.D. appraisal system has an expectation that: • All/almost all students are participating actively and successfully (Domain I). • When students are not successful, they receive specific, constructive corrective feedback (Domain III). Verbal and non-verbal communication establishes a learning climate that is positive and conducive to learning; all interactions will be courteous and respectful (Domain IV).

ESSENTIAL ELEMENTS

- **Students successfully connect new learning with prior learning, other disciplines, and/or issues in the world beyond the classroom (Domains I and II).**

Conclusions/ Judgments

Based on the data collected during my observation, you have not met these expectations.

I will be back some time during the first week in November to observe your instruction. During that observation and all future lessons, you will:

Directives for Changes in Behavior

1. **Plan and implement all lessons in such a way that all/almost all students are actively and successfully participating in the learning.**
2. **All interactions with students, staff, and parents will be courteous and respectful.**
3. **Provide corrective feedback to students who are having difficulty in such a way that they are successful.**
4. **Design and use activities in which students are actively and successfully connecting new learning with prior learning, other disciplines, and/or issues in the world beyond the classroom.**

Opportunity to Respond

My signature verifies that I have received a copy of this memorandum. It does not necessarily mean that I agree with the content. I understand that I have the right to present a written response within 10 working days.

Dated Signature of Employee

/s/ Bill Laze **Date**

NOTE: This memorandum contains comprehensive directives for changes in behavior. The directives are written in the form described in Chapter 6. While such comprehensive directives are not essential in a specific incident memorandum, you may choose to include them for the reasons previously expressed. This memorandum does not include directives for professional growth activities; they are optional in a specific incident memorandum.

Documentation of Concerns Related to Learner-Centered Instruction

Gathering and Recording Data

If you are most concerned about Mr. Laze's effectiveness in lesson design, teaching and communicating, you may choose to use the second focused observation instrument, which is designed to allow you to collect data on learner-centered instruction. A blank copy of this instrument is contained in Appendix B and also is available on the optional CD for easy downloading and use. Whether the teacher's objectives are cognitive, affective, or psychomotor, this instrument focuses attention on teaching skills. The numbers correspond with comments which pertain to each part of the instrument and follow in the next section.

FOCUSED OBSERVATION INSTRUMENT #2
Learner-Centered Instruction

- ✔ Objectives and Content of Instruction
- ✔ Interests and Varied Characteristics of Students
- ✔ Critical Thinking and Problem Solving
- ✔ Motivational Techniques
- ✔ Alignment of Objectives
- ✔ Variation of Activities and Pacing
- ✔ Value/Importance of Activity/Content
- ✔ Questioning/Inquiry Techniques
- ✔ Use of Available Technology

Name of Teacher: Bill Laze **Date of Observation:** 10/11/11

Subject/Grade Level: American History/9th **Time of Observation: Begin:** 8:30

Specific Content/Activity: **End:** 8:55 **(1)**

Civil War/Reconstruction in Texas **Number of Students in Class:** 30

Beginning of the Lesson **(2)**

Record the introduction to the lesson

"OK. Open your books to page 37. Today we're going to be talking about the South after Civil War, Reconstruction. You were supposed to read this chapter as part of last night's assignment. You need to be sure to take notes, because some of this is not in the chapter."

Concept(s)/skill(s) being taught

Teacher told students what they would be doing ("Today we're going to be talking about the South after Civil War, Reconstruction.")

Level of the learning outcome (objective)? (No specific statement of learning outcome was given.)

____ Knowledge/Comprehension ____ Synthesis

____ Application ____ Evaluation

____ Analysis

Content of the Lesson **(3)**

_✓_ New material with explanation/demonstration/modeling (describe what the teacher/students are doing)

teacher lecture; students listening; some students questioned

_✓_ Miscellaneous, unconnected data
facts about Reconstruction

____ Concepts, skills, generalizations, principles

____ Central themes/concepts of the discipline

OR

____ Practice/application/processing of material already taught (describe what the teacher/students are doing)

Connecting the New Learning **(4)**

Are the students connecting the new learning to:

____ Prior learning?

____ Future learning? No connections made

____ Students' experience?

____ Issues beyond the classroom?

____ World of work?

How is the teacher providing for students to make the connection?

____ Teacher tells students the connection. Describe:

No connections made

____ Teacher facilitates a process (student discussion, activity, etc.) whereby students make connections. Describe:

Critical Thinking and Problem Solving **(5)**

How is the teacher moving most students from knowledge/comprehension level learning to some application of the learning?

_√_ Higher-level questioning to some students

____ Small group discussion

____ Paper/pencil activity

____ Performance/demonstration

____ Producing a product(s)

____ Other (Describe)

Describe:

Ten higher-level questions to 4 students; 2 students successful.

Student Success **(6)**

What evidence is there that students are successful/unsuccessful in reaching the objective(s)?

(Susie+; Paul - and +; Audrey-; Aaron-; Matt-) 2 students successfully answered question; 4 were unsuccessful; 24 did not participate

Student Self-Direction **(7)**

Are students self-directed/self-motivated in the learning process or is student engagement/participation being manipulated/coerced by the teacher?

Describe:

All student participation teacher-directed (teacher called on students; no volunteerism).

Use of Available Technology **(8)**

What, if any, technology are the teacher and/or students using for this lesson?

No technology utilized.

Summary of Data and Judgments About Learner-Centered Instruction

Based on the data, which statements best describe what you observed?

(9)

Proficient	Below Expectations or Unsatisfactory
✓ Learning is aligned with state/district curriculum	____ Learning is not aligned with state/district curriculum
____ Most students are successfully engaged in learning	✓ Most students are not successfully engaged in learning
____ Learning is constructed around central themes/concepts of the discipline	✓ Learning is not organized around central themes/concepts of the discipline; learning is miscellaneous, unconnected data
____ Students are connecting/applying learning to other disciplines, their own lives, issues beyond classroom	✓ Students are not connecting/applying learning to other disciplines, their own lives, issues beyond classroom
____ Content and activities are related/connected with unique needs, interests, and/or characteristics of students	____ Content and activities do not relate/connect with needs, interests, and/or characteristics of students
____ Students are successfully engaged in critical thinking, problem-solving, and/or creative thinking	✓ Students are not successfully engaged in critical thinking, problem-solving, and/or creative thinking
____ Content and instructional strategies reflect current/best practices within the content area	✓ Content/instructional strategies do not reflect/ current/best practices within the content area
____ Student engagement, self-directed participation indicate content and activities are interesting, fun	✓ Lack of student engagement, self-directed participation indicate content/activities are not interesting, fun
____ Student participation/production are self-initiated	✓ Student participation/production are the result of teacher manipulation/coercion
____ Teacher uses an inquiry/discovery process for generating all/most information/critical attributes/conclusions/generalizations	✓ Teacher tells students all/most information/ critical attributes/conclusions/generalizations
____ Teacher and/or students utilized available technology	✓ Teacher and/or students did not utilize available technology
____ Other judgments	____ Other judgments

Commentary

(1) The first section of the instrument provides essential information that you will need when you are ready to document this observation and write your specific incident memorandum to the teacher (e.g., date and time of the observation, length of the observation, etc.).

(2) In these sections the exact words Mr. Laze used to begin the lesson are recorded. It is noted that the introduction did not contain a statement of the learning outcome or objective. Below is a space for recording the lesson topic and indicating whether or not the teacher is introducing new material.

(3) The lesson appeared to be presentation of new material and consisted of miscellaneous, unconnected data sets. The teacher lectured and called on six different students, two of whom were successful.

(4) There were many ways in which the teacher *could* have connected the new learning to a variety of issues. The data indicate that no connections were made.

(5-6) There were 10 questions that called for higher-level thinking; however, these questions were directed to only four of the 30 students and only two of the four were successful. [An alternate view is that the questions had the *form* of higher-level questions but were, in fact, text-book recall questions.] Note that the names of students and whether or not they were successful are noted

(7) All student participation was the result of the teacher calling on students who had not volunteered. Except for Susie, there was no evidence of self-directed or self-motivated participation.

(8) No technology was utilized in the lesson. Note that no judgment was made about this absence. Before making a judgment, an appraiser would always have to consider the availability of technology to Mr. Laze and the appropriateness of technology for this lesson.

(9) The sections labeled "Proficient" and "Below Expectations/Unsatisfactory" provide a contrast of judgments based on the data from the observation.

Formal Documentation

You are now ready to write the specific incident memorandum that addresses Mr. Laze's teaching and communication. Using the data from the structured observation instrument, our specific incident memorandum might look like the following. Note that for illustrative purposes, we have included on the left side of the memorandum the components of a specific incident memorandum related to instruction. You would not include these in the actual memorandum you send to the teacher.

ESSENTIAL ELEMENTS

Letterhead

Bestever ISD
1234 Sunny Lane
Bestever, TX 70000

TO: Mr. Bill Laze

FROM: Dr. Great Principal

Date

DATE: October 14, 2011

SUBJECT: Classroom Observation on October 10 and Conference on October 12

Nature of Allegation and Investigation

This memorandum will formally communicate information gathered during my observation of October 10, 2011, and discussed with you in our conference on October 12, 2011. I observed from 8:30 to 8:55 while you were conducting a lesson on Civil War and Reconstruction in Texas with a group of 30 ninth graders.

The observation revealed the following information.

Findings of Fact

1. You began by saying, "Open your books to page 87. Today we're going to be talking about the South after the Civil War, Reconstruction. You were supposed to read this chapter as part of last night's assignment. You need to be sure and take notes, because some of this is not in your chapter." There was no communication of the specific learning outcome.
2. The content that was presented was miscellaneous, unconnected data (e.g., vocabulary words, facts about Reconstruction in Texas, etc.).
3. Neither you nor any student connected the new content to any prior learning, to students' experiences, to other disciplines, or to issues beyond the classroom.
4. You asked 10 higher-level questions (i.e., at the application level or higher on Bloom's Taxonomy) to four different students. Two of these students (Susie and Paul) were successful.

Expectations/Basis of Authority

Domain II of the Bestever I.S.D. appraisal system has the expectation that you provide "learner-centered instruction." Within that evaluation domain, there is an expectation that you:

1. Communicate expectations for learning and that those expectations include critical thinking as well as connections to the interests and experiences of students, to

ESSENTIAL ELEMENTS

other disciplines and/or to issues beyond the classroom;

2. Utilize consistent instructional strategies that result in self-directed student participation and learning; and
3. Conduct the lesson so that most students are successful as they engage in critical thinking and in connecting the learning.

Conclusions/ Judgments

The data from my observation indicate that these expectations related to effective instruction were not met.

Directives for Changes in Behavior

I will be observing in your classroom again beginning two weeks from today. In all future lessons, you are expected to meet the district's expectations for learner-centered instruction. You will:

1. Overtly communicate expectations for learning in such a way that the students know and understand the learning outcome.
2. Organize and teach new information so that all/almost all students are successful in understanding that information.
3. Design and implement instructional activities in such as way that all/almost all students are successfully participating in critical thinking and problem-solving.
4. Design and implement activities so that students are successfully making connections to their interests and experiences, to other disciplines, and/or to issues beyond the classroom.

Opportunity to Respond

My signature verifies that I have received a copy of this memorandum. It does not necessarily mean that I agree with the content. I understand that I have the right to present a written response within 10 working days.

Dated Signature of Employee

/s/ Bill Laze ______________________ Date ____________

A Word About Subject-Matter Knowledge and Communication Skills

Our discussion has thus far highlighted compliance with the techniques of effective instruction. However, we do not want to ignore two other serious matters related to the presentation of subject matter: (1) knowledge of subject matter itself and (2) accurate communication skills (literacy in oral or written language). Obviously, both are prerequisites to effective teaching. During an observation it is not necessary to use a separate focused observation instrument for documenting in either area. Indeed, you are likely to notice subject matter or communication problems at any time during routine observations.

When the teacher exhibits weak knowledge of the teaching field or communicates poorly, it is appropriate to write a specific incident memorandum to alert the teacher to the problem and to the need for remediation. Suppose that Mr. Ziebarth is a physics teacher in your school. Some of his students and some of their parents, as well as other science teachers, have complained that Mr. Ziebarth is giving students inaccurate information in his physics class. Your concern is to follow up the complaints by gathering data to determine whether a problem exists. In order to do so, there are several sources of information that you can use:

- Ask for copies of written materials he has used in class.
- Check what is written on the board, bulletin board, and media.
- Conduct classroom observations and focus on the academic content presented orally. If there are errors in content, record what the teacher says as an exact quotation whenever possible.
- If you are not expert in the teacher's academic area, find someone who is and have that person conduct classroom observations focusing on the accuracy of academic content. The person should provide findings to you and you will write the specific incident memorandum.

Let us assume that you have used these strategies and have noted several inaccuracies in Mr. Ziebarth's presentation. First, you read on a handout that he provided to his students, "A machine's efficiency is restricted only by gravity. If it weren't for gravity, a machine could work at 100 percent efficiency. One of the reasons we do experiments in space is to show that a machine in a weightless environment can be 100 percent efficient."

On another occasion you watched Mr. Ziebarth conduct a demonstration of a pulley lifting a weight and heard him explain to his students, "The pulley in this instance has a mechanical advantage of '2.' That means that I only had to do half as much work to move the object. That's the chief advantage of simple machines."

During the same visit, after pushing against his desk, Mr. Ziebarth said, "The desk did not move. The more energy I expended in the effort, the more work was done. This is true even though the desk did not move."

The complaints about Mr. Ziebarth's accuracy have now been corroborated by data you have gathered. It is time to write a specific incident memorandum. This time, we have chosen to include a remediation directive, rather than develop a separate Teacher in Need of Assistance Plan. Note that for illustrative purposes, we have included on the left side of the memorandum the components of a specific incident memorandum related to instruction. You would not include these in the actual memorandum you send to the teacher.

ESSENTIAL ELEMENTS

Letterhead

Bestever ISD
1234 Sunny Lane
Bestever, TX 70000

TO: Mr. Ziebarth

FROM: Dr. Great Principal

Date

DATE: November 11, 2011

SUBJECT: Errors on Presentation of Subject Matter

Nature of Allegation and Investigation

I have attached a copy of a handout that you constructed and gave to students on November 1, 2011. The handout contains the following physics information that is inaccurate:

Findings of Fact

> A machine's efficiency is restricted only by gravity. If it weren't for gravity, a machine could work at 100 percent efficiency. One of the reasons we do experiments in space is to show that a machine in a weightless environment can be 100 percent efficient.

When I observed in your classroom on November 9, 2011, you conducted a demonstration of a pulley lifting a weight and gave the following explanation:

> The pulley in this instance has a mechanical advantage of '2.' That means that I only had to do half as much work to move the object. That's the chief advantage of simple machines.

During that same observation, you pushed against your desk and then stated:

> The desk did not move. The more energy I expended in the effort, the more work was done. This is true even though the desk did not move.

Conclusions/ Judgments

All these statements are inaccurate generalizations about the physics of simple machines.

Expectations/ Basis of Authority

One of the school district's basic expectations of all teachers is a thorough and accurate knowledge of subject matter. The three quotations above indicate that you are not meeting that expectation.

Directives for Changes in Behavior

You must begin immediately and at all times to teach only accurate content-related information in your classroom.

Directive for Professional Development (optional)

Both Ms. Jones, your science department chairperson, and I agree that you should attend the workshop "Science AIMS Training" at the Regional Education Service Center on Thursday and Friday, December 1-2. Accordingly, I have made arrangements for you to attend. The district will provide a substitute for your classes on these two days and will pay the workshop registration fee. You will schedule a meeting with Ms. Jones during the week following the workshop to discuss how to prevent errors of the kind described above in future classes.

Opportunity to Respond

My signature indicates that I have received a copy of this memorandum. It does not necessarily indicate that I agree with its content. I understand that I have a right to present a written response within 10 working days.

Dated Signature of Employee

______________________________ ____________

/s/ Mr. Ziebarth   Date

Note that the memorandum quotes the teacher and cites exactly the words on the handout and in the classroom presentation. Your message comes through clearly that there are errors in academic content and that they are not acceptable. But you make your point without castigating the teacher or using adjectives or adverbs that might be provocative or misleading.

The same approach is appropriate for a teacher who appears to have communication problems. After you collect samples of notes to parents, observe the written language displayed in the classroom, and/or write down samples of oral language to enable you to determine whether or not a problem exists. But proceed with caution. You will be best served by dealing *only* with grammar, punctuation, and spelling. Avoid regional or ethnic dialects and other-language accents. These should become supervision issues only if the dialect or accent interferes with students' ability to understand instruction.

A memorandum that addresses problems with communication skills will look very similar to the one directed to Mr. Ziebarth but will include statements such as:

> During my observation in your classroom on December 14, 2011, you made the following errors in grammar: (1) "The primary reason they come to this country in 1939 was to continue their research" and (2) "Einstein and von Braun was typical of German scientists." I also noticed that you misspelled "a lot" and "occurring" on the whiteboard ("alot" and "occuring").
>
> This school district expects all faculty members to be role models for students in the use of correct grammar and spelling. The errors cited above indicate that you are not meeting that expectation.

Depending upon the seriousness of the matter, it may be appropriate to have someone edit the teacher's written communication to students and parents and to review the results with the teacher. More comprehensive remediation can be addressed through a formal Teacher in Need of Assistance Plan (see Chapter 6).

Documentation of Monitoring and Assessment

Gathering and Recording Data

Assume now that your area of concern is the teacher's monitoring and assessment of student learning and that you choose the instrument that gives you information about one or more of the following issues: Physical and/or verbal monitoring and assessing of student learning, corrective feedback to students who are having difficulty, reinforcement to students who are experiencing success in learning, adjusting instruction based on the absence/presence of student success in learning, and various methods of both monitoring and assessing.

What follows is a model focused observation instrument specifically designed to allow you to collect the type of data that you want. It has been filled in with data from Mr. Laze's class on Reconstruction in Texas. As previously noted, a blank copy of each instrument is contained in Appendix B and also is available on the optional CD for easy downloading and use. Notice that there are numbers in parentheses on the form. These numbers correspond with comments which pertain to each part of the instrument and follow in the commentary section.

FOCUSED OBSERVATION INSTRUMENT #3
Evaluation and Feedback on Student Progress

- ✔ Monitoring and Assessment of Academic Progress
- ✔ Alignment of Assessment and Feedback with Objectives/Instructional Strategies
- ✔ Appropriate Assessment for Characteristics of Students
- ✔ Reinforcement and Corrective Feedback
- ✔ Reteaching and Reevaluation

Name of Teacher: Bill Laze **Date of Observation:** 10/11/11

Subject/Grade Level: American History/9th **Time of Observation: Begin:** 8:30

Specific Content/Activity: **End:** 8:55 **(1)**

Civil War/Reconstruction in Texas **Number of Students in Class:** 30

Learning Objective: none

Record the names (descriptions, seat assignment) of students who were assessed. Record the question/prompt from the teacher. Circle the + beside the name(s) of students whose participation was succussful. Circle the – beside the name(s) of students whose participation was not successful. Record the teacher's response to the student's response/performance/demonstration

STUDENT	QUESTION	SUCCESSFUL/ UNSUCCESSFUL	TEACHER RESPONSE TO STUDENT
1. Paul	"Why is this period called Reconstruction?"	+ (–) ?	"OK. Steve, do you know?"
2. Steve	(same question)	+ (–) ?	"No, not exactly. Susie, do you know?" **(2)**
3. Susie	(same question)	(+) – ?	"That's a good answer. Did everybody get that?"
4. Audrey	"Why did they disenfranchise the Southerners?"	+ (–) ?	"Didn't you read the assignment?" (Calls on Aaron)
5. Aaron	(same question)	+ (–) ?	(student asks for definition of disenfranchisement) "Look it up." (Calls on Susie)
6. Susie	(same question)	(+) – ?	"Right again, Susie. You guys better be paying attention because this stuff is going to be on the test." (Calls on Aaron: "I'm going to give you another chance.")
7. Aaron	"What was the difference between Federal fiscal policy in Texas and fiscal policy in other Southern states?"	+ (–) ?	"Not hardly, Aaron."
8. (to class)	"Does anybody know?"	+ (–) ?	(Aaron closes book and puts down pen) Calls on Susie
9. Susie	(same question)	(+) – ?	"I'm glad one person read the assignment, Susie." (Mr. L. continues to lecture)
10. Matt	"Why were former Southern troops assigned the job of fighting Indians on the frontier?"	+ (–) ?	(following Mr. L.'s question, Matt asks, "I'm sorry, what?") "You sure are." Mr. L. then calls on Paul)
11. Paul	(same question)	(+) – ?	"Right, Paul. See what happens when you pay attention?"
12.		+ – ?	
13.			

Instructional Strategies Used to Monitor and Assess

Check any techniques that the teacher used to monitor and/or assess student learning. Checking the technique does *not* necessarily mean that the technique was used effectively — it simply means that the technique was used. Make any specific notes that will help you remember what the teacher did/ failed to do.

(3)

✓ Verbally monitoring/assessing individual students (random questioning, interacting during group/seat work) Called on 6 out of 30 students

_____ Physically monitoring *individual* students (walking around, examining work) Stood at lecturn entire period

_____ Verbally monitoring/assessing *groups* of students (choral response, signal response)

_____ Physically monitoring *groups* of students

_____ Use of formative assessments (paper/pencil, performances, demonstrations)

_____ Use of summative assessments (paper/pencil, performances, demonstrations, products)

_____ Adjusting instruction/clarifying in response to monitoring/assessing

_____ Clarifying/extending in response to monitoring/assessment

_____ Reteaching (some or all students)

✓ Positive reinforcement of successful responses/performances (verbal and/or nonverbal) Reinforced Susie's responses

_____ Specific corrective feedback to students who are unsuccessful No corrective feedback provided; feedback was not courteous/respectful.

_____ Prompting/assisting students who are having difficulty responding/performing

_____ Other technique

_____ Other technique

_____ Other technique

Summary of Data and Judgments on Monitoring and Assessing

In the space below, summarize the data from the previous two pages and make judgments about the quality of instructional strategies.

Successful and Unsuccessful Students in Learning the Day's Objective **(4)**

1. How many students participated? 6 of 30 participated.
2. How many students were successful? 2 of 6 who participated.
3. How many students were unsuccessful? 4 of 6 who participated.

What was the learning objective?
"Today, we're going to be talking about the South after the Civil War, Reconstruction."

What monitoring/assessment strategies were used?
Random questioning for 6 students. 24 students not verbally monitored. Teacher stood behind lectern entire class period.

Were assessment strategies aligned with the objective?
Questions all about the South after the Civil War. No statement of objective - a statement of the activity.

Were strategies used to provide feedback to students? 1 student (Susie) received positive **(5)** reinforcement; students who were not successful received no prompting/corrective feedback; feedback comments to unsuccessful students were not courteous/respectful.

Based on the data, which statements best describe what you observed?

Proficient

_____ Learning objectives were clearly communicated

_____ Teacher monitored the learning progress of most students

_____ Teacher assessed the learning (formative and/or summative) of most students

_____ Teacher's system for obtaining and interpreting assessment data was focused on student progress in the learning objective

_____ Monitoring/assessment strategies fit the learning styles/developmental levels/other unique needs/characteristics of students

_____ Teacher acted on assessment data before moving on

__✓__ Teacher typically provided positive feedback to students who were successful

_____ Corrective feedback was positive/supportive

__✓__ Most students who received positive feedback repeated their participation and success

_____ Teacher typically provided specific corrective feedback to students who were unsuccessful

_____ Students who received corrective feedback were successful

_____ Other judgments

_____ Other judgments

Below Expectations or Unsatisfactory

__✓__ Learning objectives were unclear or not communicated

__✓__ Teacher monitored the learning progress of few/no students

__✓__ Teacher assessed the learning (formative and/or summative) of few/no students

__✓__ Teacher's system for obtaining and interpreting assessment data was mechanical and occasionally/never focused on the learning objective

_____ Monitoring/assessment strategies rarely/never fit the learning styles/developmental levels/other unique needs/characteristics of students

__✓__ Teacher rarely/never acted on assessment data before moving on

_____ Teacher rarely/never provided positive feedback to students who were successful

__✓__ Corrective feedback was negative/unsupportive

_____ Most students who received positive feedback rarely/never repeated their participation/success

__✓__ Teacher rarely/never provided specific corrective feedback to students who were unsuccessful

__✓__ Students who received corrective feedback were rarely/never successful

__✓__ Other judgments Feedback to students was not courteous/respectful

_____ Other judgments

Commentary

(1) The first section of the instrument provides essential information that you will need when you are ready to write your specific incident memorandum to Mr. Laze (e.g., date and time of the observation, length of the observation, etc.).

(2) In this section, you record each teacher/student interaction as it occurs (exactly as you need to do with Focused Observation Instrument #1). Paul's response was incorrect, and Mr. Laze called on Steve. When Steve answered incorrectly, Mr. Laze called on Susie. Susie's response was correct, and Mr. Laze told her that she had a "good answer." When Audrey did not know an answer, Mr. Laze asked, "Why not? Didn't you read the assignment?" Note again that all information is presented in objective, nonjudgmental terms.

(3) This section of the instrument is completed in the classroom during "down time," that is, when there are few teacher/student interactions and when you have time to consider other things going on in the classroom. The form indicates by check mark notations that the teacher verbally monitored and assessed students. The observer further noted that the teacher called on six of 30 students. Use of positive reinforcement also is checked, with the added note that Susie's response was reinforced. You may *later* make the judgment that these techniques were ineffective. During the observation, however, record only that these techniques were used. Students who were unsuccessful did not receive any prompting or corrective feedback; instead, they received "put-down" comments from the teacher.

(4)-(5) The final part of the focused observation instrument should be completed back in your office. It consists of a summary of the data and judgments from the previous two sections of the instrument. Remember that the preceding data were factual and objective—no judgments were made about the quality or effectiveness of the teaching behaviors. In completing this section, you may both *summarize* the data and *make judgments* about the teacher's performance. In the case of Mr. Laze, the summary reveals the following:

- Six of the 30 students were verbally monitored/assessed; none of the students were physically monitored, and it is noted that he stood behind the lectern the entire class period.
- Two of the six students who participated were successful; there are no formative assessment data on the other 24 students.
- Since Mr. Laze's exact words following unsuccessful student participation are recorded, there is strong evidence not only that he failed to provide corrective feedback, but also that the feedback he did provide was sarcastic and demeaning. It also provides documentation that there were no extensions of the four correct responses.

(5) The sections labeled "Proficient" and "Below Expectations/Unsatisfactory" provide a contrast of judgments based on the data from the observation.

Formal Documentation

Here is the memorandum to be sent to Mr. Laze. Note that for illustrative purposes, we have included on the left side of the memorandum the components of a specific incident memorandum related to instruction. You would not include these in the actual memorandum you send to the teacher.

ESSENTIAL ELEMENTS

Letterhead

Bestever ISD
1234 Sunny Lane
Bestever, TX 70000

TO: Mr. Bill Laze

FROM: Dr. Great Principal

Date

DATE: October 14, 2011

SUBJECT: Report of Classroom Observation
Classroom Observation on October 10 and
Conference on October 12

Nature of Allegation and Investigation

This memorandum will formally communicate information gathered during my observation of October 10, 2011, and discussed with you in our conference on October 12, 2011. I observed from 8:30 to 8:55 while you were conducting a lesson on Civil War and Reconstruction in Texas with a group of 30 ninth graders.

Findings of Fact

The observation revealed the following information.

- Six of 30 students were verbally monitored/assessed (Paul, Steve, Susie, Audrey, Aaron, and Matt); 24 students were not verbally monitored/assessed.
- Two of the six who were verbally monitored/assessed were successful (Paul and Susie).
- When students who were verbally monitored were not successful, you responded:

  (to Paul) "OK, Steve do you know?"

  (to Steve) "No, not exactly. Susie, do you know?"

  (to Audrey) "Why not? Didn't you read the assignment?" (then called on Aaron)

  (to Aaron) (Student asked for definition of disenfranchisement) "Look it up."

  (to Aaron) "Not hardly, Aaron. Does anybody know?" (Aaron closed book and put down pen)

  (to Matt) (Following your question, Matt asked, "I'm sorry, what?") "You sure are."
- You stood behind the lectern for the entire time I was in the classroom. No students were physically monitored.
- Reteaching did not occur.

Expectations/ Basis of Authority

Domain III of the Bestever I.S.D. appraisal system has an expectation for "evaluating and providing feedback on student progress." Within that domain, there is an expectation that you:

ESSENTIAL ELEMENTS

- **Monitor and assess all/almost all students.**
- **Provide specific and constructive corrective feedback to students who are not successful.**
- **Use effective strategies for monitoring, and assessing, and/or providing feedback on student progress.**
- **Act on assessment data before moving from one stage of instruction to the next.**

Domain IV of the Bestever Teacher Appraisal System has an expectation that all verbal and non-verbal communication establishes a learning climate that is positive and conducive to learning; all interactions will be courteous and respectful (Domain IV).

Conclusions/Judgments

Based on the data collected during my observation, you have not met these expectations.

I will be back some time during the first week in November to observe your instruction. During that observation and all future lessons you will:

Directives for Changes in Behavior

1. **Plan and use strategies to monitor and assess all/almost all students during instruction in such a way that all/almost all students are monitored and assessed.**
2. **Provide specific, constructive feedback to students who are not successful in such a way that they are successful.**
3. **Eliminate all sarcasm and negative criticism. All interactions will be courteous and respectful.**
4. **Act on assessment data to adjust instruction and/or reteach lessons in such a way that students are successful.**

Opportunity to Respond

My signature verifies that I have received a copy of this memorandum. It does not necessarily mean that I agree with the content. I understand that I have the right to present a written response within 10 working days.

Dated Signature of Employee

______________________ ______________

/s/ Bill Laze **Date**

NOTE: This memorandum contains comprehensive directives for changes in behavior. The directives are written in the form described in Chapter 6. While such comprehensive directives are not essential in a specific incident memorandum, you may choose to include them for the reasons previously expressed in this chapter.

Documentation of Classroom Management Concerns

Gathering and Recording Data

Perhaps your main concern about Mr. Laze's instructional behavior is his ability to organize and manage (1) students and their behavior, and (2) class time and materials. You will need an instrument that enables you to gather specific data about these issues. The following is a focused observation instrument designed to monitor classroom management. The data recorded on it come from Mr. Laze's same Reconstruction lesson. Once again, the numbers correspond with comments which pertain to each part of the instrument and follow in the next section. A blank copy of this instrument is contained in Appendix B and also is available on the optional CD for easy downloading and use.

FOCUSED OBSERVATION INSTRUMENT #4
Management of Student Discipline, Instructional Strategies, Time and Materials

- ✔ Implementation of Campus Discipline Management Plan
- ✔ Student Self-Discipline and Self-Directed Learning
- ✔ Fair and Equitable Interaction and Application of Rules
- ✔ Specification of Desired Behavior and Redirection of Off-Task and Inappropriate Behavior
- ✔ Selection of Materials and Management of Instructional Time and Materials

(1)

Name of Teacher: Bill Laze **Date of Observation:** 10/11/11

Subject/Grade Level: American History/9th **Time of Observation: Begin:** 8:30

Specific Content/Activity: **End:** 8:55

Civil War/Reconstruction in Texas **Number of Students in Class:** 30

Materials Used: Textbook

(2) TIME	(3) DESCRIPTION OF STUDENT BEHAVIOR	(4) TEACHER RESPONSE/BEHAVIOR
8:30	4 students enter late.	(none) Mr. L. talking with 2 students at his desk.
8:30	Mr. L. walks around room checking homework. 2 students have nothing on desks.	(none) Mr. L. makes marks in grade book.
8:40	Mr. L. begins class (10 minutes after bell)	Mr. L behind lectern
8:40	Students asked to get out books and turn to page 87. Same 2 students have nothing on their desks.	(none) Mr. L. begins asking questions over reading assignment.
8:50	When Mr. L. asks, "Did everybody get that?" 3 students nod. 6 of 30 are taking notes.	(none) Mr. L. behind the lectern. Begins lecturing.
	Same 6 students taking notes: Ron staring out window; Jason sorting papers; others looking around room.	(none)
8:55	Students in back room (Aaron, Paul, Betsy) whispering; same 6 taking notes. Angie now helping Jason sort papers. 2 students watching the observer. Marsha and Reggie talking.	(none) Mr. L. still at lectern, lecturing.

Summary of Data and Judgments About Management

The statements on the left indicate "proficient" teacher/student behaviors. The statements on the right indicate "below expectations/unsatisfactory" teacher/student behaviors. Check the statements that best describe what you have observed.

Implementation of Campus Discipline Management Plan **(5)**

____ Discipline management plan implemented	_✓_ Discipline management plan rarely/never implemented
____ Implementation of discipline management plan relies on high interest/relevant classroom instruction	_✓_ Implementation of discipline management plan rarely/never relies on high interest/relevant classroom instruction

Student Self-Discipline and Self-Directed Learning

____ Students engaged in appropriate self-direction/ self-management	_✓_ Students rarely/never engaged in appropriate self-direction/self-management
____ Teacher behavior creates safe, supportive, respectful learning environment	____ Teacher behavior creates a learning environment that is not safe, supportive, and/or respectful

Fair and Equitable Interaction and Application of Rules

____ All interactions are courteous and respectful	_✓_ Interactions are sometimes/frequently discourteous/disrespectful
____ Rules are applied consistently and fairly	_✓_ Rules are sometimes/almost always applied inconsistently/unfairly

Specification of Desired Behavior and Redirection of Off-Task and Inappropriate Behavior

_✓_ Teacher communicates expectations for behavior	____ Teacher rarely/never communicates expectations for behavior
____ Students understand and meet expectations for behavior	_✓_ Students infrequently/never meet expectations for behavior
____ Students are engaged in learning and behaving appropriately	_✓_ Students are rarely/never engaged in learning and behaving appropriately
____ Teacher successfully intervenes to stop/ redirect off-task/inappropriate behavior	_✓_ Teacher rarely/never successfully intervenes to stop/redirect off-task/inappropriate behavior

Selection of Materials and Management of Instructional Time and Materials

____ Instructional materials are equitable and reflect the varied characteristics of students	____ Instructional materials are rarely/never equitable and/or sometimes/never reflect the varied characteristics of students
_✓_ Materials are organized and managed efficiently	____ Materials are rarely/never organized and/or managed efficiently
____ Students are engaged in learning for most/all of the instructional period	_✓_ Students are infrequently/never engaged in learning for most/all of the instructional period
____ Other judgments	____ Other judgments
____ Other judgments	____ Other judgments

Commentary

(1) The first section of the instrument provides essential information that you will need when you are ready to document this observation and write your specific incident memorandum to the teacher (e.g., date and time of the observation, length of the observation, etc.).

(2) This section is used to record the time a behavior related to classroom management is observed. This information will provide increased credibility of the data when the specific incident memorandum is written. You will note that this is the only structured observation instrument that calls for recording the times that behaviors occur. When dealing with classroom management and organization, you will need to know such things as the duration of the behavior and its frequency.

(3) This column is where you record information that is related to organization of students and materials, use of time, and management of student behavior. Capturing student names for use in the specific incident memorandum lends authenticity.

Note that all information is *objective and non-judgmental.* Editorial comments are excluded. For example, when Ron was staring out the window, it is appropriate to write, "Ron staring out window" rather than making the judgment that "Ron not paying attention." Once again, stick to the facts.

(4) In the third column, you should note what the teacher is doing at the time that management or behavior problems are observed. Mr. Laze did nothing to deal with the off-task behavior you observed during your visit to his classroom, so you simply note what he *was* doing when the behavior occurred. Whether he failed to observe the behaviors or chose to ignore them, it is important that the observation data indicate Mr. Laze "still standing at lectern, lecturing."

(5) The Summary of the Data page is completed back in your office *after* the observation is over. Here you may make judgments based on the data in (1) - (4). Do not make a judgment unless the observation data support it. The judgments that you make must be linked to the data that you collected on the first two pages. For example, based on the script of the lesson, it is certainly accurate to conclude that interactions were sometimes discourteous/disrespectful. That judgment is not checked because there are no data on the previous two pages to support that judgment.

Formal Documentation

You are now ready to write the specific incident memorandum. Note that in this memorandum, Dr. Principal has chosen not to include growth activities. However, he expects the teacher to comply with the district's classroom management and organization expectations. If he finds continued noncompliance when he visits Mr. Laze's classroom in two weeks, he may choose to add directives for growth activities or to develop a formal, comprehensive professional growth plan. Note that for illustrative purposes, we have included on the left side of the memorandum the components of a specific incident memorandum related to instruction. You would not include these in the actual memorandum you send to the teacher.

ESSENTIAL ELEMENTS

Letterhead

Bestever ISD
1234 Sunny Lane
Bestever, TX 70000

TO: Mr. Bill Laze

FROM: Dr. Great Principal

Date

DATE: October 14, 2011

SUBJECT: Report of Classroom Observation on October 10 and Conference on October 12

Nature of Allegation and Investigation

This memorandum will formally communicate information gathered during my observation in your classroom on October 10, 2011, and discussed with you in our conference on October 12, 2011. I observed from 8:30 to 8:55 while you were conducting a lesson on Civil War and Reconstruction in Texas with a group of 30 ninth graders.

The observation revealed the following information.

Findings of Fact

You began by telling the students that it would be important to take notes, because much of the information was not available in the textbook. During the remainder of my visit, I observed the following:

1. Four students entered the classroom after the tardy bell. You did not say anything to these students.
2. You began instruction at 8:40 - 10 minutes after the beginning of the class period.
3. Between 8:30 and 8:45, six of 30 students were taking notes and the rest were not taking notes. Two had no books or homework.
4. At 8:45 when you asked, "Did everybody get that?" three students nodded. At 8:50 one student responded when you asked, "Does anybody know?" You continued to lecture.
5. Between 8:50 and 8:55 six students took notes. Ron stared out the window and several others looked around the room. Jason sorted papers in his notebook and after a time, Angel began to help him. Aaron, Paul, and Betsy whispered in the back of the room. Marsha and Reggie held a private conversation by the door. Two students watched me. During this time you continued to lecture and took no action to stop or redirect any of the student behaviors listed.

Expectations/Basis of Authority

The Bestever I.S.D. appraisal system has the expectation that you "manage student discipline, instructional strategies, time, and materials." Within that evaluation domain, there is an expectation that you secure and maintain student attention. It further specifies

ESSENTIAL ELEMENTS

that you "effectively and efficiently manage time." In order to accomplish this, you must establish and maintain focus and keep students engaged in the learning process (Domain V).

As part of managing student behavior, the district appraisal system expects you to (1) communicate and equitably enforce the campus management plan and your own classroom rules and (2) successfully intervene to stop or redirect off-task and inappropriate behavior (Domain V).

Conclusions/Judgments

The data from my observation indicate that these expectations related to classroom management were not met.

I will be observing in your classroom again beginning two weeks from today. In all future lessons I will expect to meet the expectations in the following ways:

Directives for Changes in Behavior

1. Implement the campus discipline management plan in such a way that all/almost all students are engaged in learning and behaving appropriately.
2. Intervene and stop/redirect off-task/inappropriate behavior in such a way that the behavior stops.
3. Plan and implement instruction in such a way that all/almost all students are engaged in learning for most/all of the instructional period.

Opportunity to Respond

My signature verifies that I have received a copy of this memorandum. It does not necessarily mean that I agree with the content. I understand that I have the right to present a written response within 10 working days.

Dated Signature of Employee

/s/ Bill Laze　　　　Date

Documentation of Learning Climate Concerns

Gathering and Recording Data

We return now to Mr. Laze's classroom to use the final focused observation instrument, which is designed to provide specific information on strategies for motivating students and maintaining a supportive environment. You will note that the use/non-use of motivational strategies and of learning environment are much more subjective that other classroom issues. The numbers on the instrument correspond to the notes in the following commentary section. As with the others, a blank copy of this form appears in Appendix B and also is available on the optional CD for easy downloading and use.

FOCUSED OBSERVATION INSTRUMENT #5
Maintaining a Supportive Learning Environment
- ✓ Uses Strategies to Motivate Students for Learning
- ✓ Maintains Positive Learning Environment

Name of Teacher: Bill Laze
Date of Observation: 10/11/11
Subject/Grade Level: American History/9th
Time of Observation: Begin: 8:30
End: 8:55 (1)
Specific Content/Activity: Civil War/Reconstruction in Texas
Number of Students in Class: 30

The following teacher behaviors are associated with learning climate.
Check any behaviors that appear and make notes/comments, as appropriate.

(2)

	Positively Associated		Negatively Associated
____	Positive reinforcement of behavior	____	Extinction (ignoring appropriate student behavior)
✓ ____	Positive reinforcement of learning	✓ ____	Not providing positive reinforcement of learning and/ or not providing corrective feedback
____	Correcting incorrect responses and preserving student dignity	✓ ____	Providing negative/demeaning corrective feedback
____	Patiently assisting students who are having difficulty	✓ ____	Ignoring or being impatient with students having difficulty
____	Using humor in a positive way to deal with a potentially negative situation (learning or behavior)	✓ ____	Using sarcasm/negative criticism in dealing with incorrect responses/ performances or with behavior
____	Relating content/activity to students' interest or experience	✓ ____	Dull, routine, or boring content/activity
____	Communicating value or importance of content or activity	✓ ____	Not communicating value or importance of content or activity
✓ ____	Using student names	____	Not using student names
____	Giving specific feedback for correct/incorrect performance	✓ ____	Telling students they are wrong without telling them why
____	Applying rules/expectations positively, consistently, and fairly	✓ ____	Applying rules/expectations negatively, inconsistently, and unfairly

Notes

Positively Associated

To Susie: "That's a good answer." "Right again."

Negatively Associated

To Paul: "Right, Paul. See what happens when you pay attention?"

No response to Paul's failure to answer question.

To Steve's incorrect response: "No, not exactly."

To Aaron: "Not hardly, Aaron. Does anybody know?" No one raised hand.

Audrey: "I don't know."

Mr. L.: "Why not? Didn't you read the assignment?" Student did not answer.

Aaron: "What's disenfranchisement?" Mr. L.: "Look it up. Susie, can you bail him out?"

Lecture/Q&A for entire period; 1 activity

Positively Associated		Negatively Associated		Notes
____	Implementing instruction that is challenging while allowing students to be successful	____	Implementing instruction that is too difficult (easy) for students to feel successful	**(2)**
____	Using positive/patient vocal tone	√	Using negative impatient vocal tone	Matt: "I'm sorry, what?" Mr. L.: "You sure are."
____	High energy/enthusiasm, moving around, animated	____	Unenthusiastic/sedentary	Mr. L.: "Didn't anybody read the assignment?"

The following student behaviors are associated with learning climate. Check any behaviors that appear and make notes/comments, as appropriate.

Positively Associated		Negatively Associated		Notes
____	Students excited/eager	____	Students bored, lethargic	Negatively Associated
____	High level of voluntary student participation	√	Low level of voluntary student participation	Students spoke only when called on.
____	Student-initiated contributions/ extensions examples/discussion	√	Few student-initiated contributions/ extensions examples/discussion	Aaron closed book and put it away after giving incorrect response.
____	Students who are having difficulty continue to make effort	√	Students who are having difficulty quit or give up	Several students engaged in off-task behaviors (sorting papers, talking, looking out the window, whispering, looking around room).
____	Students appropriately question teacher/each other	√	Students do not question or inappropriately question teacher/ each other	
____	Students having difficulty are not reluctant to ask for assistance	____	Students having difficulty are reluctant to ask for assistance	Students participated when called upon; no voluntary participation/ extension
____	Students on-task/engaged with little direction/manipulation by teacher	√	Students on-task/engaged primarily because of direction/manipulation by teacher	
____	Other behavior	____	Other behavior	

Commentary

(1) The first section of the instrument provides essential information that you will need when you are ready to document this observation and write your specific incident memorandum to Mr. Laze (e.g., date and time of the observation, length of the observation, etc.).

(2) The checklist on this page consists of teacher behaviors that are associated with learning climate. A similar checklist on the next page consists of student behaviors. The first columns on each page list behaviors positively associated with learning climate; the second columns list the opposite kinds of behaviors—those associated with a negative learning climate. Unlike the previous four focused observation instruments, this one calls for judgments to be made *during* the observation. The very nature of "learning climate" is much more subjective than the previous four areas. It is, therefore, extremely important for the observer to record such data as direct quotations from the teacher and students, and anecdotal information about teacher and student behavior. The "Notes" columns are provided for that purpose.

Formal Documentation

You are now ready to write the specific incident memorandum. Note that in this memorandum, Dr. Principal has chosen not to include growth activities. However, he expects the teacher to comply with the district's expectations for learning environment. If he finds continued noncompliance when he visits Mr. Laze's classroom in two weeks, he may choose to add directives for growth activities or to develop a formal, comprehensive intervention plan. Note that for illustrative purposes, we have included on the left side of the memorandum the components of a specific incident memorandum related to instruction. You would not include these in the actual memorandum you send to the teacher.

ESSENTIAL ELEMENTS	
Letterhead	**Bestever ISD** **1234 Sunny Lane** **Bestever, TX 70000**
	TO: Mr. Bill Laze
	FROM: Dr. Great Principal
Date	**DATE:** October 14, 2011
	SUBJECT: Report of Classroom Observation of October 10 and Conference of October 12
Nature of Allegation and Investigation	This memorandum will formally communicate information gathered during my observation in your classroom on October 10, 2011 and our conference on October 12, 2011. I observed from 8:30 to 8:55 while you conducted a lesson on Civil War Reconstruction in Texas with a group of 30 ninth graders.
Findings of Fact	During the observation there were several instances in which you exhibited behavior that is negatively associated with a supportive learning climate: 1. When Paul was unable to answer correctly, you did not respond to him – you called on another student. Later

ESSENTIAL ELEMENTS

when Paul answered correctly, you said, "Right, Paul. See what happens when you pay attention?"

2. When Steve answered incorrectly, you said, "No, not exactly."
3. When Aaron gave an incorrect response, you said, "Not hardly." Later when he asked you what disenfranchise meant, you told him to "look it up."
4. When Audrey told you she did not know the answer, you said, "Why not? Didn't you read the assignment?"
5. When Matt responded to a question with, "I'm sorry, what?" you said, "You sure are" and called on another student.

Expectations/ Basis of Authority

During this observation, I noted that students spoke only when called upon. Aaron closed his book after answering incorrectly. Several students engaged in off-task behaviors (sorting papers, whispering, looking out the window, looking around the room).

The Bestever I.S.D. appraisal system has the expectation that you "motivate the students for learning." In order to accomplish this, it is necessary to use one or more of these strategies: (1) relate the lesson to student interests or experiences, and/or (2) convey to students the value or importance of the lesson.

The district appraisal system also expects that teachers "establish and maintain a supportive environment." Teacher behaviors that promote a positive learning climate include the following: (1) avoid sarcasm and negative criticism, (2) exhibit courtesy and respect, (3) encourage slow and reluctant students, (4) maintain a positive rapport with students, and (5) provide corrective feedback to students who are having difficulty.

Conclusions/ Judgments

The data gathered during my observation indicate that these expectations were not met.

I will be observing in your classroom again later this month. In all future lessons I will expect that you:

Directives for Changes in Behavior

1. Relate each lesson to student interest or experience and communicate the value or importance of the lesson to the students in such a way that students are engaged and participating in the learning.
2. Positively reinforce or praise student effort and student success and encourage those students who are slow or reluctant.
3. Provide corrective feedback to students who are unsuccessful or having difficulty in such a way that they are successful.
4. Ensure that all interactions with students are be courteous and respectful.
5. Cease all sarcasm and negative criticism with students.

Opportunity to Respond

My signature verifies that I have received a copy of this memorandum. It does not necessarily mean that I agree with the content. I understand that I have the right to present a written response within 10 working days.

Dated Signature of Employee

/s/ Bill Laze ______________________ Date ______________

SUMMARY

Gathering classroom documentation data need not be an arduous task. The focused observation instruments presented in this chapter allow you to concentrate on particular aspects of instruction in which the teacher is having trouble. By focusing your attention, the instruments can help you document the ways in which a teacher is ineffective or marginally effective, plan improvement plan activities to improve the teacher's performance, and write clear and complete memoranda.

The use of focused observation instruments has a number of values:

- You are not burdened with non-stop note-taking.
- You are free to observe more and to detect non-verbal behaviors.
- You can concentrate your attention and data collection on the one or two areas in which a marginally effective teacher is having difficulty.

You are more likely to collect in-depth data on one area of deficiency that will aid you in writing and justifying directives for changes in behavior. School districts that use the Professional Development and Appraisal System (PDAS) will find that the focused observation instruments are tailored to the performance (i.e., classroom instruction) domains of that system. Some districts may have developed their own teacher evaluation systems using different evaluation instruments, peer coaching, portfolio assessment, teacher action research, student work products, and a host of other options. Regardless of the instrument or process used in a locally adopted teacher appraisal system, that system in all likelihood shares the same body of research on effective teaching upon which PDAS is constructed. Criteria for teacher evaluation will always include the generic teaching issues targeted by each of our focused observation instruments:

- Active, successful student participation.
- Instructional strategies.
- Monitoring and assessment of student learning.
- Classroom management.
- Learning environment.

Finally, your data collection in Domains IV-VII primarily will consist of observation outside the classroom, examination of documents and records, and/or conferences with the teacher and with other stakeholders in the school. Occasionally, data may come from classroom observation (e.g., Domain V: Professional Communication). After you have gathered your data, you will write the kinds of memoranda illustrated in this chapter and in Chapter 2. This will document and communicate to the teacher notice of your concerns related to the requirements of the job, an opportunity to improve, and directives and a time line to change the teacher's behavior.

CHAPTER FIVE: PROFESSIONAL COMMUNICATION

In recent years, communication between and among professional employees under Domain V of the Professional Development and Appraisal System (PDAS) has received greater attention in assessment. Challenges have arisen as a result. In this chapter, we first discuss the developing law in this area. Then we offer recommendations on how to document failures to meet the expectations of this domain and to direct employees to improve their ability to communicate in effective and professionally responsible ways. Domain V also encompasses communication with students. Included in our discussion is how to deal with abuses resulting from increasing teacher use of electronic communication devices (ECDs) to interact with students through social networking sites like Facebook and MySpace. ECDs encompass, but are not limited to, computers, cellular telephones, and text-messaging devices.

THE LEGAL FRAMEWORK

As we noted in Chapter One, public employees including those in both traditional public and charter schools have a constitutional right to free speech. To review, we know that school employees have a right to speak out as citizens on matters of public concern so long as they don't undermine their effectiveness as employees. However, this right does not extend to complaints about working conditions. Thus, a teacher who complains constantly about such matters as noise in the hallway outside her room, too many parental complaints, and too frequent walk-through classroom visits by school administrators is unlikely to be successful in asserting that these comments are constitutionally protected and cannot be used to support a contract termination or nonrenewal recommendation. The teacher should be directed to find a more constructive way to vent complaints (e.g., by discussing the matter with the principal in private or by following the district's grievance procedure) or to cease making them altogether.

Based on a 2006 U.S. Supreme Court ruling involving a deputy district attorney who suffered retaliation when he wrote an internal office memorandum to his supervisors noting serious deficiencies in a governmental affidavit used to obtain a search warrant, public employees who speak out on matters of public concern when acting within the scope of their employment appear to enjoy little constitutional protection.[1] Thus, a teacher who is assigned to a meeting of parents whose children will be enrolling in the school next year and opts to speak out about the lack of effective discipline procedures at the school is unlikely to find the remarks constitutionally protected. Of course, if the teacher is invited by school administrators to address this matter or if the teacher does so outside the scope of employment – for example, by writing a comment on a blog or calling into a late-night radio talk show – the speech is likely to be constitutionally protected.[2]

Also, it is important to recall from Chapter 1 that teachers in Texas have a constitutional right to lead classroom discussion on controversial matters and can't be penalized for doing so unless there is documented evidence that the teacher's ability to teach has been undermined. Of course the discussion has to be germane to the subject matter being taught. Thus, an algebra teacher who facilitates a discussion on the propriety of having American troops in Afghanistan would be unlikely to assert a constitutional right to do so. And even if germane to the subject matter, the discussion has to be age-appropriate and unbiased for the teacher to have a viable free speech claim.

While these are legal distinctions regarding constitutionally protected versus unprotected speech, it is important to note that school board members who hear employee grievances and conduct contract nonrenewal hearings often are less concerned with nuances in the law and more that employees are treated fairly. Thus, if there are other reasons related to job performance to rely upon in making a negative employment recommendation, you are best advised to use them rather than cite what a teacher says or writes. Sometimes, however, the major concerns do relate to how employees communicate with others, and you have no choice but to focus on the manner in which they do so. Just remember that much employee speech on the job is not constitutionally protected and make sure that you point this out in your documentation so that those not familiar with the law will understand that you have acted within legal boundaries. If you are uncertain about what is and is not constitutionally protected, check with the human resources department or the school attorney.

Finally, we need to note that teachers and administrators increasingly are using electronic communication devices (ECDs) on and off campus to interact with students on social networking websites. Quite often, this is part of the school's instructional delivery system. Teachers engage with students online in connection with assignments, projects, and the like. Such communication facilitates learning in that it extends face-to-face time with teachers beyond the classroom and capitalizes on student expertise in using ECDs. Clearly, the future of teaching and learning will incorporate utilization of these devices in the instructional program. But in accord with criteria of Domain V of PDAS, it is important to assure that communication between school employees and students is professional at all times whether on or off campus.

Stories now are surfacing of teachers and administrators who have crossed the line between what is professional and what is not in social networking with students. A good illustration is a case involving a Connecticut high school teacher who opened a MySpace account after students asked him to view their MySpace pages. The teacher, Jeffrey Spanierman, called one of the profiles on this account "Mr. Spiderman." He used his MySpace account to communicate with students about homework, to learn more about the students so he could relate to them better, and to conduct casual non-school related discussions. In ECD parlance, he sought to "friend" his MySpace students electronically by including them on this profile. The matter came to attention of school personnel who viewed the profile page. There they found a picture of Spanierman taken some ten years earlier when he was about the same age as the students he was friending. Also appearing were pictures of his students along with several pictures of naked men with inappropriate comments underneath them. Spanierman removed the Spiderman profile but then started another that was similar. His teaching contract was not renewed.

Spanierman sued in federal court, contending that the nonrenewal violated his right to free speech and association. The federal district court judge noted that his MySpace statements were made outside the scope of his employment and thus were not restricted by the 2006 U.S. Supreme Court decision referenced above. He noted as well that a poem Spanierman had posted on the MySpace profile expressing opposition to the Iraq war was constitutionally protected free speech. However, the judge agreed with school officials regarding the inappropriate manner in which Spanierman was communicating with students. The judge cited this exchange with a student who used the profile name "Repko."

Spanierman: "Repko and Ashley sittin in a tree.KISSING.1st comes love then marriage. HA HA HA HA HA HA HA!!!!!!!!!!!!!!!!!!!!LOL [can mean 'laughing out loud']"

Repko: "don't be jealous cuase you cant get any lol :)"

Spanierman: "What makes you think I want any? I'm not jealous. I just like to have fun and goof on you guys. If you don't like it. Kiss my brass! LMAO [can mean 'laughing my ass off']."

The judge pointed out in his decision denying Spanierman's challenge to his contract nonrenewal that it is reasonable to expect a teacher with supervisory authority over students to maintain a professional, respectful association with them. "This does not mean that the [Spanierman] could not be friendly or humorous," wrote the Judge. "However, upon review of the record, it appears that the [Spanierman] would communicate with students as if he were their peer, not their teacher." Such conduct could very well disrupt the learning atmosphere of a school, the judge observed. In short, the communication between the teacher and his students had ceased being professional. Indeed, some students maintained that they were uncomfortable with what Spanierman was saying.[3]

School districts now are beginning to educate teachers and students about appropriate conduct when engaging in communication via ECDs. In addition, districts hold teachers and students accountable when using district-hosted websites and district-owned ECDs by having them (and the parents of students) sign acceptable use policies (AUPs) that set forth the conditions and rules for doing so. Violation of the rules can result in disciplinary action against both students and school employees, with the added penalty of contract nonrenewal or termination for the latter.[4]

Controlling what teachers, other school employees, and students do with their personal ECDs on their own time away from school is more difficult, because as private citizens they have the right of free speech and association. It would be wise in our view for district officials to notify teachers that if they engage in inappropriate use of electronic communication devices off campus, doing so could jeopardize their employment status. Having a set of guidelines for off-campus use of personal ECDs would be one way of doing so. Oftentimes, such guidelines are set forth in board policies, administrative regulations, and employee handbooks. Points to make include:

- Reminding teachers that what they say on the internet could be disseminated in seconds and that they need to read carefully the privacy protections available on social communication networks.
- Pointing out that privacy protections of social communication networks do not prevent persons on the networks from forwarding pictures and messages to others. For example, critical comments about a school administrator could easily become widely known in the school community and undermine a teacher's effectiveness.
- Advising teachers that engaging in social communication with students outside of district internet access routes and not related to academic matters could easily undermine a teacher's effectiveness.
- Advising teachers to contact the school principal for advice if in doubt.

It is important to note that the Code of Ethics and Standards Practices for Texas Educators recently was revised and now contains a section specifically directed to social networking with students via cell phones, text messaging, email, instant messaging, blogging, and the like. As noted in Appendix A, Standard 3.9 sets forth factors to be considered in determining whether such networking is inappropriate. These include:

- The nature, purpose, timing, and amount of communication
- The subject matter addressed
- Whether the communication was open or secretive
- Whether a romantic relationship could be inferred
- Whether the communication was sexually explicit
- Whether the communication involves discussion of the physical or sexual attractiveness or sexual history, activities, preferences, or fantasies of either the educator or the student

School board policies usually incorporate the Code of Ethics. For districts that utilize the Texas Association of School Boards model policies, this will be found in Policy DH (Legal) and related policies. Thus, a teacher who engages in misuse of his or her own electronic communication device in the ways indicated in this standard is violating school board policies as well.

DOCUMENTING UNPROFESSIONAL TEACHER COMMUNICATION UNDER PDAS DOMAIN V

Inappropriate Written and Verbal Communication

One of the most frequent personnel issues that we encounter when we work with school administrators involves staff members who are discourteous and/or confrontational in their communication with students, other staff, and parents. They do not work and play well with others! With the increased importance of Professional Learning Communities (PLC) and collegial planning in schools, it is more important than ever for teachers to learn and to work together as a team for the best learning experiences for students. Unfortunately, a common scenario is the teacher who does not work professionally and cooperatively with other staff members.

A second facet of the issue is the teacher who is (or is perceived to be) rude, discourteous, or confrontational in the teacher's communication. Sometimes you may personally hear such communication; typically, the problem is brought to you by third parties.

Several problems emerge:

1. When a teacher is uncooperative with other staff or parents or when communication is rude or discourteous, you may not have had the opportunity to observe the uncooperative behavior or hear the rude/discourteous conversation personally. You may be relying on information from third parties, probably from other staff members or parents. Therefore, you may have to consider whether they are willing to sign a complaint form (sample in Appendix D) and/or testify to what they have seen or heard in a hearing.
2. The teacher may completely deny having been rude or discourteous. He may assert that the complaining party is overreacting or misinterpreting his behavior. You may need to meet with the teacher to point out that regardless of his intent, others are receiving his messages as rude/discourteous and that he must change his behavior. You will be the arbiter of what is or is not rude or discourteous.

3. The teacher may assert that she is merely exercising her right of free speech. As we pointed out in this chapter and in Chapter 1, not all speech is protected. When the speech is not on a matter of public concern or the speech impedes the school's functioning or the employee's job performance, you may direct her to change the content or tone of her communication.

For example, let's assume that Nick Negative is an eighth grade science teacher with many years of experience. You have an expectation that Nick participate with other teachers in designing and implementing quality lessons in all eighth grade science classes. All of the other eighth grade teachers have, at one time or another, complained to you that Nick is very difficult and unpleasant to work with. Comments from his co-workers include:

- "He's so negative about the kids—he calls them 'stupid,' says they are not capable of doing high level academic work, and says 'they just don't care and neither do their parents.' "
- "He gets angry when we try to discuss new ways of teaching. He insists that his traditional way of teaching is the best and that our 'newfangled methods' just do not work."
- "He argues and yells at us when we do not agree with him. If we argue back, he gets very rude and sarcastic."

Although you have not personally observed this behavior/language in planning meetings, you have confidence in the teachers who reported it. Two teachers agreed to complete a complaint form following a particularly confrontational meeting with Nick. Another who observed the fiery exchange completed a witness statement form (templates of both forms can be found in Appendix D). Your own experience with Nick suggests that he is entirely capable of the behavior that his co-workers have reported. You schedule a conference to talk with him about your concerns.

At the conference, he first wants to know who is doing the complaining. You explain that who is complaining is not the issue; the issue is having a productive, professional eighth grade PLC. He responds in a very loud voice, "They are just a bunch of young inexperienced teachers. I've been at this for more than 20 years, and I know what I am doing. I am not rude or sarcastic when I talk to them. I have very strong convictions and I want them to know that." At another point he says, "What do you expect me to do? Just cave in and do the Mickey Mouse lessons they come up with?" You point out that in your judgment, both the tone and content of his statement are unprofessional and sarcastic. He replies, "I'm just being honest, and I don't like being told what to do." You explain that you expect all members of the team to work together harmoniously and reach consensus on lesson planning and delivery of lessons. You also explained that you expect all team members to communicate with each other courteously and respectfully, even when they disagree with each other. You tell him that whether or not it his intention, his co-workers interpret his behavior as rude and confrontational. Finally, you tell him that his behavior is impeding his own job performance and that of his co-workers. The next day you write him a memorandum that follows the essential elements of a specific incident memorandum as set forth in Chapter 2 and in Chapter 4. The numbers in parentheses correspond with the observations in the commentary section following the memorandum.

ESSENTIAL ELEMENTS

Letterhead Stationery

PRAIRIE HIGH SCHOOL
Home of the Prairie Howlers
Coyote I.S.D.
1000 High Road

Date — October 13, 2011

TO: Nick Negative
FROM: Great Leader, Principal
RE: Planning, Working, and Communicating With Team Members

Allegation — This memorandum addresses concerns that I have expressed to you in our meeting yesterday about your work with other members of your team in cooperatively planning lessons and reports that you use loud, unprofessional language in the planning meetings. My concerns are based on my conversations I have had with you and with several members of your team. **(1)**

Findings of Fact — As I explained to you at our meeting on October 12, several members of your team have reported to me that you are uncooperative in your planning meetings. **(2)** They have also reported that when you disagree with the team that you yell at them and are rude and sarcastic. You indicated that you believed that your teaching methodologies were better than the team's ideas. You also said to me in a very loud voice, "I am not rude or sarcastic when I talk to them. I have very strong convictions and I want them to know that."

When I advised you that I expect all members of the team to work together harmoniously and reach consensus on lesson planning and delivery of lessons, you replied, "What do you expect me to do? Just cave in and do the Mickey Mouse lessons they come up with?" I told you that both the tone and content of your statement were unprofessional and sarcastic. You replied, "I'm just being honest, and I don't like being told what to do." I advised you that I expect all team members to communicate with each other courteously and respectfully, even when you disagree with each other.

Expectations/ Basis of Authority — Domain V, Criterion 6 of the Professional Development and Appraisal System (PDAS) contains the expectation that your "interactions are supportive, courteous, and respectful with students, parents, staff, community members, and other professionals." **(3)** Domain VI, Criterion 4 of PDAS has the expectation that you work "collaboratively and constructively with colleagues and other professionals toward the overall improvement of student performance."

Conclusions — I have concluded that these expectations are not being met. You are not working cooperatively and constructively with your colleagues, and your communication with me and with your colleagues is not supportive, courteous, and respectful.

Directives — Beginning immediately, I will expect you to: **(4)**

1. Interact with other staff members in a manner that is supportive, courteous, and respectful in such a way that complaints about your communication from other professionals decrease significantly and stop by the end of the semester.
2. Stop all rudeness and sarcasm in such a way that complaints from other professionals decrease significantly and stop by the end of the semester.
3. Work collaboratively and constructively with colleagues and other professionals in such a way that complaints from other professionals decrease significantly and stop by the end of the semester.

Opportunity to Respond — I have received a copy of this memorandum. I understand that my signature does not necessarily indicate that I agree with its contents. I further understand that I have a right to respond within 10 working days if I disagree.

Dated Signature — /s/______________________________ Date____________

Nick Negative

Commentary

(1) The concern/allegation is that Nick does not work cooperatively with his team and that he is rude and sarcastic in the planning meetings.

(2) You summarized your concerns about cooperative planning and professional communication and accurately reflect what he said in response to these allegations. When he wanted to know who had complained, you focused instead on your concern. You cited both the complaints from co-workers as well as your own experience in the conference. Should a contract nonrenewal or termination hearing occur over this matter, you have the complaint and witness statement forms to back up your assertions.

(3) You chose language from PDAS Domain V (Professional Communication) and Domain VI (Professional Development) as the source of your expectations. These are important because they will be the anchor/basis of authority for the directives that you write in the next section of the memorandum.

(4) Your directives are specific regarding what you expect Nick to do in the future with regard to working courteously and cooperatively with colleagues. Note that these directives follow the formula discussed in Chapter 6: teacher behavior + linking language + outcome. The teacher behaviors are anchored in the expectations from section 3 of the memorandum. The outcomes are "complaints from other professionals decrease significantly and stop by the end of the semester." This is the evidence that you will use determine whether he has complied with the directives. In addition for failure to follow directives, "failure to maintain an effective working relationship or maintain good rapport with parents, the community, or colleagues" is a cause for contract nonrenewal or termination in most district policies [see DFBB (Local) from TASB Policy Services].

Social Networking with Students with Electronic Communication Devices

Let us assume that Sterling Leader, principal of Prairie High School in Coyote I.S.D. is concerned about one of his English teachers, 24-year-old Sarah Novice. She is a good teacher, but Sterling has observed her at various school events texting a lot on her cell phone. He notes that when she finishes a text message, she often glances toward several students who also seem to be texting. Their smiles and laughter in her direction while the messaging is ongoing suggest to him that Sarah and the students are texting each other. Sterling spoke with Sarah about this after a home football game where he observed her texting on her cell phone and waving to several of her students elsewhere in the stands. They waved in response and also were busy texting. When Sterling talked with Sarah about this the following Monday, she said that she indeed was texting with her students. She said they were discussing matters related to the football game. She showed Sterling the message strings on her cell phone. He noted text exchanges over such matters as the prowess of the cheerleaders and the tripping of one of the high school band's tuba players on the field during half-time. Sterling advised Sarah to be careful about texting students, noting that what might seem innocuous communication can easily become less so. Sterling felt some unease when Sarah responded, "I just want to be friendly with my students. If they like me, they will do well in my classes." But he decided not to pursue the matter further at the time

Several weeks later, Sarah's cell phone dropped out of her purse when she was searching for a notepad as she was walking down the hall toward the school cafeteria. With the rush of students to the cafeteria and the surrounding noise, she was unaware of the incident. Several students some distance behind her found the cell phone but didn't know to whom it belonged. They checked the email, text messages, and photographs. Sarah's identity surfaced immediately. So did some other messages and images. Among the photographs was Sarah holding a glass of wine at a post-football game party attended by some of her students. The game was hosted by the parents of several football players. The students were clustered around Sarah, holding soft drinks. One student in the background was flipping his middle finger toward the camera. One of the two text messages on the phone was from a senior student who asked her if they could meet for lunch on Saturday at a nearby McDonalds to talk about his college plans. The students were laughing and hooting as they came across the photo and the message. Before they could do more searching, Sterling, who was walking down the hall, came upon them. The students told him that they had found the phone on the floor and had checked some of its contents to see whose it was. They couldn't help laughing as they pointed out the photo at the football game party. Sterling thanked them for finding the phone and told them to head on to the cafeteria.

Later that day, Sterling asked Sarah to come by the office. He handed her the phone, noting that the students had seen the photographs and read the text messages. Sarah was delighted that her cell phone was found and returned to her, but a little upset about what the students had seen. Sterling talked with her about the potential pitfalls of communicating electronically with students and then directed her to lock her cell phone and restrict her communication with students. Two days later, he sent her a follow-up memorandum. The numbers in parentheses correspond with the observations in the commentary section following the memorandum.

ESSENTIAL ELEMENTS

Letterhead Stationery

PRAIRIE HIGH SCHOOL
Home of the Prairie Howlers
Coyote I.S.D.
1000 High Road
Coyote, TX 70000

Date

November 16, 2011

TO: Sarah Novice
FROM: Sterling Leader, Principal
RE: Cell Phone Use

Allegation

This memorandum addresses concerns that I have expressed to you over use of your personal cell phone with students at this high school. My concerns are based on my own observations and well as conversations I have had with you and with several of your students. **(1)**

Findings of Fact

On Friday, October 14, I observed you at the home football game texting students in the stands with your cell phone. I spoke with you the following Monday before classes began regarding what I had observed. You acknowledged that you were texting with students. You showed me several of the text messages. I advised you to be careful in social interaction with students either by electronic or non-electronic means both on and off campus, given the potential for misuse. You responded by noting that you would be careful, adding that "I just want to be friendly with students." **(2)**

On Monday, November 14, your cell phone dropped out of your purse as you headed to the cafeteria for lunch. Four students some distance behind you

ESSENTIAL ELEMENTS

found the cell phone and were able to access its contents. They told me they did so to discover the owner. They also said they had come across a text message from another student asking you to have lunch with him at Mc-Donalds on a Saturday. They showed me the message and also a photograph of you holding a wine glass at an after-hours post-football game party hosted by several parents. You were surrounding by smiling students, one of whom displayed an obscene hand gesture to the camera.

As I explained to you at our meeting after school that day, there was nothing I could do to prevent the students who found your cell phone from accessing this material. I also advised you on how to use your cell phone appropriately at school and elsewhere. I am sending you this follow-up memorandum to make sure my directives are clear and to explain why I have made them.

Conclusions

At this time, I don't believe you have violated our district policy on communication with students via electronic means. **(3)**

Expectations/
Basis of Authority

However, as I explained to you, it is important to note that School Board Policy DH (Local) incorporates the Code of Ethics and Standard Practices for Texas Educators. Standard 3.8 states that the educator "shall maintain appropriate professional educator-student relationships and boundaries based on a reasonably prudent educator standard." Standard 3.9 goes on to address inappropriate use of electronic communication devices in social interactions with students. I am attaching both the policy provision and the Code of Ethics to this memorandum. Please pay particular attention to the components of Standard 3.9 of the Code that address conditions under which educators violate the standard in engaging in electronic communication with students. I also ask that you read our Teacher Handbook, pages 15-20 of which address use of electronic media with students. In addition, you know that Criteria 1 of Domain V of the Professional Development and Appraisal System contain the expectation that you "use appropriate and accurate written communication with students." Criteria 2 of Domain V has an expectation that you use" verbal and non-verbal communication establishes a learning climate that is positive and conducive to learning."

I am not including this matter in your appraisal for this year. I would like us to put it behind us.

Directives

At our meeting, I requested that you set a password so that you can lock your cell phone at school. That way, no one can access its contents should it not be in your possession. Second, I directed you to limit your electronic communication with students at school and school-related activities only to matters related to your professional responsibilities. These include class work, homework, and tests. I also strongly advised you to limit your communication with students off campus in a similar manner, because any misuse that undermines your effectiveness as a teacher can be grounds for disciplinary action including contract nonrenewal or termination. Both you and I agreed that you would not have any social contact with the student who requested you join him for lunch. The same is true for any other student. **(4)**

If you have any questions about communicating electronically with students, please let me know. In your first two years at Prairie High School, you have proven yourself to be a good teacher. I don't want you to do anything to jeopardize your career. The matter of communicating with students in this electronic age can be tricky. If you have any questions about this in the future, don't hesitate to contact me.

Att.

Opportunity to
Respond

I have received a copy of this letter. I understand that my signature does not necessarily indicate that I agree with its contents. I further understand that I have a right to respond within 10 working days if I disagree.

Dated Signature

/s/________________________________ Date__________________

Sarah Novice

Commentary

(1) This is less an allegation than a statement of fact, because much of what Sterling addresses is based on his own observation. However, he did talk with students and obtained information from them which he relies on in part in writing the memorandum.

(2) It probably would have been better if Sterling had directed Sarah not to text message students at all or only related to her work as a teacher when they spoke after the football game. It could be that he opted to be less directive because of Sarah's reactions and his desire not to damage their working relationship. Note that Sterling is specific as to dates, times, and substance in his findings of fact. These are based on his notes to the file. As we point out in Chapter 2, making notes to the file is essential to effective documentation where prior events are incorporated in the findings of fact. It may be that Sterling sought to have each of the students he spoke with in the hallway complete a witness statement form (see Appendix D) describing in factual terms how they fond Sarah's cell phone, what they accessed on the cell phone, and what they came across. This is a judgment call.

(3) While Sterling does not find that Sarah has violated Coyote I.S.D. policy, he takes advantage of the situation to make her fully aware of district policy and related legal sources pertaining to social communication with students via electronic means. It is extremely important for both administrators and teachers to be fully aware of the policies, rules, and procedures of the district within which they are employed. Here, the principal even broadens the scope of his discussion to include both nonelectronic social interaction and interacting with students off campus. Note that he attaches both the district policy and the Code of Ethics and Standard Practices for Texas Educators to his memorandum. He also references the teacher handbook. And he comments on Domain V of PDAS but declines to include this matter in her annual appraisal.

(4) Sterling's directives are specific regarding what he expects her to do in the future with regard to using her cell phone at school. Clearly, Sarah knows exactly what she needs to do to avoid problems in this area in the future. She also undoubtedly will be cautious in engaging in social interaction with students off campus on her own time. And the principal has left the door open should she have future concerns over the use of ECDs in interacting with students.

SUMMARY

Here is a summary of main points discussed in this chapter.

- Professional communication between and among employees is evaluated in Domain V and to a lesser extent in Domain VI (Professional Development) of PDAS. With an emphasis on professional learning communities and team planning, cooperative and professional communication is an increasingly important aspect of job responsibilities.
- Addressing communication between and among professional employees and

with the larger school community may raise the question of First Amendment free speech rights. Communication may also be a somewhat subjective issue because the problem may be rooted in judgments about volume, tone, or inflection that is interpreted as being sarcastic, rude, or discourteous.

- If employees are not communicating courteously and respectfully, direct them to meet the expectations of PDAS in their communication with students, staff, and the larger school community.
- The law dealing with communication using electronic communication devices (ECDs) is a new and still emerging field. If you are unsure how to proceed when you believe misuse has occurred, contact human resources personnel or the school attorney.
- If you know or suspect that an employee is using ECDs and social networking sites inappropriately, direct the employee to follow district policy and/ or the Code of Ethics and Standard Practices for Texas Educators.

REFERENCES

1. *Garcetti v. Ceballos*, 547 U.S. 410 (2006). Note, however that Article I, § 8 of the Texas Constitution may be more supportive of public employee speech. See endnote 62 following Chapter 1.
2. A school employee who posts a message on a personal blog about suspected violation of law by school officials and then asserts that the Texas Whistleblower Act provides protection from an adverse employment action would not likely be successful because the Act requires reporting of suspected violation of law to appropriate law enforcement personnel or to someone in the district that the employee believes is responsible for enforcing the law. Posting a message on a blog doesn't fulfill these criteria. However, the employee also would likely assert that any adverse employment action violates the employee's free speech exercised away from school and not within the scope of employment.
3. *Spanierman v. Hughes*, 576 F.Supp.2d 292 (D. Conn. 2008). The judge also rejected Spanierman's claim that his right to association was violated by the nonrenewal, questioning whether that right encompasses a medium like MySpace. MySpace, wrote the judge, doesn't express itself about anything but is merely a means to set up a private community. Even if a right of association did exist, the school had sufficient justification for its nonrenewal action in light of what Spanierman was doing with his MySpace profile.
4. Recently the U.S. Supreme Court weighed in on the matter when it ruled that police department officials could search the text messages on an officer's cell phone in compliance with an acceptable use agreement. The officer had signed the agreement. The search was conducted to determine why the officer was using the cell phone excessively while on the job. The search was judged not to be a violation of the officer's constitutional right to be free from unreasonable searches and seizures because of the agreement and because there were reasonable grounds for the officials to conduct the search. Nor was the search excessively intrusive. *Ontario v. Quon*, 130 S.Ct. 2619 (2010).

CHAPTER SIX: WRITING AND MONITORING PROFESSIONAL IMPROVEMENT PLANS

Sometimes employee deficiencies are serious enough that informal conferences and follow-up memoranda won't work. What is called for is the development of an improvement plan that sets forth deficiencies in detail and expectations for improved performance over time. In this chapter, we discuss this process.

It is important to note at the start that the terms Professional Growth Plan (PGP) and Teacher in Need of Assistance (TINA) are often used interchangeably when referring to a written plan for an employee to change or improve job performance. PGP was the terminology used in the Texas Teacher Appraisal System (TTAS), and TINA is the terminology used in PDAS. In this chapter, we use the term TINA when referring to a teacher improvement plan and PGP when referring to an improvement plan for other employees (e.g., administrators, counselors, librarian, and auxiliary personnel). The term "improvement plan" is used generically to encompass both a TINA and a PGP.

THE LEGAL DIMENSION

An improvement plan is important not only as a remedial tool for an ineffective teacher, but also as documentation in the event that you as the supervisor decide to recommend nonrenewal or termination of the teacher's contract. While the law reflects a number of reasons for a negative employment decision, your strongest and most objective rationale probably will be "failure to comply with school board policies and administrative directives," a reason cited frequently by the Texas Commissioner of Education and the courts in upholding a school district's decision to nonrenew or terminate an employment contract.[1] In the classroom context, administrative directives can best be communicated through a written improvement plan. Proving that the employee failed to follow an improvement plan is much easier and less inflammatory than proving that the employee is incompetent or ineffective. The two case summaries that follow illustrate the value of an improvement plan in defending negative employment decisions.

In 1990 the Texas Commissioner of Education was confronted with an appeal by a continuing contract teacher who was returned to probationary status. The teacher had a long history of marginal performance. Although district administrators had prepared several growth plans for the teacher and noted some improvement, deficiencies still remained. Therefore, the school board voted to place the teacher back on a probationary contract on the ground of incompetence. (As noted in Chapter 1, employment law provisions now require the employee's consent before the employee can be placed back on a probationary contract.)

The Commissioner overturned the local board's action, noting that the teacher had shown some improvement and that the school district was unable to refute the teacher's claim that she was capable of performing her duties. The board could have shown that the teacher had failed to comply with the elements of her growth plan, yet the board opted instead to list incompetence as the only basis for its action. The school board argued that the teacher had in fact *not* improved and that the improvement noted on her improvement plan was not genuine but rather was intended as a motivational technique. Nevertheless, the Commissioner rejected the board's assertion and ruled in favor of the teacher.[2] In addition to avoid focusing on "incompetency" as the basis for a negative employment decision, the lesson here is *not* to say positive things that are not justified in association with a nonrenewal or termination action. Of course, if such comments are justified, then why move forward with a contract nonrenewal or termination?

A termination case that arose several years later was decided quite differently. This time the Commissioner rejected the appeal of a continuing contract teacher whose contract was terminated for failing to meet the requirements of his improvement plan. The teacher's 1990-91 appraisal scores had decreased significantly from the previous year. The teacher's supervisor had written an improvement plan specifying six areas in which the teacher needed to improve his classroom performance. The man failed to implement the requirements set forth in the plan. In supporting the local board's decision to terminate the contract, the Commissioner found that the teacher had failed to "comply with the reasonable requirements of the board of trustees for achieving professional growth and improvement."[3] The teacher did not meet the specific directives regarding his classroom performance and rapport with students, even after the district had issued the improvement plan and provided warnings.

Two important lessons can be learned from these decisions. First, use "failure to follow an improvement plan" rather than" "incompetence" as the basis for nonrenewal or termination. Second, be honest in employee evaluation. Trying to motivate employees by inflating their performance scores works to everyone's disadvantage. This is especially true when the supervisor's goal is to move toward a recommendation of contract nonrenewal or termination. It is important to understand the circumstances in which giving employees the opportunity to improve their job performance may be a legal as well as an ethical consideration. The Commissioner of Education has issued a number of decisions over the years where remediation has come up. In a 2002 decision, he noted that the thrust of these decisions is that there is no automatic right to remediation if a teacher's conduct constitutes good cause for termination. Rather, remediation is only required if a teacher's conduct "does not rise to the level of good cause."[4] For example, the Commissioner observed that errors concerning lesson plans and grade books normally will require remediation. But serious grading infractions such as manufacturing grades will not, absent extenuating circumstances. Other behavior that does not require remediation includes violent conduct or conduct that involves significant or potentially significant emotional or physical harm to students. In the 2002 decision, the Commissioner upheld the termination of the teacher's contract after the teacher had been given ample warning that his lesson plans and grade books were unacceptable and had failed to change his behavior. The teacher also had taken excessive absences.

Basically, remediation requires advising employees of deficiencies and consequences, developing an improvement plan, assisting employees to meet the plan, and giving them a reasonable time to comply. A remediation plan also should include an assessment component so that it can be determined whether the employee has completed the components of the plan and whether improvement in performance has occurred. The section of the improvement plan "Evidence that Growth has Occurred or is Occurring" provides written notice of that assessment component. And, as we will note later in this chapter, it is important whenever possible to link expected changes in teacher behavior to improved student performance/behavior. Most districts have as one reason for contract nonrenewal a significant lack of student progress attributable to the educator. In a 2008 decision the Commissioner cited this reason in rejecting a high school math teacher's appeal of her contract nonrenewal. The teacher taught at a school in the Dallas I.S.D. that had been reconstituted after being rated unacceptable for two consecutive years. The teacher claimed that the Classroom Effectiveness Index used by the Campus Intervention Team was inappropriate and should not have been used. The Commissioner rejected the assertion, noting that the teacher had not taken advantage of opportunities to make these assertions during the time of the reconstitution. She could have filed a grievance when given notice that she would not be retained as a teacher at the campus. The Commissioner supported the decision of the Campus Intervention Team that she should not be retained because her students were not passing or showing significant improvement on the Texas Assessment of Knowledge and Skills (TAKS) tests.[5]

In another decision involving a teacher in a reconstituted school in the Dallas district, the Commissioner ruled in favor of a teacher who maintained that her contract termination for poor performance of her students on TAKS was unwarranted. The findings of fact demonstrated that the reason for poor student performance was the school environment, including the lack of discipline, and not the teacher's performance.[6]

The lesson from these decisions is to make sure that there is significant linkage between teaching behavior and student performance after taking into account intervening factors such as a high student classroom migration rate, the negative influence of a peer group, or a breakdown in campus discipline.

Remediation offers several definite dividends. First, the school board in a nonrenewal case or hearing officer in a termination case may expect that, as a matter of basic fairness, the employee should be told of his or her deficiencies and be given an opportunity to correct them. Second, the remediation plan puts the employee on notice that future employment is conditioned on complying with its components. To this extent, noncompliance later in the employment relationship will provide the groundwork for a negative employment decision. In a 1998 decision, the Commissioner noted that, while performance in a previous year cannot be used to terminate a present year contract, a previous year evaluation that includes an expectation for remediation in future years is different. As the Commissioner observed, "A failing is particularly damaging to a teacher when the error was pointed out and was not corrected."[7]

As we noted in the 1990 Commissioner's decision above, it is easier to establish failure to comply with the reasonable terms of a remediation plan than incompetence as a ground for contract nonrenewal or termination — especially when the problems are related to instruction.

WHY WRITE A TEACHER IN NEED OF ASSISTANCE OR A PROFESSIONAL GROWTH PLAN?

Remember that your primary goal is to help the employee be the best that he/she can be. The employee may be a classroom teacher, an administrator, or an at-will employee. Often, an improvement plan is viewed as punitive (especially by the person receiving it), but punishment should not be the motivation to create one. There are many reasons that you may need to write an improvement plan, and not all of these reasons reflect the employee's lack of ability.

When Job Performance Does Not Meet Expectations and More Extrinsic Motivation May Be Needed

Recall the Quadrant I and Quadrant III employees from Chapter 3. These employees share one common characteristic: low level of motivation. When formal and informal conversations fail to cause the employee to change behavior, it may be time for the supervisor to provide some more significant extrinsic motivation. Writing an improvement plan may have the triple effect of communicating to the employee:

- Job behavior does not meet expectations,
- Descriptions of what behavior is expected, and
- An indication that the deficiencies are significant — significant enough to warrant an improvement plan.

The most common purpose for an improvement plan is to formally communicate that the employee's job performance does not meet expectations. In one scenario, the employee has exhibited a pattern of behavior that does not meet job expectations. While the failures may not rise to the level of "serious job deficiencies," the supervisor has met with the employee on more than one occasion. There may be notes to the file for some of the early conversations and specific incident memoranda to document the later conversations. The specific incident memoranda may or may not have included directives for specific changes in behavior. Despite the conversations and memoranda, the employee's behavior has not changed. It may be time to write an improvement plan.

In a second scenario, there is not a history of conversations and memoranda, but the employee's failure to meet job expectations is considered serious, yet remediable. [Note: If the behavior is serious and irremedial, no notice of deficiency and no opportunity for remediation may be needed.] Even without a pattern of behavior, the employee's behavior is sufficiently serious to warrant writing an improvement plan.

When Job Expectations May Not Be Clear

You should not necessarily assume that an employee is not meeting the expectations of the job because of laxness or indifference. The employee may not be meeting job expectations because the organization has not effectively communicated them. Unfortunately, some employees in public education are hired without a job description, particularly for middle management and educational support positions. Even when job descriptions do exist, they may be "boiler-plates" that come from a personnel manual or professional organization and are not customized to the district's specific expectations for the position. This may be especially true for administrative personnel such as principals and assistant principals, central office support personnel, people who work in instructional support positions (e.g., educational technology, special education supervisors and diagnosticians, and other federally funded programs), and other personnel (e.g., counselors, librarians, and auxiliary personnel). While customizing job descriptions to the specific expectations of the district is probably the best way to communicate these expectations, writing an improvement plan also serves as a vehicle to inform the employee what specific job behaviors the district expects.

When the Supervisor Needs to Begin Laying Groundwork for Nonrenewal or Termination of Employment

You may have made a determination that the employee cannot or will not change job-related behavior. You have had conversations, provided assistance to the employee, and documented your actions through specific incident memoranda to the employee. You want to both formalize and document your efforts and the seriousness of the job-related deficiencies. Once you have determined that the employee will not or cannot change behavior, your goal is no longer growth and improvement — it is to begin laying the groundwork for a recommendation of nonrenewal or termination.

HOW TO WRITE AN IMPROVEMENT PLAN

Under the Commissioner's rule 19 TAC §150.1004(a), a teacher is designated as a "teacher in need of assistance" if (1) the teacher is evaluated as unsatisfactory in one or more domains or (2) the teacher is evaluated as below expectations in two or more domains. In either instance, an improvement plan known as a TINA in this context is required. Other employees (e.g., campus administrators, counselors, central office personnel, auxiliary personnel) may best be served by using a Professional Growth Plan (PGP). Local policies will determine when a PGP is written. Regardless of what the plan is called and regardless of who the employee is, an improvement plan should consist of these four components, each of which is explained in this section:

1. Notice of areas of job performance in which improvement or change is needed.
2. Offer of (or directive for) assistance and support through professional growth activities.
3. Time lines and evidence that will be used to determine if professional growth activities have been completed.
4. Time lines and evidence of changes in behavior that will be used to determine if professional growth has occurred or is occurring.

Step 1: Notice of Areas of Job Performance in Which Improvement or Change is Needed

The first step in creating an improvement plan is to give the employee notice of areas of job performance which need improvement or in which change is needed. You are required both ethically and legally to alert the teacher to any conduct or performance that does not meet the expectations of the school district. The improvement or change you direct the teacher to make may involve problems with instruction and classroom management and/or problems that lie outside the classroom. There are four categories of employee behavior that may require a TINA or PGP.

Classroom Instructional Issues and Student Performance

When supervising classroom teachers, the most common reason to create a TINA will most likely be performance in the classroom. This category includes both classroom instructional behavior and behaviors related to instruction such as written lesson plans, assignments for campus supervision, grading and reporting of student grades, timely arrival and departure. As we will discuss in more depth later in this chapter, language in the plan should be anchored in the language of PDAS or the locally adopted teacher appraisal system.

We are in an era of increasing student accountability within both the state and federal (No Child Left Behind) systems. An analysis of data may indicate that a teacher's students perform less well on accountability tests than other teachers who teach similar students. Your documentation of classroom observations is very important in establishing that observed behaviors do not meet district expectations. In Chapter 4, you gathered this kind of information by observing Mr. Laze's classroom. You might, therefore, include a section similar to the following in Mr. Laze's TINA.

The following areas are in need of improvement:

- Opportunities for students to participate actively and successfully.
- Feedback on student progress during instruction.
- Supportive learning environment.

You will note that these statements are broadly worded and reflect the domain-level language of PDAS. Your comments will become more specific when you write the directives for improvement in the fourth section of the TINA.

If the performance of Mr. Laze's students on the STAAR social studies test was significantly lower than the students in similarly constituted classes, the area in need of improvement might be worded:

- Increase the percentage of students who meet minimum expectations on the 9th Grade STAAR social studies test.

Compliance With Laws / Policies / Procedures

Sometimes, the job deficiency may lie in the employee's failure to comply with state or federal law or with local operating policies and procedures. The employee may be a classroom teacher, campus administrator, central office administrator, or someone who works in an instructional support program. For teachers, Domain VII of PDAS addresses Compliance with Policies, Operating Procedures, and Requirements. For other non-teaching personnel, compliance with law, policies, and procedures should be a component of their job description and/or their performance evaluation instrument. As we will discuss later in this chapter, language in the plan should be anchored in the language of the law, policy, or procedure. If an employee you supervise is deficient in one of these areas, a statement like the following will let him know what kind of change or improvement is needed:

- Following district/campus policies in reporting student grades to the office and to parents.
- Writing lesson plans according to the campus format and submit them to the principal's office by 8:00 a.m. on the first instructional day of each week.
- Being present at your assigned duty station.
- Following the state inspection requirements before the school bus is moved from the bus barn parking lot.

- Following federal law in implementing all of the provisions of the Individualized Education Program (IEP) for all special education students in your classroom.
- Following district grievance policies for complaints regarding conditions of employment.

Recall that directives similar to these were included in the specific incident memoranda illustrated in Chapters 2 and 4.

Other Job-Related Behaviors

For classroom teachers, the job deficiency may include such issues as assignments for campus supervision and timely arrival and departure. For employees who are not classroom teachers, job-related deficiencies may involve issues such as planning, producing products, meeting deadlines, and timely arrival and departure. For administrators and support personnel, the deficiencies should be anchored in the language of the employee's job description and/or the appraisal instrument. For classroom teachers, the deficiencies should be anchored in the language of the district's teacher appraisal instrument or in law/district policy. Statements like the following will let the employee know what kind of change or improvement is needed:

- Administering diagnostic tests and completing the educational diagnostician's portion of the written assessment based on state and local guidelines and the specific needs of the students (*for an educational diagnostician*).
- Preparing and implementing long- and short-range plans for district instructional technology (*for a director of technology*).
- Submitting campus PEIMS data to the central office before the district deadline *(for a PEIMS clerk)*
- Meeting deadlines for reports and documents for the agenda for local board of trustees meetings.

"Affective Issues"

The most difficult job-related issues to address in an improvement plan are what we will call "affective issues." Effective communication with stakeholders, "team work," cooperation, and negative/critical comments are all behaviors in that category. These issues were discussed more fully in Chapter 5. Statements like the following will let the employee know what kind of change or improvement is needed:

- Communicating courteously and professionally with students, staff, and parents.
- Meeting on a weekly basis and working collaboratively with grade-level team members for instructional planning.
- Following district grievance policies for complaints regarding conditions of employment.
- Communicating effectively with staff (*for administrative and support personnel*).

While these behaviors can significantly affect the quality of job performance, they are more difficult to include in the improvement plan for three reasons: (1) because of the nature of the desired behavior, it may be impossible to provide professional growth activities related to the deficiency; (2) it may not be easy to gather and objectively document the behaviors that will indicate that growth has or has not occurred; and (3) free speech issues may arise.

When identifying areas in which improvement is needed, it may be important to use language that lays a foundation for your authority to issue the directive. This may help avoid accusations that your directives are merely your subjective opinion about how things should be done or are arbitrary and capricious. When possible, use language from the following:

- The Professional Development and Appraisal System
- Locally adopted district appraisal system
- Campus plan
- The essential knowledge and skills in the state curriculum
- District (campus) policy
- Job description (especially for administrators, support staff, and at-will employees)
- Code of Ethics and Standard Practices for Texas Educators (see Appendix A)

Examples of "basis of authority" language can be found in Appendix C.

Step 2: Offer of (or Directive for) Assistance and Support Through Professional Growth Activities.

The second part of the plan encompasses a listing of improvement plan requirements (or suggestions) designed to assist the employee in meeting the specific directives you give for improvement. From an ethical and professional perspective, your concern lies in helping the employee meet the district's expectations for effectiveness. From a legal perspective, you probably will be required to demonstrate that you have attempted to help the employee improve and that you have not simply tried to get rid of him/her. Should you decide to pursue nonrenewal or termination, including this second set of administrative directives will establish a stronger basis for your decision.

Directed activities that offer support for the teacher in her efforts to improve may include training sessions, observing other teachers, submitting written lesson plans, videotaping a class, or reading journal articles (see Appendix C). Any directive should be aimed at providing information or assistance for the employee in meeting the behavioral expectations that you outlined in the first section of the plan. Examples:

1. Attend the training on TEKS-based mathematics instruction at the educational service center on November 14.
2. Schedule a meeting with me within one week of that training to discuss how you plan to implement the strategies learned in the workshop.
3. Read the book, *What Great Coaches Do Differently*. Provide a written summary and identify three to four elements discussed in the book. Submit the summary to your supervisor no later than September 15.

4. Prepare and submit to me your detailed, written lesson plans to specifically include:
    a. Texas Essential Knowledge and Skills that will be learned in each class
    b. Time allocations for activities
    c. Activities that maximize student participation and success
5. Schedule meetings and meet with me every two weeks to discuss your lesson plans and modifications/accommodations for special education students.

Note that training is not the only option in directing professional development activities. Developing plans or reports, meeting with a supervisor or team leader, and visiting/observing other professionals may be more appropriate activities. One improvement activity that you may wish seriously to consider is to assign a mentor to a marginally effective teacher or a teacher in need of assistance. As noted in the first chapter, the legislature has enacted the optional mentor program. Many districts may see the mentor program as a cost-effective way of improving teacher performance. The mentor could observe in the teacher's classroom, conduct model demonstration lessons for the teacher to observe, and assist with planning instructional and discipline management strategies. A more complete listing of other possible growth activities is found in Appendix C.

Step 3: Time Lines and Evidence That Will be Used to Determine if Professional Growth Activities Have Been Completed.

For each professional growth activity in Step 2, you will need to write a corresponding statement of evidence that you will use to determine whether or not the activity has been completed and give a time line for completion of each activity. For example:

1. Please submit a certificate of your attendance for the November 14 training session within five working days of the workshop.
2. Please schedule a meeting with me to discuss how you plan to implement the strategies learned in the workshop within five working days of the workshop.
3. Please submit lesson plans with the specifications included in #2 above by 8:00 a.m. on the first instructional day of each week.
4. Please schedule meetings and meet with me every two weeks during the school year.

Step 4: Directives for Changes in Behavior Plus Time Lines and Evidence That Will Be Used to Determine if Professional Growth Has Occurred or Is Occurring

If it seems likely that you will decide to recommend nonrenewal or termination of an employee's contract based on "failure to comply with administrative directives," you will want to consider carefully the specific set of directives you give. Because these directives form the basis for your employment decision, they should consist of behaviors that are objectively observable and should include changes in specific job-related behavior. Imagine that a hypothetical Ms. Dud is one of your teachers in the following example, which is, unfortunately, very typical.

You have just completed the third observation in Ms. Dud's classroom. In the appraisal process so far you have collected data and written memoranda documenting that Ms. Dud spends most of her time sitting at her desk while students complete workbook pages and low level work sheets. In post-observation conferences you have suggested that she use more direct instruction, engage the students in question-and-answer sessions as she presents information, and actively monitor and interact with students by walking around when they are doing paper and pencil work. You conduct a fourth classroom observation and find that nothing has changed. You write a growth plan that directs Ms. Dud to do the following:

1. Submit lesson plans that include at least 50 percent interactive instruction.
2. Observe another teacher who is an expert in conducting question-and-answer sessions and schedule an appointment with me to discuss your observation.
3. Attend a district training session on monitoring and giving feedback to students as they engage in learning activities.

Within the designated six-week time frame, Ms. Dud provides you with documentation that she has complied with all three directives. You return to visit her classroom. You observe Ms. Dud seated at her desk for thirty minutes while students complete three workbook pages. Absolutely nothing in her classroom has changed, yet Ms. Dud *did* comply with all your administrative directives and *has* fulfilled the requirements of the growth plan.

While there was nothing *wrong* with the directives you gave, they were *incomplete*. What you did was to direct the teacher to complete a series of professional growth activities but did not direct that her *teaching behavior* change. Whether your goal is to help Ms. Dud improve her teaching or, failing that, to recommend nonrenewal or termination of her contract, the growth plan should contain directives for both professional growth and changes in behavior.

In the case of classroom teachers, those could be either teacher or student behaviors, or both. Directives can be written using a cause-and-effect formula.

INSTRUCTIONAL INDICATOR		EXPECTED OUTCOME
Teacher behaves ---------------------- in a certain way	**so that ------------**	**students behave in a certain way.**
(Teacher Behavior)	**+ (Linking Words) —>**	**(Student Behavior)**

Examples:

Teacher solicits--------------- student participation	in such a way that---------	most students are participating and most are successful.
Teacher redirects --------------------- inappropriate behavior	so that ------------------	the behavior stops.

Recall the four categories of behavior that may require a TINA (see pp. 4-8). The first of those was *Classroom Instructional Issues and Student Performance.* The areas in which professional growth was needed were:

1. Providing more opportunities for students to participate actively and successfully.
2. Evaluating and providing feedback on student progress during instruction.
3. Establishing and maintaining a supportive learning environment.

The evidence which would be used to determine of growth has occurred or is occurring might be:

(Teacher Behavior)	**+ (Linking Words) —>**	**(Student Behavior)**
1. Plan and implement instruction to provide for opportunities for students to participate actively and successfully	------------------- so that -------------------	all/almost all students are actively and successfully participating in the learning for all/almost all of the instructional period.
2. When students are unsuccessful in learning, provide corrective feedback (or reteach)	------------ in such as way that ---------	they are successful.
2 & 3. When students are successful in the learning, acknowledge/reinforce that learning each time.		(no student behavior)
3. All interactions with students will be courteous and respectful.		(no student behavior)

Note that it will not be possible to write all directives to include student behavior. This is particularly true with behaviors related to learning environment. For example, research indicates that students who receive appropriate, specific positive reinforcement are more engaged, more willing to take risks, and more motivated to participate. These student behaviors tend, however, to emerge over a longer period of time. It would not be reasonable to expect immediate changes in student behavior simply because a teacher begins to use positive reinforcement. When these kinds of instructional behaviors are the directed teacher behavior, you probably will not see an immediate student response.

In the case of writing directives for administrators, instructional support employees, and at-will employees, the same basic principles apply. Instead of "student behaviors," the directives will sometimes specify the effect that the changes on employee behavior should have.

Employee Behavior	+ Linking Language —>	Expected Outcome
Communicate with staff in courteous and professional ways	--------- in such as way that ----------	complaints about rude/discourteous communication from staff are reduced and stop by the end of the semester.
Develop and implement a plan for integration of instructional technology	------- in such as way that ----------	all/almost all classrooms integrate technology into core curriculum at least two times a month.
Plan and deliver training in balanced literacy reading strategies	-------- in such as way that ----------	all K-5 teachers are trained before the beginning of the next school year.

Why Write in Terms of Teacher / Employee Behavior?

Ms. Dud's problem in her classroom is *not* that she has failed to submit lesson plans, observe other teachers, or attend workshops. Instead, her *teaching behavior* generally is at the heart of the problem that you have observed: the passive, non-interactive format and the failure to monitor students. Therefore, when you write administrative directives for her (using a cause-and-effect formula), you need to describe specific changes she must make in her teaching behavior. *These directives now form the standard against which you will conduct future classroom observations.* If Ms. Dud's teaching behavior changes, you have been effective in helping her to improve. If not, your observations and subsequent documentation build your case for a recommendation for nonrenewal or termination based on her failure to comply with administrative directives.

In the directives for administrative/support personnel, including the expected outcome is critical. For example, "developing and implementing a plan for integration of instructional technology" is all well and good. The real purpose, however, is to make certain that technology is integrated into on-going classroom instruction; therefore, it is important to include the outcome "all/almost all classrooms integrate technology into core curriculum at least two times a month."

Benefits of Using Instructional Indicators

In a hearing, you may be asked to prove that the behaviors you required were reasonable, legitimate, and job-related. Ms. Dud may allege that you are substituting "your way of doing things" for her exercise of her own unique teaching style. If you use instructional indicators as the directed teacher behavior, you will be able to defend yourself against any of these accusations for the following reasons:

1. Descriptions of teacher and student behavior like those in the Professional Development and Appraisal System (PDAS) were developed by the Texas Education Agency and published as the Commissioner of Education's recommended teacher appraisal system. In a sense, you are simply directing the teacher to meet the standards of "proficiency" as defined by the State of Texas.

2. Generic criteria such as those in PDAS (for example, "active, successful student participation" and "managing students, time, and materials") assure a strong, research-based body of teaching behaviors.
3. Many states, school districts, and professional associations have conducted validation research on a variety of instructional programs and practices. For example, you may direct a teacher to use a balanced literacy approach, including phonemic awareness and good literature, for teaching reading. Likewise, you could direct a teacher to utilize manipulatives to introduce mathematics concepts since their use is included in the Texas Essential Knowledge and Skills (TEKS) and recommended by the National Council of Teachers of Mathematics.

Why Include Student Behavior in the Directives?

Your judgment on the effectiveness of Ms. Dud's teaching practices goes beyond conformity to appraisal criteria. You are interested in the quality and effectiveness of her teaching. "Quality" and "effectiveness" are concepts, however, that are sometimes difficult to assess. From your perspective, they are best measured by a sole criterion: the impact of her teaching on her students. You want to change her classroom behaviors because they are not effective, that is, they are not having the desired impact on student learning and behavior. By including student behavior as part of your administrative directive, you help Ms. Dud to improve as a teacher, or failing that, you help yourself build an effective case for a recommendation for nonrenewing or terminating her contract. The Commissioner of Education underscored this very point in a 2008 decision upholding the contract nonrenewal of a teacher who complied with all the remediation directives set forth in the growth plan but was unable to meet an additional directive that she change her teaching behavior in the areas of classroom management and instruction so that student academic success would improve (see the endnote for a brief discussion).[8]

There are specific advantages to including student behavior in your administrative directives:

1. Student behavior has for many years been part of the state-adopted teacher appraisal system. Student behavior is significant in PDAS. Furthermore, the Texas Legislature mandates that appraisal criteria include a teacher's implementation of discipline management procedures and the performance of the teacher's students [TEC § 21.351 (a)(1) and (2)]. You are not being arbitrary or capricious when you reference student behavior and performance; you are simply directing the teacher to meet a standard of proficiency as defined by the Commissioner of Education and the Texas Education Agency. If you are using a locally developed teacher evaluation system that includes student behavior as now required, you are directing the teacher to meet the district's expectations.
2. Including student behavior reduces the likelihood of a "dog and pony show" lesson. Ms. Dud may be able to change *her* behavior when you are in the classroom, but it is less likely that she can change her *students'* behavior while you are there.
3. As we have pointed out, directives for administrative and support personnel will probably not include student behaviors. They will, however, include the anticipated outcome of the employee's behavior changes. You do not want the employee to merely create a plan. You want the plan implemented, and you want the plan to have an effect.

With classroom teachers, focus on the student behaviors that might tell you whether or not the teacher is effective. For administrative and support personnel, focus on the expected outcome of the change in behavior. We have provided numerous examples of *general* directives for teacher behavior, as well as more *specific* directives and expected outcomes, in Appendix C.

Writing Directives Related to Student Performance

The current law related to teacher appraisal requires that student performance be among the elements in both the state-adopted system and any locally developed system. There are a number of ways of looking at the issue of student performance.

Success of Students During an Observation

The first way of looking at student performance is during a single classroom walk-through observation. In this case, the observer notes the objectives or lesson outcomes and gathers evidence of student success or lack of success *during that class period.* The focused observation instruments we have provided in Appendix B provide a means of gathering these kinds of student performance data.

Most of the directives for changes in behavior in this chapter and in Appendix C are linked to student performance as observed in the classroom. For example:

Teacher Behavior	**+ Linking Language —>**	**Student Behavior/ Performance**
When students are -------------- unsuccessful in learning, provide corrective feedback (or reteach the lesson)	in such as way that-------------	they are successful.

Success of Students Over Time

A second way of looking at student performance is to look at student performance over time. Some schools require teachers to maintain portfolios of student work products that reflect student learning over an extended period of time. The success (performance) of students is then evaluated by examining the work products in the portfolio. More than half the school districts in Texas use the curriculum product C-SCOPE, designed by a consortium of 19 of the regional educational service centers. One of the assessment components of C-SCOPE is a set of "Student Performance Indicators." These indicators are typically student-designed products, performances, or demonstrations that answer the question "Have the students learned the content of the curriculum at the cognitive level of the performance standard?" The evaluator would examine these student work products and ask such questions as:

- Do the products reflect student success in learning that has depth and complexity?
- Do the products reflect student success in connecting learning to other disciplines, the world of work, and/or issues in the world beyond the classroom?
- Do the products reflect student success in critical thinking and problem solving?
- Do the products reflect improved student performance over time?

If the answer to these kinds of questions is "no," the evaluator then would write the same kinds of instructional directives contained in this chapter and in Appendix C. The only substantial difference from looking at student success/performance during a single classroom observation is the evidence of student success — in this case the student work products in the portfolio and/or the products, performances, and demonstrations contained in the C-SCOPE curriculum.

Success of Students on a Norm-Referenced or Criterion-Referenced Test

A third way of looking at student performance is evaluating the results of student performance on a norm- or criterion-referenced test. The State of Texas Assessment of Academic Readiness (STAAR) is one such criterion-referenced measure of student performance. Beginning in 2012, TAKS is replaced by STAAR examinations in most grade levels.

The Commissioner of Education some time ago upheld the nonrenewal of a term contract based, in part, on the performance of teacher's students on the TAAS mathematics test (the predecessor of the TAKS test) and on a district practice test modeled on the TAAS test specifications.[9] As a finding of fact, the Commission indicated that "Over a two-year period . . ., there is substantial evidence to support that not only was there a significant lack of student progress under Ms. Wood's tutelage, there was a significant decrease on student progress. There is subsequent evidence to support that Ms. Wood's eighth grade students were not progressing satisfactorily as they only had a pass rate of thirty-one percent (31%) in 1992-93 and on the practice test of twenty-six percent (26%)."

In this case it is significant to note that student performance on these tests was *one* of the reasons cited by the board of trustees in making its nonrenewal decision. In supporting the board's decision, the Commissioner found that, "The TAAS test is specifically designed to indicate student progress on a statewide basis and should be considered *one* of the criteria upon which a teacher's performance is evaluated (emphasis added)." The Commissioner has apparently opened the door for using performance data from the state student assessment system as one element of teacher evaluation and/or negative employment decisions.

Student performance on STAAR examinations, therefore, could be used as the "student behavior" in writing directives for change. These directives might follow the following three formats:

Teacher Behavior	**+ Linking Language —>**	**Student Behavior/ Performance**
Use models and manipulatives in teaching mathematics concepts	in such a way that	the percentage of students meeting minimum expectations on the STAAR mathematics test increases.
Use the district's balanced literacy program (phonemic awareness and whole language) on a weekly basis in teaching English Language Arts	in such a way that	the percentage of students meeting minimum expectations on the STAAR reading test increases.
Design and deliver instruction on a weekly basis that is aligned with the Texas Essential Knowledge and Skills and the district science curriculum	in such a way that	the percentage of students meeting minimum expectations on the STAAR science test increases.

The use of student performance on a criterion-referenced test as a major element of teacher evaluation has not been fully tested. Until it has been, we urge the following cautions.

1. Make student performance on STAAR *one* of the directives in an improvement plan. Include other directives related to the teacher's classroom behavior. Rely on those teaching indicators that are a part of the state-adopted teacher appraisal system or the locally adopted system.
2. Be cautious about setting specific levels of increase of the passing rate (e.g., "so that 80% of students meet the minimum expectations. . . ."). Keep the expected student performance more general, as we have indicated in the examples cited above.
3. Finally, recall that we recommend as part of writing a specific incident memorandum that you include the "basis of authority" for issuing directives for changes in behavior. In this instance, the "basis for authority" cited in a memorandum might be any of the following types:
    - The STAAR/English II has an expectation that students identify the best summary of written texts.
    - The district English language arts curriculum includes an expectation that you use a balanced literacy approach in the teaching of reading.
    - The Texas Essential Knowledge and Skills (TEKS) has an expectation that you use models and other manipulatives in teaching algebra.
    - The National Council of Teachers of Mathematics curriculum and assessment standards include the use of mathematics manipulatives in teaching mathematics concepts.

Writing Directives for Nonclassroom-Based Growth Plans

Classroom instruction will be only one of the reasons for writing a growth plan. Recall the four categories of behavior discussed earlier in this chapter which may require a TINA or PGP. The second of the four steps was *Compliance with Laws / Policies / Procedures* (see p. 6). The areas in which professional growth was needed were:

1. Following district/campus policies in reporting student grades to the office and to parents.
2. Writing lesson plans according to the campus format and submitting them to the principal's office.
3. Being present at your assigned duty station fifteen minutes before and fifteen minutes after school.
4. Following federal law in implementing all of the provisions of the Individualized Education Program (IEP) for all special education students in your classroom.
5. Following district grievance policies for complaints regarding conditions of employment.

You will need to specify the evidence that you will use to determine if growth has occurred or is occurring in each of the areas listed. That evidence could be:

1. Please submit all student progress reports and grade reports on the date/ time specified in the district calendar (progress reports: 4:00 p.m. on the third Friday of each grading period; report cards: 4:00 p.m. on the last instructional day of each grading period).
2. Please submit written lesson plans to the principal's office in the district format by 8:00 a.m. on the first instructional day of each week.
3. Please be present at your assigned duty station fifteen minutes before and fifteen minutes after school.
4. You must comply with federal law in implementing all of the provisions of the Individualized Education Program (IEP) for all special education students in your classroom.
5. You must follow district grievance policies for complaints regarding your conditions of employment. You will immediately stop all complaining about your conditions of employment to staff, students, and members of the community.

In Chapters 1 and 5, we distinguished between the difference in speaking out about matters of public policy and speaking out about conditions of employment. The last directive ("stop all complaining about your conditions of employment to staff, students, and members of the community") may raise concerns about First Amendment free speech protection. When this is the only issue related to the employee's job performance, you should exercise caution and consult with the school district's human resources director and/or the school district's attorney for guidance.

The third reason for writing an improvement plan was *Other Job-Related Behaviors* (see p. 7).

The areas in which professional growth was needed were:

1. Administration of diagnostic tests and completion of the educational diagnostician's portion of the written assessment based on state and local guidelines and the specific needs of the students (*for an educational diagnostician*).
2. Preparation and implementation of long- and short-range plans for district instructional technology (*for a director of technology*).
3. Meeting deadlines for reports and documents for local board of trustees agenda.

Once again, you will need to specify the evidence that you will use to determine if growth has occurred or is occurring in each of the areas listed. That evidence could be:

1. Please complete all assessments and assessment reports and submit them to the Director of Special Education at least *48 hours* prior to scheduled SST, PARD, and/or ARD meetings.
2. Please write a long- and short-range plan for district instructional technology using the district planning format and submit it to the superintendent no later than December 10. The plan will include detailed implementation components.
3. Please submit all reports and documents for the agenda of the board of trustees meeting no later than 12:00 noon on the Friday preceding each board of trustees meeting.

The fourth reason for writing an improvement plan was *"Affective Issues."* The areas in which professional growth was needed were:

1. Courteous, professional communication with students, staff, and parents.
2. Meeting and working collaboratively with grade-level team members for instructional planning.
3. Following district grievance policies for complaints regarding conditions of employment.

Consider the following evidence for the areas of concern noted above:

1. Beginning immediately, all of your communication with students, staff, and stakeholders will be courteous, respectful, and professional; complaints about discourteous or rude communication will drop significantly and cease altogether by the end of the semester.
2. Beginning immediately, you will meet with your grade level team each instructional day during your team planning period. All work and communication will be courteous and respectful. You will abide by the decisions made by the team and implement them in your classroom. Complaints from team members about rude/discourteous behavior from you will drop significantly and cease altogether by the end of the semester.
3. You will follow district grievance policies for complaints regarding your conditions of employment. You will immediately stop all complaining about your conditions of employment to staff, students, and members of the community.

As we noted In Chapter 5, these behaviors can significantly affect the quality of job performance. They are, however, the most difficult issues to address in a growth plan. The greatest challenge is to identify objective evidence that can be used to document whether or not the behaviors have changed and the extent to which professional growth has occurred. Decisions in this area should be made in consultation with the district director of human resources and/or the school district's attorney, particularly because free speech issues oftentimes are likely to arise.

Providing a Reasonable Time Line for Growth and Improvement

Failure to allow the teacher a fair and reasonable amount of time to correct deficiencies may lead to reinstatement of the dismissed employee.[10] In the absence of a Texas statute spelling out remediation procedures, interpretations of what constitutes "adequate time" vary. As the Texas Commissioner of Education indicated in a 1995 decision, there are no set rules on how much remediation is necessary in a particular case. Rather, each case must be judged individually.[11] In one case involving a teacher of mentally handicapped students, an Illinois court found a period of 45 days between the notice of deficiency and the final evaluation to be unreasonable since the teacher was making some improvement.[12] In another case, the same court found a 64-day remedial period a reasonable length of time for a teacher to improve instruction and classroom management.[13] However, in a contrasting Minnesota case, an eight-week time span was viewed as unreasonable when a supervisor first identified as deficient the classroom practices of a veteran teacher in the seventeenth year of the teacher's career.[14] A Louisiana court concluded in 1995 that there is no injustice in requiring a one-year probationary teacher to remediate performance sometime prior to the completion of the contract.[15]

While there is no magic number for the amount of time allowed for improvement and for complying with directives, here are some factors that administrators should consider in making this determination:

1. Complexity of Change
   - Time lines for simple changes such as developing and submitting a discipline management plan may be short.
   - Complex changes in behavior such as implementing cooperative learning will take longer.
   - Developing a district plan for a new instructional delivery system for bilingual and ESL students will take longer.
2. Previous Evaluations
   - The existence of previous negative evaluations may allow a short time line.
   - The existence of previous positive evaluations may require a longer time line.
3. Type of Contract/Length of Service
   - At-will employees may require short time lines.
   - Probationary contract teachers and administrators may require short time lines.

- Continuing contract teachers or term contract teachers/administrators with long experience may require longer time lines, especially if their previous evaluations have been positive.

4. Whether or Not Employee's Behavior is Remediable (see the first section of this chapter)
   - If behavior is remediable, a longer time line may be required.
   - If behavior is irremediable, no time line for improvement is required.
5. Local District Politics
   - Whether the person is a long-time employee.
   - Whether the person is a beloved employee.
   - Whether the person has deep roots in the community.

Supervisors also need to remember to update directives for improvement if the teacher complies with earlier directives but remains deficient in certain areas.

Sample Teacher in Need of Assistance Form

If your district uses PDAS and you are developing Ms. Dud's improvement plan because one or more PDAS domains were less than proficient, you would need to use the Teacher In Need of Assistance (TINA) form. The following sample improvement plan for Ms. Dud is based on what you already have learned about her. The numbers in parentheses correspond with the observations in the commentary that follows this improvement plan. A blank Teacher is Need of Assistance plan with this format is contained in Appendix D.

On a TINA form, Ms. Dud's improvement plan would appear as follows:

PROFESSIONAL DEVELOPMENT AND APPRAISAL SYSTEM
INTERVENTION PLAN FOR TEACHER IN NEED OF ASSISTANCE

Name: Susie Dud Appraiser: Dr. Great Principal

Campus: Fine ISD Assignment/Grade 4th Grade

Period of Intervention: From: January 3, 2011 To: May 31, 2011

1. Domain(s) in which the teacher is in need of assistance.

Domain I: Active, successful student participation in the learning process. **(1)**

Domain III: Evaluation and feedback on student progress.

2. Professional-improvement activities and dates for completion.

a. Attend district cooperative learning workshop on February 1st-2nd. District will provide substitute teacher. **(2)**

b. Observe Mrs. Cathy Coop's class within the next two weeks and schedule an appointment with the supervisor to discuss the observation.

c. Following the workshop and observation in Mrs. Coop's class, develop a lesson plan showing use of cooperative learning strategies.

3. **Evidence that will be used to determine that professional improvement activities have been completed.** **(3)**

   a. Provide certificate of completion of district workshop on cooperative learning (due in supervisor's office by February 7th).

   b. Hold conference with supervisor to discuss observation in Mrs. Coop's class (no later than February 15th).

   c. Submit lesson plan showing cooperative learning strategies (due February 21st).

4. **Directives for changes in teacher behavior and time lines.** **(4)**

   a. Domain I: Solicit student participation and interact with most/all of the students.

   b. Domain II: Monitor students by moving around the classroom and by interacting with them.

5. **Evidence that will be used to determine if teacher behavior has changed.** **(5)**

   a. Domain I: All/almost all students are actively and successfully participating in the learning.

   b. Domain II: Students who are successful will receive positive reinforcement/acknowledgement of the learning.

   c. Domain II: Unsuccessful students will receive corrective feedback in such a way that they are successful.

______________________________ ______________________________
Signature of Appraiser Date

______________________________ ______________________________
Signature of Principal Date

My appraiser, principal, and I have discussed this intervention plan. My signature does not indicate whether I agree or disagree with this plan.

______________________________ ______________________________
Signature of Teacher Date

Commentary

(1) Areas for improvement are addressed at the general *domain* level rather than at the level of the rubric which identified more *specific* teacher and student behavior. The areas of concern are the level of active student participation in the learning process and the teacher's failure to verbally or physically monitor and assess a reasonable number of students.

(2) This is the section of the plan for directing professional growth activities. These directives have nothing to do with directing changes in classroom behavior. They represent the supervisor's good faith effort to assist the teacher to improve.

(3) This section stipulates the evidence and dates for completion of the growth activities. If the plan stopped here, the teacher could simply attend the workshop, observe in Mrs. Coop's classroom, and submit a written lesson plan. Ms. Dud could successfully complete the entire growth plan and never address the real problem of her instructional shortcomings.

(4) These are the directives for changes in classroom behavior. Failure to follow directives for changes in behavior may be the basis for a future recommendation to nonrenew or terminate employment.

(5) This is the evidence that will tell the supervisor whether Ms. Dud is changing her classroom behavior. Notice that directives in the fourth and fifth sections on the TINA form combine to follow the formula we have recommended:

Teacher Behavior (in Section 4)	+	**Linking Words**	—>	**Student Behavior (in Section 5)**

Sample Professional Growth Plan Form

If you are supervising an employee who is not a teacher, you would want to use the Professional Growth Plan (PGP) form in constructing an improvement plan. The following sample PGP illustrates an improvement plan for Fred Fieldhouse, an assistant athletic director who is employed on a one-year term contract as a certificated employee. From your own observations and from interactions with district staff, you have reached the following conclusions: Mr. Fieldhouse is not meeting the expectations of his job description: e.g., he does not meet deadlines for producing UIL and other reports; on at least three occasions he has not been present at contests to make sure that officials are greeted and directed; he sits in the coaches' office when events are taking place and does not actively supervise students at the contest; and he has been absent or left early from events he was responsible for supervising. In addition, you have received frequent complaints from game official and other coaches about his "rude" and "intimidating" behavior and language. You have had two conferences with him about these issues, but his behaviors and the frequency of complaints have continued.

The following Professional Growth Plan for Mr. Fieldhouse is based on what you already have learned about him. The numbers in parentheses correspond with the observations in the commentary that follows this Professional Growth Plan. A blank PGP in this format is contained in Appendix D.

On a PGP form, Mr. Fieldhouse's PGP would appear as follows:

Professional Growth Plan

School Year 2011-2012

School District: Fine ISD **Campus:** District-Wide

Employee: Fred Fieldhouse **Assignment/Grade:** Assistant Athletic Director

1. **List area(s) related to the job description, evaluation instrument and/or campus/district policy in which professional growth is needed. Establish priorities if two or more areas are listed.** **(1)**
   - Professional communications and professional relationships
   - Fulfillment of duties of assistant athletic director (as specified in the district job description)

2. **Specify growth activities and dates for completion.**
   - Read the book, How to be a Successful Athletic Administrator. Provide a written summary of the book (no more than four pages) by August 19, 2011. As part of the summary, identify three to four lessons discussed in the book that are the most significant in your position. Schedule a conference to discuss your summary and findings with your supervisor (no later than August 26, 2011). **(2)**
   - Prepare a set of questions and interview two athletic directors and two assistant athletic directors identified by your supervisor. Determine (1) the major job responsibilities for their positions, (2) what skills and/or work habits they believe are the most valuable to their position, (3) what they do to make certain that are working professionally and courteously with others, and (4) significant mistakes that they have learned to avoid. Submit the list of questions to your supervisor prior to conducting the interviews. After conducting the interviews, provide a written summary of your findings to your supervisor no later than September 2, 2011. Schedule a conference to discuss your findings with your supervisor (no later than September 9, 2011).

3. **Specify evidence that will be used to determine whether professional growth activities have been completed.**
   - The book, How to be a Successful Athletic Administrator: A written summary of the book is submitted to your supervisor by September 15, 2011. A conference to discuss the summary and conclusions is held no later than September 30, 2011. **(3)**
   - Survey: A list of questions is submitted to the supervisor and approved prior to conducting the interviews. Interviews are conducted and the summary and findings are submitted to the supervisor no later than August 15, 2011. A meeting to discuss your findings with the supervisor is held no later than August 30, 2011.

4. **Specify evidence that will be used to determine whether growth has occurred or is occurring.**

- All schedules, reports, supervision assignments, and all other administrative tasks will be accurately completed by their due dates. **(4)**
- Perform all of the duties in your job description at all athletic events assigned by your supervisor in such a way that you have (1) introduced and made yourself available to the officials for the games, (2) moved around during the event in order to identify and assist with potential problems, and (3) act to stop or redirect problems in such a way that problems are courteously and effectively resolved.
- Report to each assigned duty on time and remain on duty until all work at each event is completed.
- Maintain positive relationships with your co-workers in such a way that complaints about your behavior are reduced and stop by the end of the semester.
- Communicate (orally and in writing) with internal district staff and external communities in a courteous, non-threatening, and respectful manner in such a way that all communications are courteous, non-threatening, and respectful and that complaints about your communication are reduced and stop by the end of the semester.
- Personally notify your supervisor no later than 7:00 a.m. in the event that you must be absent or late. Immediately and personally notify your supervisor prior to leaving an event for which you have responsibility.

My appraiser(s) and I have developed this Professional Growth Plan.

______________________________ ______________________________

Employee Signature Date

______________________________ ______________________________

Teacher's Supervisor Signature Date

______________________________ ______________________________

Other Appraiser Signature *(if applicable)* Date

Commentary

(1) Areas for improvement are identified from Mr. Fieldhouse's job description and from a general district expectation for professional communication. These areas for improvement could have come from any one or a combination of job description, evaluation instrument, district policies/handbooks, law, or general expectations for a district employee.

(2) This is the section of the plan for directing professional growth activities. These directives have nothing to do with directing changes in job behavior. They represent the supervisor's good faith effort to assist Mr. Fieldhouse to improve.

(3) This section stipulates the evidence and dates for completion of the growth activities. If the plan stopped here, Mr. Fieldhouse could simply read the book, conduct the survey, and produce the reports. He could successfully complete the entire growth plan and never address the real problem — his failure to meet the expectations in his job description and to communicate courteously and respectfully with others.

(4) This section contains a combination of directives and changes in Mr. Fieldhouse's job-related behavior and the evidence that will be used to determine whether his behavior has changed. Failure to follow directives for changes in behavior may be the basis for a future recommendation to nonrenew or terminate employment. Notice that some of the directives in the PGP follow the formula we have recommended:

Employee Behavior + Linking Words —> Outcome

A COMMENT ON COLLABORATION

While there is no state requirement regarding a non-teaching employee's participation in writing a PGP, it is good professional practice to include the employee in developing the improvement plan. The state teacher appraisal system has required that a TINA be developed in a way that includes the teacher in the process of developing the growth plan. However, the teacher does not have veto power over its content.

A Scenario That You Probably Would Lose

Ms. Dud comes to your office for a conference to develop TINA. You have prepared the form on pp. 20-21 and hand it to her to discuss and sign. She refuses to sign and files a grievance against you, claiming that the growth plan was not developed collaboratively. She probably will win the grievance because your presentation of the prepared growth plan is a strong indication that she did not collaborate in its development!

A Scenario That You Probably Would Win

Ms. Dud comes to your office to develop a TINA plan. You have a blank TINA form on your desk. You reach some early agreement that the plan will contain behavioral changes in monitoring students and in providing more interactive instruction. When you propose that she attend a no-cost workshop on cooperative learning (on a regular instruction day, with the district providing a substitute for her class), she refuses, saying "I don't believe in cooperative learning and these outlaws I have would never do it. I don't want that in the growth plan."

You explain that cooperative learning is a part of the general campus improvement plan and that you have an expectation that this approach at least be given a fair try. She still refuses to have the training included in the TINA. You then tell her, "I'm sorry that you don't agree, but this is an important part of this school's plan for improvement, and I believe that the workshop would teach you how to conduct lessons that would maximize student involvement in the learning process. Even though you don't agree, I'm still going to include this professional development activity in your growth plan." Ms. Dud then files a grievance, claiming that the TINA was not developed collaboratively — she never agreed to learn about and attempt to implement cooperative learning.

While one might argue the wisdom of requiring Ms. Dud to attend the training against her will, there is no question that you as supervisor have every right to require that she do so and to include that requirement in the TINA. You are not being arbitrary in requiring this training since it is part of the campus improvement plan and is a major instructional focus in the school district. Furthermore, you are sending her on school district time, the district is providing a substitute teacher, and there is no financial cost to her. The Commissioner rules regarding PDAS require that you include her in the process of developing the TINA form, that is, that you and she cooperate. The rules do not require that you accede to her wishes (19 TAC § 150.1004 (b)).

Reflecting a similar scenario in a 2002 decision, the Commissioner of Education held that

> A teacher must be given an opportunity to assist in the development of a growth plan. A teacher cannot preclude the development of a growth plan by refusing reasonable opportunities to assist in developing a growth plan. (19 Tex. Admin. Code § 150.1004(b)). Since Petitioner refused reasonable opportunities to help develop her growth plan, Respondent properly developed a growth plan without her input. [16]

MONITORING IMPROVEMENT PLAN ACHIEVEMENT

After the improvement plan (TINA or PGP) is developed, you will need to monitor whether or not the employee complies with its provisions. Your monitoring may result in a series of specific incident memoranda and one or more last chance memoranda. Let us take Susie Dud's growth plan and see what the process might look like. We will assume that, in the case of the second and third memoranda, you used the focused observation instruments presented in Chapter 4 to guide your documentation of classroom activities.

Writing Specific Incident Memoranda

Specific Incident Memorandum #1

Fine Independent School District
101 Wonderful Way
Fine, Texas 70000

```
TO:       Susie Dud
FROM:     Dr. Great Principal
DATE:     February 22, 2011
SUBJECT:  Non-Compliance with Teacher in Need of Assistance (TINA)
          Plan
```

As of this date I have not received your certificate of completion for the workshop on cooperative learning (due February 7th) and you have not met the deadlines for observing in Mrs. Coop's class and for scheduling a follow-up conference with me (deadline of February 15th). In addition, you have not turned in your lesson plans showing use of cooperative learning in your classroom (due February 21st). All three were requirements of your Teacher in Need of Assistance plan. This memorandum is to inform you that you have not complied with these TINA directives.

> I have received a copy of this memorandum. I understand that my signature does not necessarily indicate that I agree with its contents. I further understand that I have a right to respond within 10 working days if I disagree.

/s/______________________________ ______________

Susie Dud   Date

Specific Incident Memorandum #2

Fine Independent School District
101 Wonderful Way
Fine, Texas 70000

TO: Susie Dud
FROM: Dr. Great Principal
DATE: February 28, 2011
SUBJECT: Non-Compliance with Teacher in Need of Assistance (TINA) Plan

I observed in your classroom from 9:20-10:00 on February 24 2011. You lectured from the front of the classroom for the entire time. Three of 22 students participated in ways other than passive listening and taking notes. You have not complied with the provisions in your professional growth plan that directed you to "solicit student participation and interact with students in such a way that more students than not are actively participating and most students are successful." This memorandum is to inform you that you have not complied with these TINA directives.

> I have received a copy of this memorandum. I understand that my signature does not necessarily indicate that I agree with its contents. I further understand that I have a right to respond within 10 working days if I disagree.

/s/______________________________ ______________

Susie Dud   Date

Specific Incident Memorandum #3

Fine Independent School District
101 Wonderful Way
Fine, Texas 70000

TO: Susie Dud
FROM: Dr. Great Principal
DATE: March 7, 2011
SUBJECT: Non-Compliance with Teacher in Need of Assistance (TINA) Plan

I observed in your classroom from 1:30-2:10 on March 3, 2011. In your lesson, you introduced students to the skill of dividing common fractions. During the first 15 minutes of the observation, you told students the rules and process and then worked four problems at the board. You then assigned students to work 15 division problems. For the remaining 25 minutes you sat behind your desk and graded papers while students did written work at their desks.

During that time, I walked around the room. Seven students spent the entire time sitting and staring at the work. When I asked all seven why they were not working the problems, they told me that they did not understand how to do the assignment. I examined the work of twelve students, all of whom had worked the problems incorrectly.

Your Teacher in Need of Assistance (TINA) plan directed you to (1) "solicit student participation and interact with students in such a way that more students than not are actively participating and that most students are successful" and (2) "monitor students by moving around the classroom and by interacting with them in such a way that most students are monitored and receive feedback."

This memorandum is to inform you that you have not complied with these TINA directives.

> I have received a copy of this memorandum. I understand that my signature does not necessarily indicate that I agree with its contents. I further understand that I have a right to respond within 10 working days if I disagree.

/s/______________________________________ ________________

Susie Dud Date

Note the common elements in all three memoranda:

- Written on school letterhead stationery.
- Written within a few days of noncompliance.
- Short and specific.

- Information presented in an objective manner: what happened and what did not happen (finding of fact).
- Teacher is informed that requirements of the TINA plan have not been met (conclusions/judgments).
- Teacher signature to acknowledge receipt of memorandum.

NOTE: In Memorandum #3, the appraiser focused both on student active participation and on student success in learning that day's objective. In order to make a determination about student success, the appraiser walked around the room, examined student work, and interacted with students. You may need to do the same to determine if students are on task and are learning. Use common sense and good professional judgment as to when to move around. If the teacher needs all student attention focused on him or her, you should remain seated and unobtrusive. Sit so that you can see the students. At the side of the room near the front is a good position. It is best to move around the room when the teacher is not involved in delivering direct instruction.

Writing a Last Chance Memorandum

Following these three memoranda, you held a conference with Ms. Dud. It is reasonably apparent that she either cannot or will not do the things that she was directed to do. This is an appropriate time to write a last chance memorandum. The numbers in parentheses correspond with the comments that follow the memorandum.

Fine Independent School District
101 Wonderful Way
Fine, Texas 70000

TO: Susie Dud
FROM: Dr. Great Principal
DATE: March 23, 2011
SUBJECT: Follow-Up to Our Conference of March 21, 2011

This memorandum is a follow-up to our March 21, 2011 meeting during which I expressed my concerns regarding your failure to comply with the directives contained in your Teacher in Need of Assistance (TINA) plan. **(1)**

As you will recall, we first discussed my memorandum of February 22nd informing you of your failure to document attendance at the cooperative learning workshop, to turn in your lesson plans, and to observe cooperative learning in Mrs. Cathy Coop's classroom. I told you that your explanation that "I simply was too busy and did not have time" is not acceptable. **(2)**

I explained to you that my observations in your classroom on February 24th and March 3rd revealed the same pattern of instruction that led to our creating the TINA plan. I expressed my continuing concern that students still were not actively and successfully participating in the learning process and that you were not monitoring student learning and providing them with feedback. I told you that your stated reasons for not complying – "My students are not **(3)** sufficiently motivated" and "Six-weeks grades were due that week" — are not acceptable. I reminded you that active, successful student participation, together with teacher monitoring and feedback, are expectations in all Fine I.S.D. classrooms. I further reminded you that both issues were addressed as specific directives in your TINA plan.

Failure to follow the directives in your Teacher in Need of Assistance plan constitutes failure to follow administrative directives and will result in my recommendation that your contract not be renewed. If I do not see immediate efforts to comply with the terms of your growth plan and consequent change in student behavior, I will have no alternative but to take this action. **(4)**

If you disagree with the content of this memorandum, please respond to me in writing within 10 working days. I will be pleased to talk with you further about this matter if you wish. **(5)**

Copy: Personnel File

Dr. Paul Peopleprocessor, Director of Personnel

> I have received a copy of this memorandum. I understand that my signature does not necessarily indicate that I agree with its contents. I further understand that I have a right to respond within 10 working days if I disagree. **(6)**

/s/________________________________ ________________

Susie Dud Date

Commentary

(1) Notice how promptly Dr. Principal acted on these incidents. Following each incident (February 22nd, February 24th, and March 3rd), he wrote a specific incident memorandum. Immediately following the third incident, he held a conference with Ms. Dud. It is clear that he considers this a serious matter.

(2) He first deals with the failures (1) to document attendance at the staff development session, (2) to observe in Mrs. Coop's classroom, and (3) to submit the lesson plan. He also includes Ms. Dud's explanation of these failures.

(3) He spends considerable time spelling out exactly what was observed in the two classroom observations. He presents this information in an objective and non-judgmental manner. He then explains that the behaviors observed did not meet the expectations for the school district and did not comply with the directives of the TINA plan.

(4) He unambiguously informs Ms. Dud (1) that she has not followed the directives in the TINA plan, (2) that failure to do so constitutes a failure to follow an administrative directive, and (3) that failure to follow administrative directives will lead to a recommendation of contract nonrenewal.

(5) He reminds Ms. Dud that she may respond in writing if she disagrees with the content of the memorandum. It is important that Dr. Principal set a reasonable deadline to respond, rather than leave the response date open-ended.

(6) Ms. Dud does not have to agree with the content of the memorandum; she just has to acknowledge that she received it.

SUMMARY

In writing both Teacher in Need of Assistance plans and Professional Growth Plans and their directives for improvement, remember the following:

1. Give written notice that improvement or change is needed.
2. Provide specific written directives for improvement. Make certain that these directives include teacher behavior linked with student behavior when appropriate.
3. Provide assistance and support to demonstrate a good-faith effort to help the teacher improve.
4. Establish reasonable time lines for growth and improvement to occur. Consider the complexity of the changes directed, previous evaluations, years of experience, and type of employment contract in determining a standard for what is reasonable.
5. Periodically monitor the teacher's progress toward complying with the terms of the improvement plan, using the focused observation instruments discussed in Chapter 4 during classroom observations. Follow-up with written memoranda indicating areas of deficiency. If improvement does not occur, send the teacher a last chance memorandum delineating the continuing problems and stating that a recommendation of contract nonrenewal or termination is likely if improvement is not forthcoming.

REFERENCES

1. See, for example, *Roberts v. San Benito C.I.S.D.*, Dkt. No. 102-R1-598 (Comm'r Educ. 1998); *Foley v. Houston I.S.D.*, Dkt. No. 034-R2-1097 (Comm'r Educ. 1997); *Hernandez v. Asherton I.S.D.*, Dkt. No. 028(2)-R2-1079 (Comm'r Educ. 1983); *Lopez v. Edinburg C.I.S.D.*, Dkt. No. 122-R2-481 (Comm'r Educ. 1982); *Phillips v. Houston I.S.D.*, Dkt. No. 026-R2-1081 (Comm'r Educ. 1983); *McConnell v. Alamo Heights I.S.D.*, 576 S.W.2d 470 (Tex. App. — San Antonio 1978, writ ref'd n.r.e.).
2. *Brandhorst v. Northside I.S.D.*, Dkt. No. 034-R3-1088 (Comm'r Educ. 1990).
3. *Fetchin v. Lewisville I.S.D.*, Dkt. No. 348-R2-691 (Comm'r Educ. 1993). See also *McGrath v. Webb C.I.S.D.*, Dkt. No. 171-R 2-294 (Comm'r Educ. 1997).
4. *Johnson v. Houston I.S.D.*, Dkt. No. 074-R2-402 (Comm'r Educ. 2002).
5. *Strickland v. Dallas I.S.D.*, Dkt. No. 075-R1-0808 (Comm'r Educ. 2008).
6. *Toussaint v. Dallas I.S.D.*, Dkt.No.071 R-2-0708 (Comm'r Educ. 2008).
7. *Wooten v. Dallas I.S.D.*, Dkt. No. 018-R2-997 (Comm'r Educ. 1998).
8. *Lyman v. Blooming Grove I.S.D.*, Dkt. No. 046-R1-0508 (Comm'r Educ. 2008). In his findings of fact, the Commissioner stated that the teacher complied with her intervention plan directives to attend a workshop, observe one teacher per week for the first 12 weeks of school and complete an observation form on each, and meet with her principal bi-weekly for critique and discussion about the improvement plan. But he went on to note that her intervention plan also contained directives for changes in teacher behavior, including improving classroom management and altering instructional strategies so that students would be on task and their academic success would increase. These directives were not complied with. The evidence established that

after the intervention plan was in place, students continued to wander freely about the classroom and were off-task. Students shoved each other and threw paper clips, coins, and paper wads at each other. Throughout the year, less than 70 percent of the teacher's students were on task during instructional time. Students had "zero response" to teacher's re-direction attempts, and the students demonstrated that it was routine to ignore the teacher. In addition, the teacher was observed at least twice a week throughout the school year yelling at students in an effort to maintain discipline. The teacher excessively referred students to lunch detention. Based on the inability of the teacher to change her classroom behavior in such a way that students were on task and improving academically, the Commissioner upheld the teacher's contract nonrenewal.

9. *Wood v. Post I.S.D.*, Dkt. No. 335-R1-794 (Comm'r Educ. 1996).
10. *Trimboli v. Board of Education of Wayne Cnty.*, 280 S.E.2d 686 (W. Va. 1981).
11. *Baker v. Rice C.I.S.D.*, Dkt. No. 227-R2-493 (Comm'r Educ. 1995).
12. *Board of Education of School District No. 131 v. Illinois State Board of Education,* 403 N.E.2d 277 (Ill. App. 2d 1980).
13. *Community School District No. 60 v. Maclin,* 435 N.E.2d 845 (Ill. App. 2d 1982).
14. *Ganyo v. Independent School District No. 832,* 311 N.W.2d 497 (Minn. 1981).
15. *McKenzie v. Webster Parish School Board,* 653 S.2d 215 (La. App. 2 Cir., 1995).
16. *Michael v. Houston I.S.D.*, Dkt. No. 012-R10-1000 (Comm'r Educ. 2002).

APPENDIX A

Code of Ethics and Standard Practices for Texas Educators[1]

STATEMENT OF PURPOSE

The Texas educator shall comply with standard practices and ethical conduct toward students, professional colleagues, school officials, parents, and members of the community and shall safeguard academic freedom. The Texas educator, in maintaining the dignity of the profession, shall respect and obey the law, demonstrate personal integrity, and exemplify honesty and good moral character. The Texas educator, in exemplifying ethical relations with colleagues, shall extend just and equitable treatment to all members of the profession. The Texas educator, in accepting a position of public trust, shall measure success by the progress of each student toward realization of his or her potential as an effective citizen. The Texas educator, in fulfilling responsibilities in the community, shall cooperate with parents and others to improve the public schools of the community. This chapter shall apply to educators and candidates for certification.

The State Board for Educator Certification (SBEC) is solely responsible for enforcing the Educators' Code of Ethics for purposes related to certification disciplinary proceedings.

ENFORCEABLE STANDARDS.

I. Professional Ethical Conduct, Practices and Performance.

Standard 1.1. The educator shall not intentionally, knowingly, or recklessly engage in deceptive practices regarding official policies of the school district, educational institution, educator preparation program, the Texas Education Agency, or the State Board for Educator Certification (SBEC) and its certification process.

Standard 1.2. The educator shall not knowingly misappropriate, divert, or use monies, personnel, property, or equipment committed to his or her charge for personal gain or advantage.

Standard 1.3. The educator shall not submit fraudulent requests for reimbursement, expenses, or pay.

Standard 1.4. The educator shall not use institutional or professional privileges for personal or partisan advantage.

---

1. Texas Education Code § 21.041(b)(8) requires the State Board for Educator Certification (SBEC) to set forth an educators' code of ethics. The Code of Ethics and Standard Practices set forth here was adopted in December 2010 and is used by SBEC for educator certification and discipline. Most school districts incorporate the Code through one or more policies relating to employee standards of conduct (e.g., Policy DH-Legal, Policy DH-Local, and Policy DH-Exhibit), thus making them part of the district's conditions of employment. Here we include a key paragraph from the "Purpose and Definitions" of the Code and then its entire "Enforceable Standards."

Standard 1.5. The educator shall neither accept nor offer gratuities, gifts, or favors that impair professional judgment or to obtain special advantage. This standard shall not restrict the acceptance of gifts or tokens offered and accepted openly from students, parents of students, or other persons or organizations in recognition or appreciation of service.
Standard 1.6. The educator shall not falsify records, or direct or coerce others to do so.
Standard 1.7. The educator shall comply with state regulations, written local school board policies, and other state and federal laws.
Standard 1.8. The educator shall apply for, accept, offer, or assign a position or a responsibility on the basis of professional qualifications.
Standard 1.9. The educator shall not make threats of violence against school district employees, school board members, students, or parents of students.
Standard 1.10. The educator shall be of good moral character and be worthy to instruct or supervise the youth of this state.
Standard 1.11. The educator shall not intentionally or knowingly misrepresent his or her employment history, criminal history, and/or disciplinary record when applying for subsequent employment.
Standard 1.12. The educator shall refrain from the illegal use or distribution of controlled substances and/or abuse of prescription drugs and toxic inhalants.
Standard 1.13. The educator shall not consume alcoholic beverages on school property or during school activities when students are present.

II. Ethical Conduct Toward Professional Colleagues.

Standard 2.1. The educator shall not reveal confidential health or personnel information concerning colleagues unless disclosure serves lawful professional purposes or is required by law.
Standard 2.2. The educator shall not harm others by knowingly making false statements about a colleague or the school system.
Standard 2.3. The educator shall adhere to written local school board policies and state and federal laws regarding the hiring, evaluation, and dismissal of personnel.
Standard 2.4. The educator shall not interfere with a colleague's exercise of political, professional, or citizenship rights and responsibilities.
Standard 2.5. The educator shall not discriminate against or coerce a colleague on the basis of race, color, religion, national origin, age, gender, disability, family status, or sexual orientation.
Standard 2.6. The educator shall not use coercive means or promise of special treatment in order to influence professional decisions or colleagues.
Standard 2.7. The educator shall not retaliate against any individual who has filed a complaint with the SBEC or who provides information for a disciplinary investigation or proceeding under this chapter.

III. Ethical Conduct Toward Students.

Standard 3.1. The educator shall not reveal confidential information concerning students unless disclosure serves lawful professional purposes or is required by law.

Standard 3.2. The educator shall not intentionally, knowingly, or recklessly treat a student or minor in a manner that adversely affects or endangers the learning, physical health, mental health, or safety of the student or minor.

Standard 3.3. The educator shall not intentionally, knowingly, or recklessly misrepresent facts regarding a student.

Standard 3.4. The educator shall not exclude a student from participation in a program, deny benefits to a student, or grant an advantage to a student on the basis of race, color, gender, disability, national origin, religion, family status, or sexual orientation.

Standard 3.5. The educator shall not intentionally, knowingly, or recklessly engage in physical mistreatment, neglect, or abuse of a student or minor.

Standard 3.6. The educator shall not solicit or engage in sexual conduct or a romantic relationship with a student or minor.

Standard 3.7. The educator shall not furnish alcohol or illegal/unauthorized drugs to any person under 21 years of age unless the educator is a parent or guardian of that child or knowingly allow any person under 21 years of age unless the educator is a parent or guardian of that child to consume alcohol or illegal/unauthorized drugs in the presence of the educator.

Standard 3.8. The educator shall maintain appropriate professional educator-student relationships and boundaries based on a reasonably prudent educator standard.

Standard 3.9. The educator shall refrain from inappropriate communication with a student or minor, including, but not limited to, electronic communication such as cell phone, text messaging, email, instant messaging, blogging, or other social network communication. Factors that may be considered in assessing whether the communication is inappropriate include, but are not limited to:

(i) The nature, purpose, timing, and amount of the communication;

(ii) The subject matter of the communication;

(iii) Whether the communication was made openly or the educator attempted to conceal the communication;

(iv) Whether the communication could be reasonably interpreted as soliciting sexual contact or a romantic relationship;

(v) Whether the communication was sexually explicit; and

(vi) Whether the communication involved discussion(s) of the physical or sexual attractiveness or the sexual history, activities, preferences, or fantasies of either the educator or the student.

APPENDIX B

Appendix B includes blank versions of the five focused observation instruments discussed and completed in Chapter 4. The copyright for this book has been waived to the extent that purchasers may want to make copies of the forms for their use. Alternatively, purchasers may wish to purchase the accompanying CD that contains these forms, along with those in Appendix D, for easy computer downloading and use. Neither the authors nor the publisher assumes responsibility for any liability that may arise from use of the forms.

FOCUSED OBSERVATION INSTRUMENT #1
Active, Successful Student Participation in Learning

- ✔ Active Student Engagement/Participation
- ✔ Student Success
- ✔ Cognitive Level/Complexity of Instruction
- ✔ Students Connecting Learning

Name of Teacher: ________________ **Date of Observation:** ______________

Subject/Grade Level: ________________ **Time of Observation:** **Begin:** ___

Specific Content/Activity: **End:** ____

Number of Students in Class: ______

Learning Objective:

Record the names (descriptions, seat assignment) of students who participated in ways other than passive listening. Record the question/prompt from the teacher. Circle the + beside the name(s) of students whose participation was successful. Circle the – beside the name(s) of students whose participation was not successful. Record the teacher's response to the student's response/ performance/demonstration.

STUDENT	QUESTION	SUCCESSFUL/ UNSUCCESSFUL	TEACHER RESPONSE TO STUDENT
1.		+ – ?	
2.		+ – ?	
3.		+ – ?	
4.		+ – ?	
5.		+ – ?	
6.		+ – ?	
7.		+ – ?	
8.		+ – ?	
9.		+ – ?	
10.		+ – ?	
11.		+ – ?	
12.		+ – ?	
13.		+ – ?	

Instructional Strategies Used to Promote Participation

Check any techniques that the teacher used to promote active, successful student participation. Checking the technique does not necessarily mean that the technique was used effectively — it simply means that the technique was used. Make any specific notes that will help you remember what the teacher did/failed to do.

_____ Used random calling

_____ Sent students to board/chart/map

_____ Instructional activities allowed/encouraged students to interact with each other

_____ Provided application/lab activity

_____ Varied activities

_____ Made lesson relevant/interesting to student experience

_____ Positively reinforced student participation and/or success

_____ Corrected incorrect responses/performances in a way that preserved student dignity

_____ Encouraged slow/reluctant students

_____ Instructional activities provided for students to produce products

_____ Instructional strategies provided for students to make connections of new learning (e.g., prior/future learning within the discipline, other disciplines, world beyond the classroom)

_____ Provided opportunities for students to interact with each other

_____ Provided opportunities for students to volunteer, offer feedback, make independent choices

_____ Other technique

_____ Other technique

Summary of Data and Judgments on Use of Instructional Strategies

In the space below, summarize the data from the previous two pages and make judgments about the quality of instructional strategies.

Active, Successful Student Participation

1. How many students participated? _____ of _____ participated.
2. How many students were successful? _____ of _____ who participated.
3. How many students were unsuccessful? _____ of _____ who participated.

What was the learning objective?

What instructional activities, strategies, and resources were used in teaching this lesson?

Based on the data, which statements best describe what you observed?

Proficient

_____ Most students were engaged and successful

_____ Student engagement/participation was self-directed/self-motivated

_____ Instructional activities were aligned with instructional objectives

_____ Most students were successful in learning at the application level or higher on Bloom's Taxonomy of Cognitive Learning

_____ Most students successfully produced products which represented complex learning

_____ Most students successfully connected new learning with the discipline, with other disciplines, and/or with the world beyond the classroom

_____ Instructional strategies reflected the unique needs/characteristics of students

_____ Other judgment

_____ Other judgment

Below Expectations or Unsatisfactory

____ Few/no students were engaged and successful

____ Student engagement/participation was externally manipulated by the teacher

____ Instructional activities were not aligned with instructional objectives

____ Few/no students were successful in learning at the application level or higher on Bloom's Taxonomy of Cognitive Learning

____ Few/no students successfully produced products which represented complex learning

____ Few/no students successfully connected new learning within the discipline, with other disciplines, and/or with the world beyond the classroom

____ Instructional strategies do not reflect the unique needs/characteristics of students

____ Other judgment

____ Other judgment

FOCUSED OBSERVATION INSTRUMENT #2
Learner-Centered Instruction

- ✔ Objectives and Content of Instruction
- ✔ Interests and Varied Characteristics of Students
- ✔ Critical Thinking and Problem Solving
- ✔ Motivational Techniques
- ✔ Alignment of Objectives
- ✔ Variation of Activities and Pacing
- ✔ Value/Importance of Activity/Content
- ✔ Questioning/Inquiry Techniques
- ✔ Use of Available Technology

Name of Teacher: ______________

Subject/Grade Level: ______________

Specific Content/Activity: ______________

____

Date of Observation: ______________

Time of Observation: Begin: _______

End: _______

Number of Students in Class: _______

Beginning of the Lesson

Record the introduction to the lesson

Concept(s)/skill(s) being taught

Level of the learning outcome (objective)?

____ Knowledge/Comprehension

____ Application

____ Analysis

____ Synthesis

____ Evaluation

Content of the Lesson

____ New material with explanation/ demonstration/modeling (describe what the teacher/students are doing)

____ Miscellaneous, unconnected data

____ Concepts, skills, generalizations, principles

____ Central themes/concepts of the discipline

OR

____ Practice/application/processing of material already taught (describe what the teacher/students are doing)

Connecting the New Learning

Are the students connecting the new learning to:

____ Prior learning?

____ Future learning?

____ Students' experience?

____ Issues beyond the classroom?

____ World of work?

How is the teacher providing for students to make the connection?

____ Teacher tells students the connection. Describe:

____ Teacher facilitates a process (student discussion, activity, etc.) whereby students make connections. Describe:

Critical Thinking and Problem Solving

How is the teacher moving most students from knowledge/comprehension level learning to some application of the learning?

____ Higher-level questioning to most students

____ Small group discussion

____ Paper/pencil activity

____ Performance/demonstration

____ Producing a product(s)

____ Other (Describe)

Describe:

Student Success

What evidence is there that students are successful/unsuccessful in reaching the objective(s)?

Student Self-Direction

Are students self-directed/self-motivated in the learning process or is student engagement/ participation being manipulated/coerced by the teacher?

Describe:

Use of Available Technology

What, if any, technology is the teacher and/or students using for this lesson?

Summary of Data and Judgments About Learner-Centered Instruction

Based on the data, which statements best describe what you observed?

Proficient	**Below Expectations or Unsatisfactory**
_____ Learning is aligned with state/district curriculum	____ Learning is not aligned with state/district curriculum
_____ Most students are successfully engaged in learning	____ Most students are not successfully engaged in learning
_____ Learning is constructed around central themes/concepts of the discipline	____ Learning is not organized around central themes/concepts of the discipline; learning is miscellaneous, unconnected data
_____ Students are connecting/applying learning to other disciplines, their own lives, issues beyond classroom	____ Students are not connecting/applying learning to other disciplines, their own lives, issues beyond classroom
_____ Content and activities are related/connected with unique needs, interests, and/or characteristics of students	____ Content and activities do not relate/connect with needs, interests, and/or characteristics of students
_____ Students are successfully engaged in critical thinking, problem-solving, and/or creative thinking	____ Students are not successfully engaged in critical thinking, problem-solving, and/or creative thinking
_____ Content and instructional strategies reflect current/best practices within the content area	____ Content/instructional strategies do not reflect/ current/best practices within the content area
_____ Student engagement, self-directed participation indicate content and activities are interesting, fun	____ Lack of student engagement, self-directed participation indicate content/activities are not interesting, fun
_____ Student participation/production are self-initiated	____ Student participation/production are the result of teacher manipulation/coercion
_____ Teacher uses an inquiry/discovery process for generating all/most information/critical attributes/conclusions/generalizations	____ Teacher tells students all/most information/ critical attributes/conclusions/generalizations
_____ Teacher and/or students utilized available technology	____ Teacher and/or students did not utilize available technology
_____ Other judgments	____ Other judgments

FOCUSED OBSERVATION INSTRUMENT #3
Evaluation and Feedback on Student Progress
- ✔ Monitoring and Assessment of Academic Progress
- ✔ Alignment of Assessment and Feedback with Objectives/Instructional Strategies
- ✔ Appropriate Assessment for Characteristics of Students
- ✔ Reinforcement and Corrective Feedback
- ✔ Reteaching and Reevaluation

Name of Teacher: **Date of Observation:**

Subject/Grade Level: **Time of Observation: Begin:** _______

Specific Content/Activity: **End:** _______

Number of Students in Class: _______

Learning Objective:

Record the names (descriptions, seat assignment) of students who were assessed. Record the question/prompt from the teacher. Circle the + beside the name(s) of students whose participation was succussful. Circle the – beside the name(s) of students whose participation was not successful. Record the teacher's response to the student's response/performance/demonstration.

STUDENT	QUESTION	SUCCESSFUL/ UNSUCCESSFUL	TEACHER RESPONSE TO STUDENT
1.		+ – ?	
2.		+ – ?	
3.		+ – ?	
4.		+ – ?	
5.		+ – ?	
6.		+ – ?	
7.		+ – ?	
8.		+ – ?	
9.		+ – ?	
10.		+ – ?	
11.		+ – ?	
12.		+ – ?	
13.		+ – ?	

Instructional Strategies Used to Monitor and Assess

Check any techniques that the teacher used to monitor and/or assess student learning. Checking the technique does *not* necessarily mean that the technique was used effectively — it simply means that the technique was used. Make any specific notes that will help you remember what the teacher did/ failed to do.

_____ Verbally monitoring/assessing individual students (random questioning, interacting during group/seat work)

_____ Physically monitoring *individual* students (walking around, examining work)

_____ Verbally monitoring/assessing *groups* of students (choral response, signal response)

_____ Physically monitoring *groups* of students

_____ Use of formative assessments (paper/pencil, performances, demonstrations)

_____ Use of summative assessments (paper/pencil, performances, demonstrations, products)

_____ Adjusting instruction/clarifying in response to monitoring/assessing

_____ Clarifying/extending in response to monitoring/assessment

_____ Reteaching (some or all students)

_____ Positive reinforcement of successful responses/performances (verbal and/or nonverbal)

_____ Specific corrective feedback to students who are unsuccessful

_____ Prompting/assisting students who are having difficulty responding/performing

_____ Other technique

_____ Other technique

_____ Other technique

Summary of Data and Judgments on Monitoring and Assessing

In the space below, summarize the data from the previous two pages and make judgments about the quality of instructional strategies.

Successful and Unsuccessful Students in Learning the Day's Objective

1. How many students participated? _____ of _____ participated.
2. How many students were successful? _____ of _____ who participated.
3. How many students were unsuccessful? _____ of _____ who participated.

What was the learning objective?

What monitoring/assessment strategies were used?

Were assessment strategies aligned with the objective?

Were strategies used to provide feedback to students?

Based on the data, which statements best describe what you observed?

Proficient

_____ Learning objectives were clearly communicated

_____ Teacher monitored the learning progress of most students

_____ Teacher assessed the learning (formative and/or summative) of most students

_____ Teacher's system for obtaining and interpreting assessment data was focused on student progress in the learning objective

_____ Monitoring/assessment strategies fit the learning styles/developmental levels/other unique needs/characteristics of students

_____ Teacher acted on assessment data before moving on

_____ Teacher typically provided positive feedback to students who were successful

_____ Corrective feedback was positive/supportive

_____ Most students who received positive feedback repeated their participation and success

_____ Teacher typically provided specific corrective feedback to students who were unsuccessful

_____ Students who received corrective feedback were successful

_____ Other judgments

_____ Other judgments

Below Expectations or Unsatisfactory

_____ Learning objectives were unclear or not communicated

_____ Teacher monitored the learning progress of few/no students

_____ Teacher assessed the learning (formative and/or summative) of few/no students

_____ Teacher's system for obtaining and interpreting assessment data was mechanical and occasionally/never focused on the learning objective

_____ Monitoring/assessment strategies rarely/never fit the learning styles/developmental levels/other unique needs/characteristics of students

_____ Teacher rarely/never acted on assessment data before moving on

_____ Teacher rarely/never provided positive feedback to students who were successful

_____ Corrective feedback was negative/unsupportive

_____ Most students who received positive feedback rarely/never repeated their participation/success

_____ Teacher rarely/never provided specific corrective feedback to students who were unsuccessful

_____ Students who received corrective feedback were rarely/never successful

_____ Other judgments

_____ Other judgments

FOCUSED OBSERVATION INSTRUMENT #4
Management of Student Discipline, Instructional Strategies, Time and Materials

- ✔ Implementation of Campus Discipline Management Plan
- ✔ Student Self-Discipline and Self-Directed Learning
- ✔ Fair and Equitable Interaction and Application of Rules
- ✔ Specification of Desired Behavior and Redirection of Off-Task and Inappropriate Behavior
- ✔ Selection of Materials and Management of Instructional Time and Materials

Name of Teacher: ______________ **Date of Observation:**

Subject/Grade Level: ______________ **Time of Observation: Begin:** ________

Specific Content/Activity: ______________ **End:** ________

______________ **Number of Students in Class:** ________

Materials Used:

TIME	DESCRIPTION OF STUDENT BEHAVIOR	TEACHER RESPONSE/BEHAVIOR

Summary of Data and Judgments About Management

The statements on the left indicate "proficient" teacher/student behaviors. The statements on the right indicate "below expectations/unsatisfactory" teacher/student behaviors. Check the statements that best describe what you have observed.

Implementation of Campus Discipline Management Plan

_____ Discipline management plan implemented	____ Discipline management plan rarely/never implemented
_____ Implementation of discipline management plan relies on high-interest/relevant instruction	____ Implementation of discipline management plan rarely/never relies on high-interest/relevant classroom instruction

Student Self-Discipline and Self-Directed Learning

_____ Students engaged in appropriate self-direction/ self-management	____ Students rarely/never engaged in appropriate self-direction/self-management
_____ Teacher creates safe, supportive, respectful learning environment	____ Teacher creates a learning environment that is not safe, supportive, and/or respectful

Fair and Equitable Interaction and Application of Rules

_____ All interactions are courteous and respectful	____ Interactions are sometimes/frequently discourteous/disrespectful
_____ Rules are applied consistently and fairly	____ Rules are sometimes/almost always applied inconsistently/unfairly

Specification of Desired Behavior and Redirection of Off-Task and Inappropriate Behavior

_____ Teacher communicates expectations for behavior	____ Teacher rarely/never communicates expectations for behavior
_____ Students understand and meet expectations for behavior	____ Students infrequently/never meet expectations for behavior
_____ Students are engaged in learning and behaving appropriately	____ Students are rarely/never engaged in learning and behaving appropriately
_____ Teacher successfully intervenes to stop/ redirect off-task/inappropriate behavior	____ Teacher rarely/never successfully intervenes to stop/redirect off-task/inappropriate behavior

Selection of Materials and Management of Instructional Time and Materials

_____ Instructional materials are equitable and reflect the varied characteristics of students	____ Instructional materials are rarely/never equitable and/or sometimes/never reflect the varied characteristics of students
_____ Materials are organized and managed efficiently	____ Materials are rarely/never organized and/or managed efficiently
_____ Students are engaged in learning for most/all of the instructional period	____ Students are infrequently/never engaged in learning for most/all of the instructional period
_____ Other judgments	____ Other judgments
_____ Other judgments	____ Other judgments

FOCUSED OBSERVATION INSTRUMENT #5
Maintaining a Supportive Learning Environment

✔ Uses Strategies to Motivate Students for Learning
✔ Maintains Positive Learning Environment

Name of Teacher: ______________ **Date of Observation:**

Subject/Grade Level: ______________ **Time of Observation: Begin:** ________

Specific Content/Activity: ______________ **End:** ________

______________ **Number of Students in Class:** ________

The following teacher behaviors are associated with learning climate.
Check any behaviors that appear and make notes/comments, as appropriate.

Positively Associated	Negatively Associated	Notes
____ Positive reinforcement of behavior	____ Extinction (ignoring appropriate student behavior)	
____ Positive reinforcement of learning	____ Not providing positive reinforcement of learning and/or not providing corrective feedback	
____ Correcting incorrect responses and preserving student dignity	____ Providing negative/demeaning corrective feedback	
____ Patiently assisting students who are having difficulty	____ Ignoring or being impatient with students having difficulty	
____ Using humor in a positive way to deal with a potentially negative situation (learning or behavior)	____ Using sarcasm/negative criticism in dealing with incorrect responses/ performances or with behavior	
____ Relating content/activity to students' interest or experience	____ Dull, routine, or boring content/activity	
____ Communicating value or importance of content or activity	____ Not communicating value or importance of content or activity	
____ Using student names	____ Not using student names	
____ Giving specific feedback for correct/incorrect performance	____ Telling students they are wrong without telling them why	
____ Applying rules/expectations positively, consistently, and fairly	____ Applying rules/expectations negatively, inconsistently, and unfairly	

Positively Associated	Negatively Associated	Notes
_____ Implementing instruction that is challenging while allowing students to be successful	_____ Implementing instruction that is too difficult (easy) for students to feel successful	
_____ Using positive/patient vocal tone	____ Using negative impatient vocal tone	
_____ High energy/enthusiasm, moving around, animated	_____ Unenthusiastic/sedentary	

The following student behaviors are associated with learning climate. Check any behaviors that appear and make notes/comments, as appropriate.

Positively Associated	Negatively Associated	Notes
_____ Students excited/eager	_____ Students bored, lethargic	
_____ High level of voluntary student participation	_____ Low level of voluntary student participation	
_____ Student-initiated contributions/ extensions examples/discussion	_____ Few student-initiated contributions/ extensions examples/discussion	
_____ Students who are having difficulty continue to make effort	_____ Students who are having difficulty quit or give up	
_____ Students appropriately question teacher/each other	_____ Students do not question or inappropriately question teacher/ each other	
_____ Students having difficulty not reluctant to ask for assistance	_____ Students having difficulty are reluctant to ask for assistance	
_____ Students on-task/engaged with little direction/manipulation by teacher	_____ Students on-task/engaged primarily because of direction/manipulation by teacher	
_____ Other behavior	_____ Other behavior	

APPENDIX C

Appendix C contains a generic list of remediation activities and a set of sample directives for changes in teacher behavior.

I. A Generic List of Remediation Activities

THE TEACHER WILL . . .

- Develop a written strategy to . . .
- Develop a list of ways to . . .
- Provide a list of guided practice activities for . . .
- Prepare a list of directions for . . .
- List appropriate sponge activities to accompany . . .
- Develop and teach a lesson that . . .
- Review and summarize a list of possible techniques for . . .
- Tape record a class evidencing . . .
- Videotape a class evidencing . . .
- Watch and write a review of the teaching film, __________.
- Complete the following instrument, __________.
- Review selected instructional leadership materials in the area of remediation and write:
  - a summary statement of content.
  - a critique including how this information specifically can apply to teacher's classroom.
- Develop a task analysis . . .
- Define and give a rationale for the sequence of instruction.
- Outline a step-by-step plan for improving . . .
- Develop a schedule for . . .
- Prepare a list of . . . (e.g., positive feedback remarks).
- Develop a system of . . . (e.g., scheduled feedback, rewards).
- Create a sample list of questions that . . . (e.g., extend students' responses).
- Develop a questioning strategy based on Bloom's Taxonomy.
- Write instructional objectives, methods/procedures, student activities, and evaluation strategies.
- Write behavioral objectives in relation to . . .
- Review objectives and determine which are relevant to the ability level(s) of the students.
- Review available classroom materials and submit a chart determining which materials are relevant to the ability level(s) of the students.
- Prepare a list of materials to be used and state a rationale for each.

- Prepare a list of supplementary materials.
- Develop and implement a questionnaire for students concerning . . .
- Survey students' interests and abilities and group them for instruction.
- Identify the ability levels of your students.
- Develop a plan to determine the instructional needs of the students.
- Discuss the students' needs with the resource teacher.
- Establish rules, procedures, and consequences with students.
- Post in the room . . . (e.g., rules and consequences).
- Schedule to observe other teachers who . . .
- Attend a workshop on . . .
- Attend an on-campus meeting of teachers to brainstorm ways to improve . . .
- Invite the supervisor to visit . . .
- Develop a plan following these steps:
    - review and discuss curriculum goals
    - identify content focus and learning outcomes
    - identify student needs
    - select materials.
- Write a summary statement of how the lesson fits the focus and desired learner outcomes.
- Write objectives, methods, student activities, and evaluation strategy.
- Submit ________ to the evaluator.
- Write and submit lesson plans that include . . . (e.g. time allocations).
- Write and submit lesson plans designed to . . . (e.g. motivate students for learning).
- Write a self-critique or evaluation after the next three lessons, emphasizing . . .

II. Sample Directives for Changes in Teacher Behavior

Stems for Directives:

- In all future classroom observations, I will expect to observe the following:
- In the future, you will . . .
- In all classroom instruction you will . . .
- Beginning immediately, you will . . .
- Beginning *(date)* you will . . .
- As of *(date)* you will . . .

General Directives Linked to Educational Behaviors

One of the stems above, plus linking language to outcomes.

FORMULA:

Teacher behaves in a certain way —>	(Linking Words) —>	Outcome/Effectiveness (usually, student behavior)
• Provide opportunities for students to participate in instruction	in such a way that	most students are participating in learning that has depth/complexity.
• Evaluate and provide feedback to students who are not successful	in such a way that	they are successful.
• Monitor all students when they are engaged in individual and/or group learning activities.		No student behavior*
• Manage time and materials	with the result that	• administrative tasks consume very little time. • 85% of the students are engaged in learning for 85% of the instructional period. • most students are attending when they should be. • most students are self-directed/ self-managed.

***CAUTION:** Some areas of instructional behavior may *not* have a *student* behavior that is always objectively observable. In that case, your directive will only include teacher behavior.

• Manage Student Behavior	so that	• most students are self-directed/ self-managed. • most students are on-task and behave appropriately. • off-task/inappropriate behavior stops when the teacher immediately and appropriately intervenes.
• Teach the daily objective (cognitive, affective, psychomotor)	with the result that	• most/almost all students are successful in learning that has depth/complexity/connectivity. • most/almost all students are successful in applying learning/ engaged in critical thinking/ problem solving. • most/almost all students are successful in learning that has depth/complexity/connectivity.
• Use strategies to motivate students	so that	• most/almost all students are engaged and, when appropriate, participate in the learning process. • most/almost all students are consistently engaged in the learning process.
• Stop/redirect inappropriate/ off-task/disruptive behavior	in such a way that	off-task/inappropriate behavior behavior is stopped promptly.
• All interactions with students (staff, parents) will be courteous and respectful.		No student behavior.*
• Teach the daily objective	in such a way that	• most/almost all students are successful in learning that has depth/complexity/connectivity. • most/almost all students are successful in applying learning/ engaged in critical thinking.

***CAUTION:** Some areas of instructional behavior may *not* have a *student* behavior that is always objectively observable. In that case, your directive will only include teacher behavior.

• Use effective communication with students (staff, parents).		No student behavior.*
• Do not make significant errors in content, grammar, or language.		No student behavior.*
• Use strategies to motivate students	in such a way that	• students are engaged in learning. • students comply with classroom rules and procedures.
• Establish and maintain a supportive learning environment	so that	all interactions with students are courteous, supportive and helpful.
• Plan and deliver instruction	in such a way that	• all/almost all students are successful in learning that has depth/complexity. • all/almost all students connect learning to other disciplines and/or issues beyond the classroom.

Linking Instructional Behaviors with TAKS Results

Teacher Behavior/Performance +	**Linking Language ---->**	**Student Behavior/Performance**
• (any of the teaching behaviors listed in PDAS and Appendix C)	in such a way that or that results in	the percentage of students meeting minimum expectations (i.e., passing) on the TAKS/EOC reading test increases.
• Plan and deliver instruction on measurement (*or any specific student expectation)* in the Texas Essential Knowledge and Skills (TEKS)	so that	students are successful in learning. (all/almost all students are successful in demonstrating their knowledge of that student expectation).

***CAUTION:** Some areas of instructional behavior may *not* have a *student* behavior that is always objectively observable. In that case, your directive will only include teacher behavior.

Linking Specific Instructional Programs/Materials/Best Practices with TAKS Results

Teacher Behavior- +	Linking Language ---->	Student Behavior/Performance
• Use models and manipulatives in teaching Algebra	in such a way that	the percentage of students meeting minimum expectations (i.e., passing) on the Algebra I EOC increases.
• Use the district's balanced literacy program (phonemic awareness, model reading, guided reading, independent reading, reading/writing connection) on a weekly basis in teaching English Language Arts	in such a way that	the percentage of students meeting minimum expectations (i.e., passing) on the TAKS reading increases.
• Design and deliver instruction that is aligned with the student expectations and specifications of the TAKS/ EOC reading *(math, science, social studies)* test	in such a way that	the percentage of students meeting minimum expectations (i.e., passing) on the TAKS/EOC reading *(math, science, social studies)* increases.
• Design and deliver science instruction using at least 60% active, laboratory activities	in such a way that	students are using the science process skills specified in the Texas Essential Knowledge and Skills.

Other Kinds of Behaviors:

General Directives, Including Directives to Non-Instructional Personnel

- Plan for and engage in professional development (specify the professional development).
- Comply with:
    - (district or campus) *policies* (specify policy) OR
    - (district or campus) *operating procedures* (specify the operating procedures)
    - (district or campus) *requirements* (specify requirements)
    - (state/district) *law / requirements* (specify law/requirements)
- Plan and implement instruction (usually a written lesson plan or planning with another teacher/administrator) in conformity to campus/district policy.
- Document (may be: student progress/grades, curriculum or attendance records, reports, etc.) in conformity to campus/district policy.
- Report student progress *(e.g., to parents, to administration, to the media)* in conformity to campus/district policy.
- Align daily instruction with the Texas Essential Knowledge and Skills.
- Align daily instruction with the instructional targets and specifications of the Texas Assessment of Knowledge and Skills.
- Design and implement a plan for *(e.g., instructional technology, bilingual education, disaggregating and reporting student performance).*
- Design a time line for communicating *(e.g., district / campus expectations, reporting procedures, budgeting, purchasing)* to all stakeholders.
- Conduct and write/deliver the report of all special education *(504, ADA, dyslexia, ESL)* assessments to the program director within *(time frame)* of receiving the referral.
- Schedule, notify all participants, and conduct all Admission, Review, and Dismissal (ARD) Committee meetings within the time frame required by law.
- Follow all provisions of the Individualized Education Program (IEP) for all special education students in your class *(on your campus).*

APPENDIX D: SAMPLE FORMS

The following sample forms are included in this section:

Complaint Form. This form is to be completed by persons who have a complaint about a school employee. Its purpose is to provide detailed information in writing that will enable the administrator to conduct an effective investigation. For the reasons set forth in Chapter 2, no guarantee is made on the form or should be made orally that the contents of the complaint form will remain confidential, though every effort will be made to do so and at the same time to follow the requirements of the Texas Public Information Act and the Family Educational Rights and Privacy Act.

Witness Statement Form. This simple form formalizes the process of securing a statement from witnesses to incidents that are being investigated. For the reasons set forth in Chapter 2, no guarantee is made on the form or should be made orally that the contents of the witness form will remain confidential, though every effort will be made to do so and at the same time to follow the requirements of the Texas Public Information Act and the Family Educational Rights and Privacy Act.

Template for a Specific Incident Memorandum Related to Instruction. This form is designed to guide you through the development of a simple focused observation follow-up memorandum and can be placed on a computer file for this purpose. Thereafter, all you need to do is fill in the necessary information. The result is uniformity in writing this kind of instructional memorandum.

Professional Growth Plan Form. This form can be utilized effectively with the Texas Teacher Appraisal System or a locally adopted variation.

Teacher in Need of Assistance Form. This form is appropriate for use with the Professional Development and Assistance (PDAS) system or a locally adopted variation.

The copyright protection for this handbook has been modified to the extent that purchasers of the book may reproduce the forms in this section for their own use. We advise that you contact the school district's human resources director and/or school attorney before doing so to make sure that the forms are consistent with local policy and practice. Note that these forms, along with those in Appendix B, are available on a CD for easy computer downloading and use. Neither the authors nor the publisher assumes any responsibility for liability associated with their use.

COMPLAINT FORM

Name of person filing this complaint: ______________________________

Address: ______________________________

Statement involves complaint against whom: ______________________________

Please state your specific complaint or complaints. Please describe in detail the events surrounding the complaint against the above-named person. Please include dates, times, locations, persons present, substance of statements, and conversations, etc. Please be as factual as possible. If you must express an opinion, please make it clear that you are doing so. Attach additional pages if necessary. ______________________________

Please refer us to any persons having personal knowledge of the facts stated in this complaint.

Please state the individual harm alleged and identify the person or persons alleged to be harmed, if other than yourself.

Please state what specific relief or resolution you are requesting.

Please attach copies of any written documentation that may assist us in resolving this complaint.

Note: When you are finished, please reread your statement in its entirety. Make any necessary changes and initial those changes. Then initial each sheet in the bottom righthand corner. Sign and date below.

"I affirm that the above statement is the truth to the best of my knowledge."

______________________________	______________________________
Signature Date	Signature Date
Person making statement	Person receiving statement

WITNESS STATEMENT FORM

Please describe in your own words and handwriting what you observed. Be as factual and specific as you can. Try not to reach conclusions or make judgments.

Please provide the names of other witnesses if you know them, or descriptions if you do not.

Your Name (Please Print)

Date

Signature

TEMPLATE FOR SPECIFIC INCIDENT MEMORANDUM RELATED TO INSTRUCTION

Your Independent School District
1995 Southeast Loop
Your Town, Texas 70000

____

(date of memorandum)

____

(name of teacher/employee

____

(campus/site assigned)

Dear ________________________ :

This memorandum is to formally communicate information gathered during my observation in your classroom on _______________________ *(Date)* . I observed from __________ *(Beginning Time)* to __________ *(Ending Time)* .

During that time you were ____ *(Brief Description of Content and Activity)*

____ to/with __________ *(# of students)* students. During that

observation I observed the following:

- *Objective narrative*
- *Free of judgmental language*
- *"Sgt. Joe Friday Rule" – "Nothing but the facts, ma'am."*
- *What the teacher said and did and what the students said and did*

Domain ____ on the Professional Development and Appraisal System has an expectation that you

Your job description has an expectation that you:

Our campus improvement plan has an expectation that you *(component/initiative in campus improvement plan).*

District (Campus) Policy *(cite policy number)* has an expectation that you *(summary or quotation from policy).*

The data from my observation indicate that these expectations were not met.

In future classroom observations I will expect to see expectations met in the following ways:

1. Teacher Behavior	Linking Language	Student Behavior
2. Teacher Behavior	Linking Language	Student Behavior
3. Teacher Behavior	Linking Language	Student Behavior

Finally, I have arranged (I recommend) the following as support for your efforts to meet these expectations. You will (you may wish to consider):

1. Professional Development Activity
2. Professional Development Activity

Sincerely,

/ S /

Principal

My signature verifies that I have received a copy of this memorandum. My signature does not necessarily indicate agreement with the content. I understand that I have a right to respond in writing within ten (10) working days.

____ ____________________

Signature of Teacher */ S /* Date

PROFESSIONAL GROWTH PLAN

School Year 20 ____ - ____

School District: ________________________ Campus: ______________________________

Teacher: ______________________________ Assignment/Grade: ____________________

1. **List area(s) related to the job description, evaluation instrument and/or campus/district policy in which professional growth is needed. Establish priorities if two or more areas are listed.**

2. **Specify growth activities and dates for completion.**

3. **Specify evidence that will be used to determine whether professional growth activities have been completed.**

4. **Specify evidence that will be used to determine whether growth has occurred or is occurring.**

My appraiser(s) and I have developed this Professional Growth Plan.

Teacher Signature ______________________________________ Date ______________

Supervisor Signature ___________________________________ Date ______________

Other Appraiser Signature ______________________________ Date ______________
(if applicable)

PROFESSIONAL DEVELOPMENT AND APPRAISAL SYSTEM
INTERVENTION PLAN FOR TEACHER IN NEED OF ASSISTANCE

Name: ______________________ Appraiser: ______________________

Campus: ______________________ Assignment/Grade ______________________

Period of Intervention:

From: ______________ To: ______________

1. Domain(s) in which the teacher is in need of assistance.

2. Professional-improvement activities and dates for completion.

3. Evidence that will be used to determine that professional improvement activities have been completed.

4. Directives for changes in teacher behavior and time lines.

5. Evidence that will be used to determine if teacher behavior has changed.

______________________ ______________________

Signature of Appraiser Date

______________________ ______________________

Signature of Principal Date

My appraiser, principal, and I have discussed this intervention plan. My signature does not indicate whether I agree or disagree with this plan.

______________________ ______________________

Signature of Teacher Date